GPS *for the* Soul

A clear, easy–to–understand exploration of the *Tanya's* essential concepts

Original Hebrew author:
Rabbi Nadav Cohen

©

© 2014 by Chish Printing and Nadav Cohen

Author: Rabbi Nadav Cohen
Translator: Rabbi Zalman Nelson
Editor: Chava Dumas
Copy editor: Suri Brand
Consultation: Rabbi Yaakov Rapoport

Sales:
Chish Printing
Kfar Chabad, Israel
Office: +972-9600770 | **Fax:** +972-3-9606761
www.chish.co.il | chish770@gmail.com

ISBN: 978-965-7498-37-8

Foreword

It is a merit and honor to have had a part in producing *GPS for the Soul* and to help make the timeless, relevant wisdom of the *Tanya* more accessible to English speakers everywhere. The need for this book is clear—the passage of time has only proven the *Tanya* ever more applicable to our daily lives—yet countless souls who have sought its sagely advice have struggled to grasp and understand it. The currently available works in English have helped, but more had to be done.

My personal connection to this need began after years of learning *Tanya* and *Chassidut*, when I began my training as a social worker in an addiction rehab center for young Jewish people. The addicts I worked with faced intense battles with their Animal Souls. At that time, I began to look deeper into the *Tanya*'s message, seeking practical guidance and inspiration that could help them in their daily wars.

It worked. The more I sought such an understanding, the more I found applicable answers. I was grateful to see that the ideas I shared in new ways could be grasped and applied to their recoveries. Many were able to return to a joyful life of committed Jewish observance.

I continued the journey while working with private counseling clients, as well as the hundreds of people I corresponded with as part of Chabad.org's "Ask the Rabbi" team. The clear message from *Tanya* about our inner being and psyche, and how to grow and succeed, proved immensely helpful to people dealing with depression, anxieties, traumas, and a whole array of life issues and struggles.

The need for a book like *GPS for the Soul* became even clearer when I began teaching *Tanya* to seminary students in Machon Alte in Safed,

Israel. As newly observant Jewish women, they appreciated the *Tanya*'s timeless wisdom, and their insightful questions brought new clarity.

However, the concepts and language continued to present a barrier to learners. More needed to be done to help people engage the *Tanya*, grasp its message, and put its guidance into practice.

GPS for the Soul is an enormous step toward making this a reality. Rabbi Cohen's book was crafted from his successful lecture series that engaged students by rendering the material more accessible to a wider range of people. His words were easy to follow and brought readers into the world of the *Tanya* in an entirely new way. It was a pleasure translating his Hebrew book into English, and as a result, I personally deepened my own understanding of *Tanya*.

Enjoy and *hatzlachah* in your efforts to live the *Tanya*! Feel free to be in touch with your comments and questions.

Zalman Nelson, LMSW
zalnelson@gmail.com
www.zalmannelson.com

Introduction

It has been three hundred years since the Baal Shem Tov established the Chassidic movement. He started by teaching the inner, mystical secrets of the Torah to the masses using stories and analogies everyone could understand. As a result, he breathed new life and enthusiasm into the Jewish people. He inspired them to not be satisfied with dry, technical study of the Torah and performance of *mitzvot*, but rather to seek out deeper, inner meaning in everything they did: to be Jewish with fire, passion, excitement, and feeling.

Following his passing, he was succeeded by his student Rabbi Dov Ber, the Maggid of Mezeritch. The Maggid continued the Baal Shem Tov's path, spreading powerful concepts and ideas from the Torah's inner dimension among the Jewish masses in order to inspire them to live their lives with a deeper sense of purpose. *Chassidut* infused new meaning, joy, and vitality into every aspect of Jewish life: prayer, Torah study, *ahavat Yisrael*, Shabbat, holidays, and more.

After the Maggid's passing, there was no successor who was accepted by all of his students. This led to there being many Rebbes—the highest spiritual standing accorded in *Chassidut*. Rabbi Shneur Zalman from the village of Liadi—known as the Alter Rebbe—was one of those students. He was responsible for creating the Chabad branch of Chassidism, named after the acronym formed from our three intellectual attributes: **Chochmah, Binah**, and **Da'at**. The uniqueness of his approach, in comparison to his predecessors, the Baal Shem Tov and the Maggid of Mezeritch and his fellow students, is broadly and clearly outlined in the *Tanya*—the core, fundamental work on the teachings of *Chassidut*.

The *Tanya* provides us with a full picture of man's soul, the uniquely Jewish soul, the structure of the worlds, the meaning behind the

v

mitzvot, our purpose in this world, and much more. The Alter Rebbe's masterpiece enables us to understand the loftiest of spiritual concepts intellectually and logically. Besides discussing the great importance of pure and wholesome faith, the *Tanya* emphasizes the importance of grasping deep concepts with our intellectual attributes of *Chochmah* and *Binah*, internalizing them, and then putting them into practice via *Da'at*. It is specifically our intellect that serves as our tool of connection to spirituality and G-dliness, enabling us to make true and powerful changes on the soul level.

Along with growing worldwide interest in spirituality has come an increasing demand to learn and grasp the *Tanya's* two-hundred-year-old wisdom. But despite their initial excitement and enthusiasm, many students struggle to understand and give up. Why? The *Tanya* is long and can be difficult to fathom. Even though commentaries on the *Tanya* exist, most of them are so deep that new students feel overwhelmed and are scared off from further attempts to study it.

In an effort to make the *Tanya's* incredible wisdom and guidance more accessible, the Ascent Institute in Safed tried a new approach: on-line courses covering the first twelve chapters of the *Tanya* that featured a more oral, experiential approach. Reading, translating, and explaining the text was replaced with summaries, general commentary on themes and subjects, and stories and examples from daily life. This unprecedented initiative was very successful and enjoyed fabulous feedback.

This book is an easy-to-read summary of those courses.

Just remember one thing: reading this book is not a replacement for studying the *Tanya* in its original Hebrew. But it does serve as a great introduction to this classic work of *Chassidut*. Hopefully this taste will inspire you to join a local class or study the original commentaries to delve deeper into the *Tanya's* wisdom.

Table of Contents

The First Gate – The Long Way
Tanya, Chapters 1-17

The Second Gate – The Shorter Way
Tanya, Chapters 18-25

Table of Contents

The Third Gate – Being Joyful
Tanya, Chapters 26-34

The Fourth Gate – It's All about Doing
Tanya, Chapters 35-37

The Fifth Gate – Intention
Tanya, Chapters 38-50

Table of Contents

The Sixth Gate – "Make for Me a Sanctuary"
Tanya, Chapters 51-53

The Seventh Gate – The Gate of Unity and Faith
Tanya, Sha'ar Hayichud Veha'emunah, Chapters 1-12

The Eighth Gate – The Gate of Repentance
Iggeret Hateshuvah, Chapters 1-12

The First Gate

The Long Way

Tanya, Chapters 1-17

Chapter One
Who Am I?

Every Jew has two souls. The categories of *Tzaddik*, *rasha*, and *beinoni* relate to the state of the interaction between the two souls.

(Tanya, chap. 1)

Sefer shel Beinonim

The *Tanya* opens with a title page where Rabbi Shneur Zalman shares the book's mission statement. But instead of calling it *"Tanya,"* it's called *"Sefer shel Beinonim,"* the Book for the Average Person.

That seems so insulting! Only average? That's all we can aspire to be?

I remember one occasion when I started teaching *Tanya* to someone for the first time. After reading these words, he closed the book and asked me to bring the *"Sefer shel Tzaddikim,"* the Book for the Righteous.

Tzaddik, Rasha, and Beinoni

What's the first thing you think of when you hear the categories *Tzaddik*, *rasha*, and *beinoni*-righteous, wicked, and average? Most people envision the *Tzaddik* as someone who does many righteous deeds and very few bad ones. The *rasha* does very few good deeds and many evil ones, and then comes the *beinoni* who is somewhere in the middle with a 50-50 balance. This is the common, familiar use of these terms. Even the *Talmud* uses these terms when discussing how all of us are judged by G-d according to our deeds on Rosh Hashanah.

Delving deeper, however, we come to see that these commonly held definitions are merely simple, superficial meanings. In truth, *Tzaddik*, *rasha*, and *beinoni* mean something much more comprehensive.

In general, every concept in the Torah can be understood on many levels, and by nature we constantly seek out the deepest explanation and innermost understanding. In this sense, the Torah is very similar to a person. We are comprised of body and soul, external and inner dimensions, and so too are the levels of Torah comprehension.

When we encounter another person, we know there is more to him than just his outer appearance. If we want to strive to know him and reach his inner soul, we need to go beyond the superficial. The same goes for the Torah and its many levels of explanation.

Borrowed Names

When we describe a smart person as being "clever as a fox," does that mean he walks on four legs, is furry, and has a tail like a real fox? Of course that's not what we mean.

The same thinking applies when we call someone a *Tzaddik*. Is that who he truly is, or are we using this word to describe the fact that he just did something nice for us, fulfilled a mitzvah, or performed a good deed?

Clearly, we "borrowed" the idea of the cunning fox or the righteous *Tzaddik* in order to describe a particular aspect of that individual's character, but not that they are, in fact, a fox or a *Tzaddik*.

Accurate Names

In contrast to a borrowed name (*shem hamushal*) is an accurate name (*shem ha'etzem*). When we call someone a *chacham* (wise person), and intend it as an accurate description of the essence of this person, we mean that he is truly a *chacham* in everything he does, just as we call a person who practices medicine a doctor. The *Tanya* refers to these as accurate names.

When we apply the accurate name *Tzaddik* to someone, it means that this is his entire essence and it finds expression in everything he does.

Inner vs. Superficial

Based on this, we can better understand the difference between the way *Tzaddik* is commonly used and its precise definition. According to the Torah's simple and basic level of interpretation, a person is judged only according to his deeds-i.e., that which we can see on the surface. As such, all he has to do is perform more *mitzvot* than sins to be considered a *Tzaddik*.

But the accurate usage of the title *Tzaddik* means that the person is a *Tzaddik* in his entire essence and being. According to the Torah's deeper and more inner level of interpretation, a person is measured by his true nature. Which means we now have a completely different scale for judging who is a *Tzaddik* and who is a *beinoni*.

But before we can comprehend this new scale or actually start progressing on the path of righteousness, we need to know more about who we are-the makeup of our inner world, the parts of the psyche, and the nature of our soul.

The Structure of the Soul

Each one of has not just one, but two souls.

Let's meet them.

The first soul is responsible for animating our bodies, and it is this soul that we sense and feel most of the time. It is also called the "Animal Soul." This doesn't mean we are literally animals, G-d forbid; this is just the name that describes its inner essence, which is animalistic, driven by physical needs and desires.

Animals primarily worry only about themselves and spend most of their time in pursuit of material, physical things (eating, sleeping, etc.). This makes the Animal Soul's focus chiefly itself. It sees itself as the center of the world, and therefore believes that everything exists for it and it deserves everything. Sometimes this nature is crude, expressed outright in words and actions, without sugar coating. Other times it acts more subtly, with tact and without brazenness. But either way, this nature is always present. In modern language, we would associate this soul with the ego.

The Animal Soul drives a person to be primarily concerned with himself and act out of self-interest.

It may seem harsh to say such a thing. But what would we answer if we take an honest, deep look at ourselves and ask, "Would I do something for someone else before I do it for myself? Am I willing to give to others even if I get nothing out of it? Am I willing to sacrifice for other people without receiving money, honor, or satisfaction for my efforts?"

Or, here is another option: test yourself by trying to go an entire day without saying the words "me" or "I," or thinking about oneself at all.

Is It Possible to Overcome Our Animal Nature?

The Animal Soul is the source of all our negative personality traits: I am angry-because someone bruised my ego. I am jealous-because my ego is threatened. I even love because of my own ego! In such circumstances, even the love we express toward others can bounce back at us like a boomerang and seek vengeance against us. Why? Because we really acted out of self-love, thinking about what we get out of the relationship, and not out of true care and concern for the other person. Eventually the fraud is revealed.

We can safely assume that every reasonable person who wants to grow would like to break free of this animalistic cycle, which lies at the heart of all our problems. The Animal Soul is responsible for the blockages and interference we encounter in all we do. This self-interest simply will not let go and let us progress spiritually in life.

But we have a second soul-a G-dly Soul. Without it, we would be hopeless; our entire life would be exclusively focused on our ego. However, the G-dly Soul's presence changes the picture.

The Second Soul

Every Jew has another soul, a G-dly Soul, which is literally a "part of G-d above." In other words, a very real piece of G-d comes into this world and is embedded inside us. This soul is selfless and desires only to be connected to its source-G-d.

The way these two souls behave inside us can be compared to the two parts of a candle-the wax and the flame. On one hand, the flame surges upward toward its source: the supernal source of fire (which is why flames always reach upward regardless of how the candle is held). The flame wants to rise and is willing to give up its very existence for it. At the same time, the wax drips downward.

The same tendencies are found in our two souls. The G-dly Soul longs for an ever-deeper connection with the Creator, while the Animal Soul pulls us downward with a single-minded interest in meeting its needs and enjoying the pleasures of this world.

An Inner Definition of Self

These two souls wage an intense, constant battle deep within us, yet they strike a different balance in each person. This provides us with new parameters for understanding who is a *Tzaddik, rasha*, and *beinoni*. The *beinoni* is actually on such a high level that we're grateful if we can reach this level!

In a *Tzaddik*, the battle between the two souls is over and the winner is the G-dly Soul. It subdued the Animal Soul, took it prisoner, and gave it a completely new identity. Not only has it stopped opposing the G-dly Soul, it actually changed sides! As a result, the *Tzaddik*

never sins,

does only good deeds and *mitzvot* throughout the day, and

has absolutely no desire or interest in anything outside the realm of holiness, *mitzvot*, and goodness-not in his actions, words, or even a single *thought*.

The *Beinoni*

The *beinoni* is more complicated. According to the *Tanya*, he never sins and spends his whole day doing good deeds and *mitzvot*-just like the *Tzaddik*. So why isn't he considered a *Tzaddik*? How are they different?

The answer is found inside. Deep within the *beinoni*, the battle between the G-dly and Animal Souls not only continues to rage on, it gets even *more intense* with time. The *beinoni*'s drive in life is not pure and focused like the *Tzaddik*, and he is distracted by attractions to physical things. However, each round of battle ends with a decisive win for the G-dly Soul: no sins in *action and deed*. In terms of his behavior, he remains someone who never sins.

In fact, the very notion of sin, even the tiniest of sins, is completely foreign to the *beinoni* in the same way that we would never consider committing murder, G-d forbid. Just as it is perfectly clear to us that all the money in the world couldn't get us to murder someone, so is committing even the slightest of sins totally foreign to the *beinoni*. Just as a normal person would never willingly ingest poison, because a normal person deeply desires to stay alive, so too a *beinoni* would never commit a sin: he sees it as spiritually poisonous.

In other words, the *beinoni*'s level of knowledge, awareness, and self-control is so great that he is able to maintain constant control over his urges despite the raging inner battle. He is the absolute boss when it comes to the deeds he performs, the words he says, and the thoughts he thinks.

Sounds like a *Tzaddik*, right? But he's not. He still experiences an inner struggle. He wins every single battle and exercises full control of his three modes of expression, but there is no dominant force in the realm of inner drives and feelings. The war goes on. The *beinoni* has not yet completely uprooted his natural attraction to worldly, physical pleasures.

Then Who Is a *Rasha*?

It is clear to us now that the *rasha* is also more than we traditionally believed. He is not necessary the wicked, evil, mean person who we imagine sins all the time. When using definitions that speak to a person's inner reality, a *rasha* can even be on a *very high* level. A *rasha* might sin only once a year!

However, his lack of total self-control regarding his thoughts, words, and actions can lead him to lose the countless inner battles he faces. At any moment his *yetzer hara*, his inner evil inclination, has the potential to overcome his *yetzer tov*, his good inclination. Based on the state of his inner world, which may lead to expression in his thoughts, words, and actions, he is called a *rasha*.

For the *rasha*, drinking "spiritual poison" is not such a far-fetched idea. His commitment and loyalty to the King is still not yet one hundred percent. It's possible for him to give in to temptation and falter. So we call him a *rasha*, but not a *rasha* like we are used to thinking a *rasha* is-someone who sins all the time. Rather, "*rasha*" defines the state of the person's inner world and where he is holding in the battle between the two souls.

If Only I Were a *Beinoni*

At this point, you are probably entertaining noble fantasies of being a *beinoni*, or at least moving your spiritual life in that direction. That alone is already a high level...

The *Tanya*'s early chapters help us do just that, by providing practical tools for getting started on this path and moving in the right direction. To begin, we first need to understand the structure and makeup of the souls and how each one operates.

The *Tanya* starts with the G-dly Soul, discussing its essence, faculties, garments (i.e., methods of expression), and overall aspirations and desires. Then there is an analysis of the Animal Soul. After dissecting both souls, it's possible to better discern the interaction between the two.

Fight Darkness with Light

Don't beat back the darkness with a stick, teaches *Chassidut*. Light a candle and add more light instead. Then the darkness flees on its own. The same approach applies to the battle between the souls.

Instead of attacking your Animal Soul head-on, increase the light of your G-dly Soul. The darkness of the Animal Soul will automatically disappear. For this reason, the *Tanya* teaches us to start our exploration and discovery with the G-dly Soul.

Changing Our Approach

Reb Chaim was a Chassid who made his living buying and selling merchandise in the European markets. Every free moment he had was devoted to studying Torah. Once a year he would travel to spend time with his Rebbe and fill up on inspiration and encouragement.

Known as a scholar and righteous man, Reb Chaim was always greeted with great respect. On Shabbat, they honored him by calling him up for the final aliyah of the Torah reading, maftir. And everyone knew that Reb Chaim's aliyah to the Torah would be followed by a generous contribution to the synagogue.

On one such trip, Chaim entered his Rebbe's private study for "yechidut"-a highly personal and precious soul-to-soul meeting time of deep connection.

When they were together, Chaim poured out his heart, telling his Rebbe of an extremely difficult challenge he was facing in his Torah observance.

"Every day my service to G-d is disturbed," he began. "I am hot-tempered, and I easily get angry and upset.

"And I don't get upset just about big things. Even the small stuff sets me off. When things don't go as planned, or people don't do what I asked them to do-in short, when I don't get my way-I blow up!"

He finished his heartfelt description and eagerly waited for his Rebbe's response. Chaim had been in yechidut many times before and merited receiving answers and instructions on a variety of matters. This time, however, was different.

The Rebbe barely addressed the question. Instead, he waved his hand dismissively and said, "Your problem is really very small and insignificant. In fact, it isn't really a problem at all."

Chaim was shocked. He'd waited a long time to tell his Rebbe this problem and longed to hear a good solution. "But Rebbe! For me this is a big problem! I feel terrible every time I explode, and yet, I do it again and again."

The Rebbe waved his hand again. "That is a very small issue, and really it's not a problem at all."

Chaim refused to give up and described the whole problem again, emphasizing how hard it was for him and how it pained him and those around him.

"Maybe now the Rebbe will answer me," Chaim added hopefully.

"It's a tiny problem, and in fact it's not really a problem at all," the Rebbe repeated.

Even a fourth time of explaining the problem was met with the exact same response!

There was nothing left to do, and Chaim left the Rebbe's room dejected and disappointed. "I can't believe I didn't get an answer," he muttered.

After Chaim left the room, the Rebbe called in his shamash

(administrator) and instructed him not to give Reb Chaim his customary honor of maftir that Shabbat.

"Instead, give him gelilah" (the retying of the Torah scroll at the end of the reading that was usually given to children).

The shamash was astonished by the Rebbe's request as he imagined what the reaction would be in synagogue...

As Shabbat approached, the shamash became increasingly worried about what he had to do.

It's best to tell the truth and warn him, he thought. He met with Chaim and told him that he would be honored with gelilah instead of his customary maftir.

Naturally, Chaim began to complain and loudly voiced his opposition. When the shamash explained that it was a directive straight from the Rebbe, he calmed down.

Ah, the Rebbe must be testing me, Chaim decided.

Shabbat arrived, and as the local Chassidim greeted Chaim, they assumed he would have the usual honor and give his usual generous donation.

Everyone was stunned when someone else was honored with maftir. They all turned to look at Chaim, and their shock grew even greater. Chaim just stood there, completely calm. Shortly afterward, when he was honored with gelilah, the congregants were certain that Chaim would get angry. Yet he strode up to the Torah with a little smile on his face and a niggun on his lips. He tied the Torah scroll and quietly returned to his seat.

"What's going on?" everyone wondered.

When the prayers ended, Chaim remained in the synagogue to talk with the Rebbe. He approached him and the Rebbe smiled. Chaim smiled back.

"I see that your problem is not as great as you said it was," the Rebbe began. *"They tried to dishonor you in front of everyone, but you didn't get angry."*

"Of course not, Rebbe," said Chaim. *"I didn't get angry because I knew it was a test from you. Now, had they really wanted to make me angry, you can't imagine how I would have reacted."*

"Well, that was exactly my intention," the Rebbe responded. *"Listen to me carefully: it is always just a test! G-d is constantly testing and assessing you. He sits up in Heaven, with all the angels who are watching you to see your reaction. The whole world looks very different when viewed from that perspective.*

"G-d has many messengers-everyone around you, the people who annoy you. They are all His emissaries and part of the test He is conducting to see your reaction. Always look at it this way, and the world will appear completely different. You won't have to overcome your anger, since you won't even have a reason to be angry."

When Chaim realized that the Rebbe was testing him to see if he would get angry, he was able to stay calm. If we look at our life through the lenses of the Animal Soul, we become the center of attention, easily offended, easily angered, and self-righteous. However, when we wear the lenses of the G-dly Soul, everywhere we look we see *hashgachah pratit*-G-d personally overseeing every individual detail of our life, including the things that irritate us. How will we react? In a G-dly way or in an ego-centered way?

When we identify with our G-dly Soul, the world will start to look very different.

In Conclusion

The titles *Tzaddik*, *rasha*, and *beinoni* can apply to a person's conduct alone, or to the state of his inner world. The coming chapters will give us a deeper explanation of the makeup of our inner world and empower us to choose the upward path.

Chapter Two

The Second Soul

The G-dly Soul is literally a part of G-d. It has a
parent-child relationship with G-d that constitutes a
deep, essence-level, eternal connection with Him.

(Tanya, chap. 2)

A Game of Chess

You can't play chess unless you know how all the pieces are allowed to move, their roles, their advantages, and their weaknesses. Only then can you start.

The same applies to working with your soul.

In the previous chapter, we explained that we have a constant battle between our two souls going on inside us. And since the goal here is to learn how to win that battle, we first have to learn all we can about the attributes, capabilities, and natures of our two souls.

An Actual Part of G-d Above

The G-dly Soul is an actual piece of the Creator of the universe! Yes, a sliver of holiness-like an apple cut into separate pieces. Just as every aspect and characteristic of an apple can be found in each individual slice, so is every character trait and nature of G-d present in a Jewish soul.

But this fact is tough to visualize and even harder to put into practice. Let's make it easier by looking at some analogies from the teachings of *Chassidut*.

Before we start, we need to keep something in mind. All of these examples share a common idea: the world is comprised of three categories: Creator, creation, and the intermediary between them-the G-dly Soul. In other words, the G-dly Soul was not created like the rest of creation. Rather, it is a part of the Creator that is sent down into this physical world, hidden within a physical body.

Speaking vs. Exhaling

In the beginning of *sefer Bereshit* (1:3), where the Torah discusses the way the world was created, we read, "G-d said, 'Let there be light...'" This means that the world was created through speech-G-dly speech.

"He spoke and the world came into being" (as explained in depth in the second section of the *Tanya*, "*Sha'ar Yichud Veha'emunah*").

However, when the Torah later describes the creation of man and the formation of his soul, it uses different language-"G-d breathed [*vayipach*] a living soul into him" (ibid. 2:7)-which is related to the word *nifuach* (to blow or breath out). This illustrates that the soul is not spoken into existence like everything else in creation; it is forcefully breathed into existence.

What is the difference between speaking and breathing?

Think about your own personal experience with balloons. Two things happen while you're blowing one up: it's difficult to do anything else at the same time, and you tire quickly. Why? While you are blowing up the balloon, your breathing comes from deep within you and draws on many of your internal faculties.

Speaking, on the other hand, comes from a more external source, and therefore it's relatively easy to speak. We don't usually tire quickly from conversations with people.

Similarly, our soul comes from the innermost dimension of G-d, whereas the rest of creation comes from more external levels.

Thought and Speech

Another way to appreciate the uniqueness of the Divine soul's creation is by examining the difference between thought and speech.

Speech is only an external expression of ourselves, not who we truly are. Our thoughts, however, are much more unified with our soul and reveal its essence.

This difference also explains why we can stop speaking whenever we want, but our thought processes are constantly flowing, never stopping for even a moment.

This analogy further demonstrates why the Divine soul is closer to

G-d than any of His other creations, since it derives from the level of Divine thought and not speech.

The External and Internal Will

This idea can be understood even better by taking a look at a fundamental concept that is frequently discussed in the teachings of *Kabbalah* and *Chassidut*. Each of us has desires-things that we want. All our desires are either internal desires or external desires. And here's the difference between them: an internal desire is something that I truly want, while an external desire is something that I want as a means to achieve what I truly want.

For example, let's say that I want to attend a Shabbat learning seminar that's being offered somewhere. First I have to clarify the technical details: where it is located, how to get there, and how much it will cost for travel and lodging. Then, of course, I actually have to travel for a few hours until I arrive.

But these are merely the steps that I have to go through to achieve what I truly want. What I'm really interested in, and the reason why I am going through all the steps, is to get to the seminar and enjoy the Shabbat experience. Therefore, since all the preparatory steps only serve as a means to an end, they are called "external desires." The purpose for which all those steps are taken is called an "internal desire."

Incidentally, if we apply this concept to our lives, we will see that the majority of our days are invested in external desires-things we have to do. Meanwhile, the things we want to do-the internal desires-happen far less frequently.

The difference between internal and external desire can also be applied to G-d. His innermost desire is our G-dly Soul-everything else is secondary and subordinate. In other words, the only reason G-d created an entire world full of plants, animals, and inanimate matter was in order to reach the ultimate goal and purpose: the G-dly Soul of every Jew.

Parent and Child

The third and final analogy that we will look at in order to deepen our understanding of the nature of the G-dly Soul is that of a parent and child. There is a deep, essence-level connection between a parent and child that isn't dependent on any external reason or cause. Ideally, a father doesn't love his son only because he is successful, nor does he love one of his children more than the others because of his academic achievement. Rather, a father's love is the same for all his children because it flows from the very fact that they come from his essence.

Even in less than ideal situations, where there are difficulties and struggles in the parent-child relationship, there still remains an inexplicable connection between parent and child.

However, there are differences regarding the more external feelings of pleasure and satisfaction that a father derives from his children. For example, a father gets great pleasure when he sees his son following in his footsteps. The opposite also holds true when the child doesn't do so. And while the mood of the father is affected by his child's choices and decisions, this is only a reflection of the external dimension of their relationship. The internal love and connection remains the same no matter what the child does.

We see the external-internal difference even more clearly in a situation where the father's son has been taken captive. The father doesn't want his son back because that child is the most successful of all his children. He simply wants his son back whatever the cost. It doesn't even matter how this particular child may or may not behave in the future.

Why? Because this situation brings out the deep, essential connection shared between a father and son, which transcends all of the external characteristics of their relationship.

G-d's connection with the G-dly Soul is similar: a deep, core-essence bond. And while it's true that this fact is not always consciously seen and felt-just as a father's love for his son is not always openly expressed-it is internally always there.

A Story from India

An Israeli girl walked into one of the Chabad centers in India. She had grown up on a kibbutz and had very little knowledge of Judaism, Torah, and mitzvot. She believed that the Chabad center in India was funded by her taxes in Israel. Some Israelis even think that Jews who become baalei teshuvah (returnees to Judaism) begin receiving monthly payments of ten thousand Israeli shekels every month!

So in she walked, and right away she started voicing her complaints against Chabad, religion, and Judaism in general. "I am enlightened, educated, and do not believe in G-d or His Torah," she proclaimed with pride.

The Chabad rabbi in charge of the center was in a particularly cheery mood that day and decided to go with the flow instead of arguing.

"Are you sure you don't believe?" he asked her.

"Absolutely," she said with certainty.

"Well, if that's the case, then prove it. There is a Torah scroll in the ark in our synagogue here. Let's see you take it out and throw it on the floor."

"Oh, I can't do that," she answered immediately.

"Why not? What's the problem? You just said you don't believe it's true, that it's all made up and the Torah is not holy. Why can't you throw it on the floor?"

She couldn't come up with an answer. Instead, she tried to make excuses. "I feel uncomfortable doing that. I may not believe, but I still don't want to show disrespect to it."

The rabbi replied that if respect was the problem then he was formally putting aside his own pride, and she was welcome to throw the Torah scroll on the floor.

Still she squirmed and spouted that she didn't want to make a bad name for people from a kibbutz.

"Oh, that can be solved as well," he replied. "Take the Torah and go into a closed room with no windows. No one will see you. Throw it on the ground and then come out and tell us about it."

After this suggestion she was speechless.

Finally, she confessed that though she had no explanation why, she simply could not do it.

"I'm not surprised," said the rabbi. "You have a G-dly Soul just like the rest of us. It's true that it's been asleep for a long time, perhaps even knocked out unconscious, but when it's pushed, it awakens and asserts its absolute refusal to do anything that could separate it from its Father in Heaven."

It's not just this Israeli girl: all of our souls are "dozing," and the only question is what will have to be done to wake them up. Some people wake up immediately in the morning when you call their name. Some need to be shaken gently and others firmly, and some even need to be splashed with water.

Waking up our souls is similar. Some souls wake up easily, unwilling to allow transgression of even the smallest of sins. Others are harder to wake up, and only when they feel they have reached the outermost boundaries of sin, separation, and distance from their G-dly source do they suddenly awaken.

Back to the Analogy: The Child Soul

Now we can better understand the nature and character of the Divine soul. Our G-dly Souls make us all His children: "You are the children of the L-rd, your G-d" (*Devarim* 14:1). As a result, all Jews are "believers and the children of believers," and no one can take that away from us. Even when a Jew speaks or acts inappropriately, deep inside he remains connected to G-d. The only question is how deeply buried that inner connection is.

This is also why there have been many cases throughout history when Jews suddenly experienced an awakening and great longing for G-d that was not connected to learning or increased understanding. If our relationship with G-d was based only on logic and intellect-if we loved Him and were connected to Him only because it makes sense-then we would drop it as soon as we felt it wasn't right for us or it no longer made sense. But the bond is an essence-level one and thus cannot be broken.

A Deeper Look at the Parent and Child

Beyond what we learn from the essential bond that a parent and child ideally share, let us examine the way a child comes into being. The process of bringing a child into the world begins in the thoughts of the parents. That first thought travels down the spine of the father, is incorporated into the semen, which is then transferred into the mother for fertilization. This thought is now transformed into an embryo that develops and matures in the mother's womb. After months of development, the fetus becomes a viable life and is born.

This demonstrates how the source and root from which a child is derived is (even physically speaking) in the mind of the parent. Furthermore, after the baby is born, the child's mind is the main organ that controls his entire body-everything he feels, everything he thinks, every move he makes, all the organs of his body are functioning due to his brain. Every part of the body receives its energy and life force directly from the brain.

Since every part of the child's body is connected to the brain, and the child's brain is the organ that most closely resembles its original source-the parent's brain-the entire body of the child, through his brain, remains connected to its source in the parent's brain.

In the same way, our G-dly Soul is continuously connected to G-d.

One Nation, One Soul

Earlier, we quoted the verse "You are the children of the L-rd, your G-d," and discussed how this means that every Jew, because of his unique soul, has a parent-child relationship with G-d.

According to the works of *Kabbalah* and *Chassidut*, the verse also teaches us that the Jewish people collectively constitute one soul and one child; that we are not separate entities from one another.

Imagine that we were looking at the earth from outer space through a special telescope that enables us to see souls. We would see that the Jewish people constitute one massive, collective soul comprised of many organs and limbs-similar to the way a body is designed. Some souls are "legs," others are the "heart" or the "spine," and the mighty and lofty souls-the souls of the *Tzaddikim*-represent the "brain."

With this idea in mind, let's revisit our discussion of the way a son derives from his father's essence and remains connected to it.

All of the son's organs and limbs (i.e., all the souls) are connected to his mind (i.e., the souls of the *Tzaddikim*), and the mind connects them back to the mind of the father (i.e., G-d). The result: every Jew is deeply and powerfully connected to G-d via the *Tzaddikim* of the generation, like the organs of the son's body connect to the father's brain by way of the son's brain and its inherent connection with the father's brain.

There is yet another thing we can learn from our investigation of the parent-child relationship. When the child was still in the potential stage, he had no form or actual existence. His physical body, organs, and limbs came into being only during the long process of development inside his mother's womb and eventual emergence at birth.

Similarly, the G-dly Soul descended, developed, and transformed from on high starting at the level of G-dly thought. Then it developed (i.e., becoming physical) and came down into the physical world and entered the body of a Jew.

At this point, it should be clear to us that every Jew is connected to G-d since, as we said before, all the Jews are "believers and the children of believers." At the same time, the more we strive to be connected to "the mind" (i.e., the *Tzaddik* who is the leader of the generation and the other *Tzaddikim* of the generation), the more this connection is internalized and revealed.

Our Connection to the *Tzaddik*

Tzaddikim do not see the world as ordinary people see it. Even if our faith in G-d is strong, when we look around, we first and foremost see a physical world and then we have faith that a spiritual world exists behind the physicality we see.

When a *Tzaddik* looks at the world, he sees first the spiritual reality that infuses the entire physical world. The *Tzaddik* sees G-dliness everywhere and is keenly aware that the physical world is not the true reality. By being connected to a *Tzaddik*, we are given an opportunity to glimpse the world through the view of the *Tzaddik*.

In Conclusion

Every Jew has a G-dly Soul, which relates to G-d like a child with a parent. The soul's connection to G-d is eternal and unbreakable.

Chapter Three

The Structure of the Soul: The Ten Sefirot

The G-dly Soul has ten attributes that subdivide into two groups: the intellectual and the emotional. The intellectual attributes give birth to the emotional attributes. This process is primarily accomplished via *Da'at*, in which we deeply unite with what we understand to the point where we can feel the concepts and they truly come alive for us.

(Tanya, chap. 3)

In the previous chapter, we looked at the essence of the G-dly Soul and found that it was literally "a piece of G-d above," connected to Him with a deep, powerful bond. In this chapter, we will further analyze the G-dly Soul's characteristics and attributes.

The Structure of the G-dly Soul

Before we look at the structure of the soul according to the teachings of *Kabbalah* and *Chassidut*, it's important to consider an interesting point. Modern psychology also discusses the internal makeup of a person. What's so unique about the Torah's approach and why do we need to learn it?

It goes without saying that there is a vast difference between the two approaches.

The map of the psyche discussed in psychology is the product of human research. That means researchers analyzed and compared all kinds of human behaviors, studied and reviewed their data, and arrived at various conclusions. While many of their conclusions may be correct and informative, the kabbalistic perspective of human behavior as it stems from a G-dly Soul comes from a completely different angle.

According to the *Tanya*, the soul's attributes derive from the ten *sefirot* from which G-d created the world (this concept will be explained in greater detail later on). When G-d tells us in the Torah that He "created man in His image," it means that our souls were created with ten attributes that mirror the ten *sefirot* by which G-d created the world.

But how does *Kabbalah* know this? How did the Alter Rebbe discover G-d's ten powers?

It wasn't through research or laboratory testing-he simply saw it and *experienced it in real time*. It is said that the Alter Rebbe lived and experienced everything he wrote about, but because of this, he couldn't always fully write very lofty and holy spiritual terms because he was experiencing what he wrote about as it occurred. Instead, he chose to write in spiritual "shorthand" that made it possible for him to express his involvement and excitement in the concepts.

To truly comprehend the soul, its functions and attributes, we need to learn about them from the source: the illuminating teachings of *Kabbalah* and *Chassidut*. By studying G-d's Torah, which contains the most accurate depiction of His creation, we will have access to a greater awareness of our G-d-given souls.

The Intellect and the Emotions

Many books have been written about the makeup of the soul, and a few mere lines on the subject are certainly insufficient to sum it up entirely. Here the Alter Rebbe focuses on the most relevant attributes and characteristics of the soul in order to provide us with the tools we need to overcome our animal nature.

As mentioned before, each soul can be divided into two main aspects: the intellect and the emotions.

The intellect further subdivides into three cognitive powers: *Chochmah* (wisdom), *Binah* (insight), and *Da'at* (knowledge) (from which comes the acronym *CHaBaD*).

The emotions subdivide into seven faculties: *Chesed* (kindness), *Gevurah* (severity or restraint), *Tiferet* (beauty or mercy), *Netzach* (victory), *Hod* (surrender), *Yesod* (foundation), and *Malchut* (kingship or royalty). (These form the acronym *CHaGaT* and *NaHYM*.)

Before we begin describing each one, it's important to understand a fundamental principle in *Kabbalah* and *Chassidut* that applies to each of us in our individual service to G-d in our daily lives: that in the G-dly Soul, the intellect dominates the emotions.

The Mind Rules over the Heart

Not only does the intellect rule over the emotions in the world of the Divine soul, it is even the root source of the emotions. In other words, deep contemplation of G-d's greatness gives rise to feelings of *yirah* (awe) and *ahavah* (love) for G-d. And, as we will soon discuss, deeper and more intimate contemplation produces stronger and more intense emotions.

It's completely understandable if at first this seems like a foreign and unfamiliar idea. Most of us strongly identify with our Animal Souls, and emotions dominate the Animal Soul. The emotions that arise from the Animal Soul are very intense and tend to subjugate the mind into its service.

For example, when your heart produces a strong craving for something, it convinces the mind that it is a good and worthwhile thing to pursue. A person who desires to eat something unhealthy, despite his doctor's dire warning to avoid this food, can convince himself that he can eat it. This is what happens when we give in to our Animal Soul.

However, when the G-dly Soul is in charge, the mind dominates the emotions. Here's a common example of how a person's intellectual view of the world influences his emotions:

A person who believes that animals and humans are essentially equal, and loves animals as if they were people, may naturally feel repulsed at the thought of eating meat. These heartfelt emotions are an outgrowth of the person's *intellect*: the mind is directing the heart.

The Mind

Let's take a look at the three attributes that comprise the intellect: *Chochmah*, *Binah*, and *Da'at*.

What is unique about each of them?

Chochmah is called a "lightning flash" in the teachings of *Kabbalah*. This refers to the first flash of an insight that enters the mind-the initial moments of a new idea (like the lightbulb that suddenly appears above a cartoon character's head). At this stage, however, the idea is still so completely abstract that one may not yet even be able to explain it to others or even to oneself. But it is most definitely "there."

Binah is the next step in the process. In this stage, the initial insight is broadened and developed in all its details.

Because *Chochmah* and *Binah* have this type of working relationship, they are often compared to a father and mother. In the creation of a child, the father contributes a drop of semen that contains the entire child in abstract potential-free of form or dimension. The mother then absorbs the drop and develops it for nine months, drawing out its form in detail until a child is produced with all the necessary functional bodily organs: head, feet, hands, etc.

Let's further clarify this concept with an analogy. When a person has a flash of inspiration and conceives a new product, his first attempt to capture his innovation generally fits on a single page. Then, in order to develop the idea and turn it into an actual product, he drafts lengthier plans and proposals that fully develop every detail of the original concept. The original idea is like *Chochmah*, and the developmental process is *Binah*.

The attribute of **Da'at** is assigned the task of bringing the lofty, developed concepts produced by *Chochmah* and *Binah* into our emotions. It's possible to learn something, and transform it from a flash of insight into a detailed vision, and yet remain aloof, cold, and detached from the conclusion. In such a case, a person's understanding fails to inspire change in his attributes and emotions and naturally leaves his behavior unaffected.

Da'at is the power to internalize and become united with your learning-to feel it, to make it true for you. It moves a person from being a passive bystander to an engaged and involved participant who takes the issue personally and seriously.

An illiterate man entered the post office to pick up a telegram. Since he could not read, the postal clerk read the message to him: horrible things had happened to members of his family. The man was shaken to the core and burst into tears, yet the clerk remained unfazed.

How could the clerk be so cold and unaffected? Simple: it wasn't *his* family and had nothing to do with him, even though he fully understood the message. This is the great importance of *Da'at*. It transforms comprehension into feelings and makes it come alive.

Applying *Da'at* in Our Lives

When the Alter Rebbe returned home after an extended period of learning with his teacher, the Maggid of Mezeritch, his father-in-law asked him, "What did you learn there? What new knowledge did you acquire that you did not know before?"

The Alter Rebbe replied, "Now I know that there is a Creator of the world."

Disappointed, his father-in-law asked the housemaid to join them and asked her if there was a Creator of the world.

"Of course there is," she said, surprised at the question.

"You see?" his father-in-law challenged. "She also says that the world has a Creator. You had to go so far away to learn that?!"

*"She **says** the world has a Creator, but I **know** it," replied the Alter Rebbe.*

How can we practically apply *Da'at* in our lives?

After learning and studying something, take a break and deeply contemplate all the details and points of what you just covered. Don't just think about it briefly, go into it deeply and keep your mind firmly focused on it.

During prayer, use the opportunity to try to be completely focused. This is the essence of prayer-the application of *Da'at* in a meaningful way. Our daily, specially designated times for prayers are meant for arousing and developing our feelings of love and awe for the Creator of the world. Prayer is when we contemplate His greatness and His wondrous deeds.

Shacharit (the morning prayer service) begins with chapters from *Tehillim* that describe G-d's greatness, His wonders and miracles, and how He interacts with the world. This is in order to awaken our feelings of awe.

Next, the order of the *tefillah* takes us through a contemplation of the angels and the spiritual worlds.

Finally, we reach the pinnacle of prayer, the *Shema*: "Hear, O Israel, the L-rd, our G-d, the L-rd is One." By saying the *Shema*, which is primarily a contemplation of how G-d's oneness fills the universe, this naturally leads to feelings of love for Him. It leads to the next words that we say in the *Shema*, "And you shall love the L-rd, your G-d, with all your heart..." (*Devarim* 6:4).

Only after all these steps of contemplative preparation are we truly able to stand before G-d's presence-the *Shechinah*-in the silent *Amidah* prayer.

This is why *Da'at* is so crucial, and it is why the *Zohar* refers to it as the "key to the *middot* (emotional attributes)." Without deep contemplation, observation, knowledge, and awareness, a person will never develop true feelings and emotions toward G-d.

Mind, Heart, Liver

When all is in order, and the mind (*Mo'ach*) is ruling over the heart (*Lev*) and producing actions via the liver (*Kaved*), it forms the acronym "*MeLeCh*," king. The person is king of his own body and desires.

But when the heart (*Lev*) comes first and drags the mind (*Mo'ach*) in its wake before leading to actions in the liver (*Kaved*), the acronym formed is "*LeMeCh*"-fool.

Emotional Faculties = Feelings

If *Chochmah* and *Binah* are like a father and mother, who are the children? Our feelings and emotions-our "*middot*," as they are called in the teachings of *Kabbalah* and *Chassidut*.

There are six emotional attributes. First we will focus on the two primary *middot*: *yirah* (awe) and *ahavah* (love).

Yirah

The *yirah* that we are discussing here is not fear, such as the fear of punishment-where a person fears G-dly punishment and therefore avoids transgression. Although such fear has positive qualities, it renders a person stuck in a neutral or perhaps worse place, because he is primarily concerned with himself and his ego. *He* is afraid and therefore tries to avoid various negative behaviors.

We are more interested in striving to achieve a loftier level of *yirah*, where our relationship with G-d is so consciously important that we fear harming or severing it.

Through contemplation, we get in touch with G-d's infiniteness, the extent to which we are constantly dependent upon Him for existence, and how our personal connection with Him is so crucial to our existence. As a result, we automatically have no desire to go against His will and weaken or sever our connection, or even "disappoint" Him.

Ahavah

After awe blossoms in our hearts, feelings of love are born.

"Love" refers to a desire and aspiration to become one with our beloved. Proper contemplation of G-d's greatness fills us with a desire and thirst to become united with Him-to transcend the material world and be joined with the Creator of the world.

The stronger and deeper our contemplation, the greater the love we feel, as King David said, "My soul thirsts for G-d" (*Tehillim* 63:2), and "For You my soul thirsts" (ibid. 42:3). Our soul thirsts and yearns for holiness and G-dliness.

This is similar to how we feel when we have some new love or interest in our lives that we can't stop thinking about. The same applies here: when you truly "fall in love" with G-d, it is difficult to think of anything but Him, and your mind constantly seeks ways to make the bond even stronger.

All the rest of our emotional experiences are offshoots of love and fear.

In Conclusion

We explained that intellect gives birth to emotions in the G-dly Soul. *Da'at* is the bridge between the contemplation of the mind and the feelings of the heart.

Chapter Four

The Structure of the Soul: Garments

The soul's attributes find expression in its garments: thought, speech, and action. The garments, more than the attributes, make the greatest connection between the soul and G-d.

(Tanya, chap. 4)

In the previous chapters, we looked at some of the intellectual and emotional powers of the soul, and how the intellect gives birth to the emotions and guides them. In this chapter, we will take a look at the next step: the soul's garments-the tools through which the intellect and the emotions find expression.

The Garments

After we deepen our awareness and begin to intellectually understand better the attributes of the soul, our emotions can be guided to feel more deeply. Next comes the expression of the soul-the "garments" of thought, speech, and action.

As much as we may like clothes, they are not our essence. We adjust our clothes according to our environment to be in harmony with it. Clothes worn to work are not the same as those worn to a wedding or on a hike.

The clothes we choose to wear are also an expression of the way we want to be viewed by others. Formal, fine-tailored, expensive clothes can be a status symbol-expressing wealth, importance, elegance, and rank-when we want to appear cool and aloof. Casual clothing can convey that we want to be seen as easy going, friendly, down-to-earth, and approachable.

However, our clothes and the messages they convey to the world are not necessarily compatible with our *true, inner* character. There are simple, unrefined people who prefer to wear elegant, dignified clothing, and some very aristocratic people who prefer to dress casually. Our choice of clothing is a channel for broadcasting messages, but it's not our essence. It is only an outer garment.

The words we choose to speak serve a similar role to our clothing: we get people's attention and publicly express ourselves through the power of speech. And just like clothing, the words we choose to say may not necessarily express who we truly are or what we really think. Rather, they impart how we want others to see us. They express what we want to "publicize" to those around us. For this reason, our speech is also called a "garment."

This concept applies to our thoughts and deeds as well.

The soul's garments are how we communicate with the world. The garment of *action* connects us with the physical world. The garment of *speech* connects us with others who speak our language. The garment of *thought* enables us to communicate with ourselves-thinking is our inner dialogue.

Why "Garments"?

The soul's attributes-the intellect and the emotions-are united with the soul. However, thought, speech, and action are like garments for the soul. In other words, they can be taken off and replaced like clothes.

This means that our actions are not who we truly are, since it's possible to act in a way that is inconsistent with our personality. The same goes for speech: you can speak words that do not truly represent yourself.

Furthermore, your style of speech and the way you act are changeable, just like clothes. The way you speak at home in a familiar environment is different from the way you speak in a different, less friendly environment.

But the great shocker is that even our thoughts are not who we truly are! A person can live in a fantasy world and imagine things about himself and his life that are not true. And although our thoughts are far more consistent, aligned, and united with our soul than speech or action (which is why it's impossible to stop thinking), they are still not who we truly are deep down.

The Garments of the Divine Soul

Since we have been discussing the G-dly Soul, let's explain what its garments look like.

In the previous chapter, we discussed the soul's intellectual and emotional attributes: the mind contemplates the greatness of G-d and gives rise to the heartfelt emotions of love and awe for G-d. These feelings are then expressed through the "garments"-thought, speech, and action.

Step 1: Meditating on G-d's greatness.

Step 2: Feelings of love and fear toward G-d are aroused.

Step 3: The feelings can now be expressed through the garments.

Because the intellect is primarily expressed in thought and speech, Torah study is accomplished via mainly thought and speech.

The emotions are primarily expressed in action. Therefore, the G-dly Soul's feelings of love are invested in the performance of the positive commandments, while its feelings of awe are found in one's avoidance of the Torah's prohibitions.

For an action to be real and complete, it must be motivated and powered by feelings of love. Actions that are free of feeling are empty, external shells.

Husband and Wife: Four Scenarios

In order to appreciate the crucial importance of connecting feelings and deeds, let's compare different states of married life:

First scenario: The husband loves his wife but is unwilling to express his love in words or deeds. Naturally, his wife is unhappy. "If you really love me, then say it," she tells him. "Don't just rely on signs and hints." Since we live in a world of action and not only emotion, a woman expects her husband to express his feelings in words and actions.

Second scenario: The husband loves his wife and expresses it in action, but not in the way she hopes. He does it *his* way. For example, for her fortieth birthday, he buys her a very special gift-a lawnmower.

This is something he would really like, so he assumes his wife wants the same thing. She is *not* pleased; she doesn't appreciate his gift to himself. "When I asked you to express your love in actions, I meant things that *I* appreciate, not things you want and love."

Third scenario: Our husband finally understands that he needs to give his wife something that *she* wants, so he buys her a piece of jewelry. But when he arrives at home, he casually tosses the gift on the table and says, "Here! I hope you like it!" Once again, she is not happy. She wants his gift to be given as a wholehearted, loving expression of meaningful, conscious intent, not this obligatory action devoid of feeling!

Fourth scenario: Now that he has ruled out all the less successful options, the husband is ready for the best approach: he buys his wife a gift that she wants and presents it to her lovingly, accompanied by warm words of affection.

The Creator of the Universe and Us

Our husband-and-wife scenarios apply to our performance of *mitzvot*. Sometimes we tell G-d that we love Him, but "only" in our hearts-it doesn't get expressed in speech and action.

Other times we love Him and even express it in action, but not the kinds of actions He asked us to do.

It's also possible to fulfill everything He asks of us, but in a casual manner, without care and intention. It's like we're doing G-d a favor and can't wait to get it over with.

However, when we do the *mitzvot* with loving feelings, with passion, care, and focused intention, our entire being is acting in total harmony. When we contemplate G-d's greatness, this gives birth to feelings of love and awe for G-d, which result in learning Torah (thought, speech) and fulfilling *mitzvot* (action) with passionate dedication.

With this in mind, let's look at two different perspectives on the performance of *mitzvot*.

An Exercise in Discipline or a Direct Connection?

There are several ways of relating to the *mitzvot* that G-d gave us in His Torah.

There are those who think G-d doesn't really care about the *mitzvot* we do. They think the action itself is meaningless. G-d is just testing our loyalty and wants to see if we will fulfill His commands or not. But we think that the *mitzvot* themselves have no impact on the world.

Then there is a deeper way of looking at the *mitzvot*. Beyond testing our loyalty, they are "*mitzavtot*" (from the word "*tzevet*," team)-i.e., they put us on His team, binding us and G-d together. In effect, *mitzvot* are the tools for connecting to Him. He is somewhere up above, we are down below, and the *mitzvot* elevate us to Him.

But there is an even deeper way of looking at this.

A *mitzvah* is not just a vehicle for connection to G-d; rather, *the mitzvah itself is connection to Him.* In other words, G-d compressed and squeezed Himself into the *mitzvah*, so that in fulfilling the *mitzvah* we are actually one with Him.

The Limbs of the King

The *Zohar* encapsulates this idea in an analogy. It says that the *mitzvot* are like G-d's "limbs." (Obviously, this is only a metaphor since the Creator of the universe has no physical body.) Why does the *Zohar* use the example of limbs?

A limb is something physical and inanimate that draws light and life force into itself- i.e., the "energy" of the soul. As expressed in the teachings of *Kabbalah*, a limb is a *vessel* that contains *light*.

Just as the human body contains 248 limbs that contain the soul, so does G-d have 248 positive commandments that draw His holy light into the world. Therefore, every *mitzvah* we do draws Divine light into the world. And since the body's 248 limbs correspond to 248 dimensions of the soul, observing all the *mitzvot* in thought, speech, and deed unites the "limbs" of the soul with the "limbs" of the Torah, and thereby to G-d's "limbs." The *mitzvot* directly connect us to G-d.

When viewed this way, it doesn't matter if we understand the *mitzvah* or whether we feel "connected" to it. The primary point of each and every *mitzvah* we do is to connect us directly to G-d. He compressed and compacted Himself into that particular *mitzvah*, into the very physical thing being used to perform the *mitzvah*, so that by fulfilling it we are connected to Him.

Based on this explanation, we can conclude that the *mitzvot* are much more than a bunch of traditions or tools for making order in the universe. Above all, they are literally G-dliness, a direct connection to the Creator of the universe! Any other benefit we receive by keeping the *mitzvot*, such as nice family rituals, stability, or order in our lives, is a bonus of secondary importance.

Love and Awe Are the Motivation

The motivating, driving force behind our performance of the positive commandments is love of G-d: our love is expressed in our positive actions. Similarly, the motivating, driving force behind our adherence to the negative commandments, or prohibitions, is awe of G-d: our awe is expressed by avoiding transgression.

Previously we explained that love is the hope to unite with our beloved. We naturally want to fulfill and do what our beloved desires of us. When we like our friends, we want to help them and do things for them.

Awe, on the other hand, is the desire to preserve the relationship and not weaken or damage it. This motivates us to avoid actions that are undesirable to our loved one. With this perspective, we can understand that awe is the driving force behind observing the negative commandments.

Focused contemplation of G-d's greatness also produces feelings of awe, fear of being disconnected, and-on a higher level-concern for not disappointing or angering G-d. Then we are inspired to make sure to avoid doing things He doesn't want us to do-which is anything that *might* displease Him.

365 Prohibitions, 365 Veins and Sinews

We compared the positive *mitzvot* to limbs that draw in vitality and G-dly light. The prohibitions are compared to veins. This is because their role is to preserve this vitality and keep it from "escaping" to the outside.

We draw G-dly light onto ourselves when we perform a positive commandment. But when we transgress a negative commandment, it makes a hole in our spiritual body that enables the *kelipot* (the powers of impurity, which will be discussed in the coming chapters) to come and siphon off the vitality and G-dly light we possess.

Imagine a person who earns a lot of money and keeps it in his home. Thieves are lurking outside and waiting for the moment he leaves a door or window open so they can enter and steal his money. He does not suffice with merely locking his safe; he even locks the doors and windows.

The analogy is clear. By observing the positive commandments, we "earn" and store G-dly light. However, if we do not protect it by avoiding misdeeds (transgressions), the thieves (powers of impurity) will come and try to take the light away from us.

Thus, our spiritual and physical health depends on our actual performance of *mitzvot*. This is why a *Tzaddik*, who sees spirituality, is able to pinpoint our issues, discern their spiritual causes, and instruct us which *mitzvah* needs reinforcement in order to restore our health.

Who's In Charge: Attributes or Garments?

In the structure of the soul, it is clear that emotions and intellect are loftier than the garments, since they are far more united with the soul. But in terms of which one connects us to G-d more-intellect and emotions, or the garments of thought, speech, and action-the answer is the opposite.

As lofty as the intellect and emotions can possibly be, they are still a part of the person. And since a person is limited, his intellect and emotions are also limited. On the other hand, the observance of the *mitzvot* is the direct will of the Creator, Who is unlimited. Thus the *mitzvot* offer us an unlimited, direct connection to Him.

As it says in the *Zohar,* "The Torah and G-d are one." Fulfilling a physical *mitzvah* by way of the garments connects us to the Torah, which then connects us to G-d in that very same moment.

In Conclusion

With our minds we can grasp, understand, and know G-d's greatness. With our hearts we love Him and long to be connected with Him. We are also in awe of Him and yearn to preserve and protect our connection with G-d.

With the garments of the soul-thought, speech, and deed-we directly connect to Him. We do this by fulfilling the *mitzvot* (action) and learning Torah (thought, speech) with the appropriate intellectual thoughts and emotional feelings.

Chapter Five

The Structure of the Soul:
The Secret of Tzimtzum

The bond between the soul and G-d is greater in
Torah study than in the performance of *mitzvot*.

(Tanya, chap. 5)

In the previous chapter, we discussed how our emotions are clothed in our physical actions and thereby connect us with the Creator of the universe. We saw how the soul's attributes of intellect and emotions are on a higher level than the garments (thought, speech, and action) in terms of the structure of the soul. However, the garments enjoy superiority in terms of connecting a person with G-d.

G-d and His Torah

Learning Torah and doing *mitzvot* with our thoughts, speech, and actions are a powerful way to connect to G-d because Torah and *mitzvot* are completely united and one with G-d. Since the garments are how the soul plugs into Torah and *mitzvot*, they in effect facilitate a direct connection with G-d.

On the other hand, the soul's attributes of intellect and emotion-even at their highest and fullest level (i.e., full with the powerful feeling of love for G-d)-can't reach the same level of connection as the garments. For this reason, the Torah instructs us, "Action, not study, is of the greatest importance."

Even if we had in mind all the powerful *kavanot* (intentions) that a person could possibly intend and felt the most passionate emotions, it still would not compare to the degree of connection our physical performance of *mitzvot* can provide for our souls. And the *Tanya* tells us that out of all of the *mitzvot* that we can do, Torah study creates the strongest connection.

We will examine the difference between physically doing *mitzvot* and learning Torah deeply, and gain an understanding of Torah study's advantage over practical *mitzvot*. But before we get to that, there still remains a question from the previous chapter: how did the infinite, unlimited Creator "compress" and "squeeze" Himself into the finite, limited form of a physical action-the *mitzvot*?

The Secret of *Tzimtzum*

Here are three viewpoints on how we perceive the Creator.

First viewpoint: G-d is very, very big-the biggest Being there can possibly be. But He also has limitations.

Second viewpoint: G-d is unlimited and infinite.

The second viewpoint is more correct than the first, but it still leaves room for a mistaken assumption: G-d is unlimited and the world is limited, but He doesn't care what happens here. Or, an even more extreme way of saying it: G-d's infinite being and unlimited nature prevent Him from "entering" the limited and finite aspects of creation. As such, the only way to "grasp" Him is to rid oneself of the physical world's restrictions and deal only with spirituality.

Beyond the problem that this perception would discourage us from performing *mitzvot*, it also puts limitations on G-d by saying He is infinite and nothing else-unable to also be finite or relate to His finite creations.

Third viewpoint: G-d is not limited to being either infinite or finite. He is above both and thus able to simultaneously be both. When G-d views us from His perspective on high, the finite and the infinite look alike. It is only our limited perspective that sees the infinite as being loftier than the finite. G-d, however, is so exalted above both levels that in comparison to Him they are completely the same.

It's similar to the way two government ministers (defense and education) may argue who is more important, yet when the king walks into the room they are both equally nothing in comparison to him.

By perceiving G-d according to the third viewpoint, we understand that He has the ability to compress and squeeze Himself into the finite forms of our physical world as He wishes and without any restrictions. And this is exactly what G-d did when He gave us the Torah. He made a "zip file" of Himself, so to speak, and inserted His entire essence into the Torah's letters, stories, and instructions, so that by following its guidance and directives we can access His very essence.

Compression, Not Removal

When we say that G-d underwent a *tzimtzum* and compressed Himself into the *mitzvot*, it's possible to make a mistake and think that means some parts of Him were left out. However, that is not what *tzimtzum* means.

Let's understand it with an analogy. When astronauts go into space, they need to take food with them. However, the spaceship does not have enough space to store the amount of food they need for the length of such a trip. To deal with this issue, NASA created capsules of special concentrated food that contain the nourishment a person needs for an entire day.

Tzimtzum means to *concentrate* and *distill* the essence, and not leave anything out. It's like taking a vast library of books and compressing scans of their pages so they will fit on a single memory card.

Ice Cubes

How do we transfer a large quantity of water from one location to another if we don't have appropriate containers? We freeze it and then we can move the entire amount as ice. G-d did the same thing with His Torah. He wanted to transfer to us His infinite, unlimited wisdom, but we are limited beings, with limited minds that can't "contain" the infinite. So He "froze" His wisdom, so to speak, compressing and condensing every drop of it into the finite, graspable form of the Torah and *mitzvot* that we have today.

Now imagine someone who never saw ice before. They have no idea that the clear block of ice they are seeing is really water. When they hold it in their hands, they don't realize that they are, in fact, holding water.

Torah is the same. A person could look at the Torah and its *mitzvot* and believe that G-d is not inside them, since he denies the fact that G-d "froze" Himself into them. But the truth remains: by learning Torah and fulfilling its *mitzvot* we have direct access to G-d Himself!

Let's clarify this further. Although it's a "concentrated" form of G-d that's found in the study of Torah and performance of *mitzvot*, we're getting direct access to G-d. It's like meeting a long-lost friend from our past. When we embrace each other joyfully, we know that we're not only hugging the many layers of outer clothing he may be wearing, we're hugging our friend! He is there!

So too, when we learn Torah and do *mitzvot*, we are at one with G-d.

Mitzvot in This World or Pleasure in the Next

What's greater-doing *mitzvot* and good deeds in this world, or enjoying the "G-dly radiance" that shines on souls dwelling in the World to Come?

When the soul ascends to Heaven, it enjoys the results of all the work it accomplished when it was embodied in a physical form during its lifetime in this physical world. In addition, the soul keenly perceives the Divine light that it drew down into the world with every bit of Torah it learned and every *mitzvah* it fulfilled.

Throughout the soul's time in Heaven, it continually ascends to even higher levels, and there is no greater pleasure than this, to bask in the light of G-d's presence. Nevertheless, even a soul that has been ascending for thousands of years (such as the soul of Rabbi Shimon Bar Yochai, the author of the *Zohar*, who has been in Heaven for two thousand years and receives more exalted light each year) is ultimately only enjoying G-d's light. It doesn't have G-d Himself. It's like someone partaking of the king's feast. As enjoyable as this is, he still hasn't met or embraced the king himself.

On the other hand, when anyone performs a *mitzvah*-even the simplest one-in this world, in that moment he is grasping G-d Himself and the souls in Heaven are jealous! Based on this teaching, if we truly fathomed what this means, it's clear that we would feel great joy with each *mitzvah* we do.

Mitzvot vs. Torah

Both *mitzvot* and Torah study connect us to G-d. However, the way we connect through each venue is different.

When we do *mitzvot*, G-d surrounds and envelops us, as though we are wrapped inside a *tallit*.

Torah study works differently and offers an additional benefit. Unlike *mitzvot*, Torah study does not require a physical object-only our intellect. And because it is spiritual, the intellect is able to do something unique: "grasp" and "be grasped."

When we study *Mishnah*, *Talmud*, or *halachah*, our minds comprehend, grasp, and envelop the subject matter. At the very same time, the holy subject matter surrounds and grasps our minds. This kind of two-way connection, in which we simultaneously surround and are surrounded, is impossible to achieve with something physical.

In the physical realm you *either* envelop *or* you are enveloped (it's impossible for us to surround the *tallit* that is currently enwrapped around us). As such, the great advantage of studying Torah is that it unites us with the Giver of the Torah from both directions simultaneously! There is no union greater than this.

And this occurs regardless of what part of Torah we study, or if our learning gets translated into action or not. The study itself brings about this incredible union.

Mitzvot = Garments; Torah = Food

This also explains why *mitzvot* are compared to garments: their main role is to surround us. Torah, meanwhile, is compared to food that we ingest in order to provide ourselves with nourishment. Just as bread nourishes the body, the study of Torah nourishes the soul.

It should be mentioned that mitzvot also have an advantage over Torah study. The Tanya discusses each of their unique qualities and advantages in later chapters.

Studying Torah *Lishmah*

There is a prerequisite for Torah study to be able to generate such a holy union: the study must be *lishmah*, "for its own sake."

Torah should not be studied for personal gain, such as acquiring knowledge and obtaining honor, but rather for a higher, holier purpose-i.e., to connect with the Creator. When we learn for such a pure purpose, in order to bring about a perfect connection with G-d, this draws down the aforementioned G-dly light.

It is worthwhile to point out that you can't start right off with the level of learning called "*lishmah*." But since you have to start somewhere, it's acceptable to begin studying with an intention that's not "for its own sake," as long as the ultimate goal is to achieve *lishmah* learning. For we say that "from performing something not for its own sake, one eventually does do it for its own sake." *Chassidut* adds that this means that within one's non-*lishmah* learning is found the *lishmah* learning, since all Jews ultimately want to be connected with G-d.

In Conclusion

Since G-d inserted Himself into the Torah, our Torah study and performance of *mitzvot* enable us to connect with Him. The advantage of Torah study over *mitzvot* is that it unites us more completely with G-d.

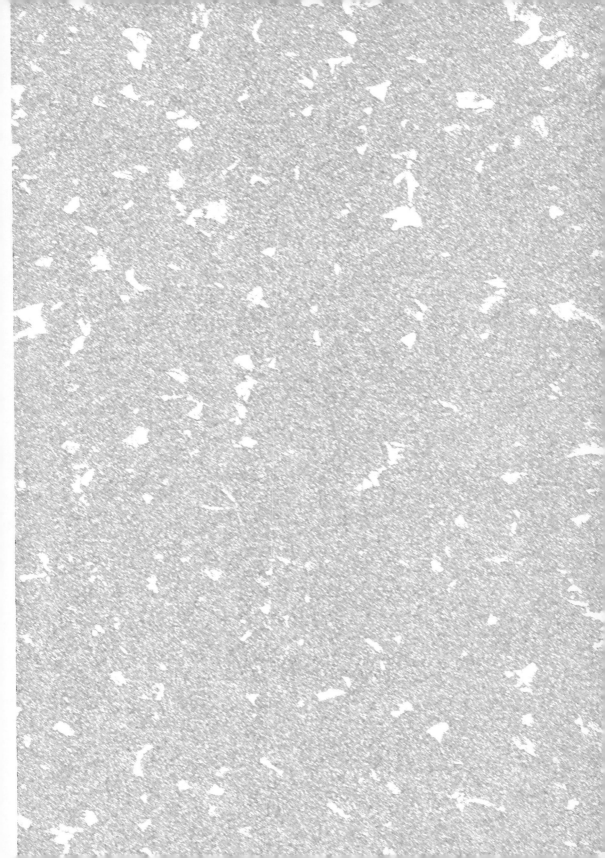

Chapter Six

The Other Side: The Animal Soul

The Animal Soul also has attributes and garments. Its essence is the ego and self-importance, which separate us from G-d.

(Tanya, chap. 6)

The *Tanya*'s initial chapters deal primarily with the G-dly Soul. The G-dly Soul's essence is to be fundamentally unified with G-d. Its attributes (the structure of the soul and the ten *sefirot*) and its garments (Torah and *mitzvot* observance in thought, speech, and deed) are the ways in which the G-dly Soul becomes united with holiness and G-dliness.

Now we will move on and take a look at the Animal Soul. Here, too, we will explore its essence, attributes, and garments.

The Animal Soul-Its Essence

The Animal Soul's negative nature starts long before its attributes and garments. It's part of its essence. In other words, the Animal Soul isn't associated with the opposite of holiness only because its attributes and garments get used in unholy ways. Rather, its problematic nature derives from the very fact that it exists, and that it experiences that existence as something separate from the Creator.

Simply put, the source of a person's spiritual conflicts is that he sees himself as the center of the world, believes he is the most important element, and feels exalted above others. From this point come all the rest of a person's negative traits and the start of his separation from G-d.

The Test of Smell

A story is told of a scholarly Jew who lived in the times of the Baal Shem Tov. He studied Torah constantly and devoted his life to serving G-d. One day, he overheard people talking about the Baal Shem Tov, how he was a great Tzaddik who performed miracles.

I think I'll go meet him and learn more about him, the scholar decided.

During the trip, he began to wonder, How will I know whether or not the Baal Shem Tov is truly a Tzaddik? Torah knowledge can be tested with questions, but how do you determine if someone has Divine inspiration?

Finally, he decided that he would accept the Baal Shem Tov if he could "smell" and sense that he was a learned Jew whose life was dedicated to serving G-d. If he couldn't, then he was probably not a Tzaddik.

The scholarly Jew arrived at the Baal Shem Tov's home and knocked on the door.

"Who's there?" asked the Baal Shem Tov.

"Me," the Jew replied.

The Jew's response prompted the Baal Shem Tov to quote a verse from the Torah: " 'Can a man hide in a hiding place and I will not see him?' says G-d."

The Jew immediately understood what the Baal Shem Tov meant.

The simple meaning of the verse is that G-d asks this question to tell us that it's impossible to hide from Him. "Do you really think you can hide from Me and I won't see you?"

But the Baal Shem Tov offered a different way to read and interpret the verse: "'If a man will hide in a hiding place as 'I-I will not see him,' says G-d."

One who conceals himself and has an "ani," an "I," regarding such a person G-d says, "He is not seen."

The Jew grasped what the Baal Shem Tov was saying to him: when a person's "I," or ego, is the most important thing in his life, then even if he leads a religious life devoted to prayer and Torah study, it remains unsure if he's truly connected to the realm of holiness. He's serving himself, not G-d. It's as if he is arrogantly "hiding" from the world behind his religious observances.

Without even opening the door, the Baal Shem Tov had interpreted *this verse to precisely sum up the scholar's state of personal growth and Divine service, teaching him that ego and arrogance renders one invisible to G-d.*

The Baal Shem Tov's keen "sense of smell" was so apparent, he had perceived his guest more accurately than the Jew had assessed himself!

The Jew stayed on with the Baal Shem Tov and become his devoted Chassid.

After a year of learning, growth, and renewed effort to improve his service to G-d, they read the verse together again: "'If a man hides in a hiding place and "I am not"-I will see him,' says G-d." When a person is in a state of "I am not"-i.e., humility and ego nullification-then he is seen by G-d.

It takes hard work and effort to draw holiness into our lives and truly absorb it. In many areas of life, we need to push aside what we want and dedicate ourselves to what G-d wants. The realm of holiness follows the principle "By the sweat of your brow will you eat bread"- meaning that it takes hard work and effort to earn "profits." Nothing is given out for free.

This is why we are usually suspicious of anything that's obtained easily, without effort. As our Sages said, "If someone claims he obtained his goal, yet he did not work hard for it-do not believe him. But if he says he worked hard and he achieved his goal-believe him."

Rotten Traits (For the Most Part...)

Because the Animal Soul perceives itself as an independent entity that's separate from G-d, its emotional traits are also twisted and distorted. These traits can be classified into four categories, each aligned with one of the four elements:

The element of fire in the Animal Soul is the source of our anger and pride. Both a flame and an arrogant person constantly reach upward-pride is a person's efforts to raise himself above others. And both a flame and an angry person burn red hot. Furthermore, pride and anger are connected in that pride leads to anger. A person who feels he is above others is often angry, since he perceives everything done by those around him as being directed against him.

The element of water in the Animal Soul generates cravings and desires for pleasure. Water aids the growth of many pleasurable things (such as food).

The element of wind in the Animal Soul produces foolishness, mockery, ridicule, boasting, and idle chatter. They are all connected to the element of air since they represent a person "making hot air" that lacks real, tangible content.

The element of earth in the Animal Soul leads to laziness and depression. As the heaviest of the four elements, the element of earth drags us downward. Similarly, laziness is when we are physically being dragged down, while depression is akin to being spiritually and mentally dragged down. These two traits are also connected, exerting a negative influence on each other. A lazy, fatigued person is on the path to depression, and sometimes a depressed person becomes fatigued and lazy.

But don't give up! It's not as bad as it seems. Our Animal Soul also has good traits, such as compassion, bashfulness, and a desire to be helpful to others. Let's learn more.

The Attributes of the Animal Soul

G-d created all things with a counterbalance. In other words, everything you find in the realm of holiness has its parallel in the other side.

Just as we started our discussion of the G-dly Soul by analyzing its essential nature, and then we moved on to its attributes, so too will we approach the Animal Soul. Now that we've touched on its essence, let's analyze its attributes.

The Animal Soul also has ten attributes that subdivide into two groups: intellect and emotions.

The intellectual attributes are *Chochmah* (wisdom), *Binah* (insight), and *Da'at* (knowledge). And the emotional attributes include *Chesed* (kindness), *Gevurah* (severity or restraint), *Tiferet* (beauty or mercy), *Netzach* (victory), *Hod* (surrender), *Yesod* (foundation), and *Malchut* (kingship or royalty).

In the Animal Soul, however, these powers have a different focus than the G-dly Soul.

Chochmah, in the realm of holiness, leads a person to humility and modesty. But in the realm of *kelipah* (concealment that covers up the G-dliness and holiness in the world), *Chochmah* leads to the very opposite: arrogance, ego, and an overblown sense of self-importance.

The more a person studies Torah and uses his *Chochmah* for holy purposes, the greater will be his humility before G-d. As he grows in understanding, he comprehends better just how small and insignificant he is in comparison to G-d. He is able to more easily push aside his own opinions and desires in favor of G-d's. On the other hand, when a person studies other kinds of wisdom and uses his Animal Soul's *Chochmah*, the more he learns, the more pride and arrogance he feels.

The emotional traits work in a similar way. For example, *Chesed* in the realm of holiness is expressed in one's love for G-d and giving to others. But in the realm of *kelipah* and impurity, *Chesed* is expressed in a love for material pleasures. This perversion of holiness is also found with the other emotional traits of *Gevurah*, *Tiferet*, *Netzach*, *Hod*, *Yesod*, and *Malchut*.

The biggest difference between the structures of the two souls is that the intellect draws out and directs the emotions in the G-dly Soul-the mind rules the heart. In the Animal Soul, the emotions dominate the intellect and use it to justify and validate its cravings and passions.

Moreover, the Animal Soul's cravings are in accordance with the level of one's intellect. For example, children have less developed intellects and tend to be attracted to simpler pleasures, like candy, treats, and toys. When the child grows up and his intellect develops, he is attracted to more sophisticated pleasures: money, cars, honor, etc. Children want toy motorcycles. and young adults want real motorcycles. The trait is the same, but gets directed toward different things as the intellect matures and develops.

The Garments of the Animal Soul

The two souls also parallel each other in the realm of the garments. They both have thoughts, speech, and actions, but only the G-dly Soul's garments are in Torah and *mitzvot*. By putting its attributes into its holy garments, the G-dly Soul becomes united with G-d.

The Animal Soul works similarly: by inserting its attributes into its garments-anger, arrogance, or cravings in thought, speech, or action- it becomes connected to the realm of impurity, known as the "*sitra achra*," the Other Side.

The Other Side

People generally believe that we are always found in one of three possible states:

1. Connected to the Creator when our G-dly Soul's attributes are invested into Torah and *mitzvot* through thoughts, words, and actions.

2. Connected to the Other Side when our Animal Soul's attributes are expressed in forbidden thoughts, speech, and actions. (This is why doing something forbidden is called an "*aveirah*"-because we *ma'avir*, or "transfer," our capacity for holiness to the Other Side.)

3. Connected to neither G-d nor the Other Side when we are engaged

in "neutral" activities that don't qualify as a *mitzvah* or a sin-a kind of middle ground.

Kabbalah and *Chassidut* see it differently.

There are only two options: we are either connected to holiness or it's opposite. There is no middle ground! Doing G-d's *ratzon*-will-unites us with the realm of holiness. *Anything else* attaches us to *kelipah* and spiritual impurity.

Making Room for G-d

Although G-d is everywhere, when we say that something is holy, it means that G-d's presence is found there in a revealed, conscious manner. And that only occurs in those things that are self-nullified and dedicated to Him.

In other words, by transcending one's desires and instead fulfilling what G-d wants, space is made for G-d to dwell and be present.

Pride, arrogance, and an overemphasized sense of self prevent G-dly revelation from occurring. Sense of self and holiness are in opposition, and arrogance pushes away G-d's revealed presence. This is why a person would do well to stay far away from false humility.

A yeshivah student reached marriageable age. He was considered a learned student from a respected family, and he arrogantly looked down on all the matches that were suggested to him. They are not on my level, he thought.

The head of his yeshivah saw that the student's perspective was twisted by his arrogance. He decided to send him away to a yeshivah where they focused on learning the "Gateway of Modesty," in the hope that this would lessen his ego.

After a year of study, he returned and was offered the last proposal made to him before he left.

Turning to the matchmaker, the young man said, "A year ago, when

I was a learned student, a Talmud scholar from a well-to-do family, you offered me this match and I turned it down. And now that I have all these qualities as well as modesty-do you really think I would be interested?"

With our ego in check, we can dwell on the side of holiness. But when we are filled with self-importance, we are pushed over to the Other Side and G-d's presence moves away.

Shechintah Begaluta-the Secret of G-d's Presence in Exile

How can it be that G-d created something that opposes Him and refuses to be self-nullified before Him?

Since G-d is everywhere, how can parts of creation not do His will, or even do the opposite of what He wants? Why would G-d sustain something that rebels against Him?

The answer is simple. G-d is indeed everywhere, and it is He who gives life to everything in creation. But G-d's reality is concealed and undetected. The vitality He provides is deeply buried under layers of concealing *kelipot*, so that it is undetected by an outside observer. When we observe creation, especially those entities that oppose G-d's will, we do not see how G-d is giving them life. Even we ourselves do not feel how G-d is giving us life and vitality at every moment and how without Him we would not exist.

The *Zohar* explains that those creations that nullify themselves before the Creator receive their vitality from Him directly. It's compared to a person giving a beloved friend a gift with all his heart, face to face, with a big smile. On the other hand, those who oppose and rebel against Him receive their vitality indirectly, "in an offhanded way."

When you have to give something to someone against your will, it's done with resentment, without any joy or willingness, tossed to the person without looking at him. Or if someone needs to pay a traffic ticket-he'll do it because he has to, but he waits until the last possible date and throws in a few nasty words to the clerk. Similarly, creations who do not nullify themselves to G-d receive vitality indirectly, in a more concealed and hidden way.

The World of *Kelipot*

Our world is called a "world of *kelipot*" and the "Other Side"-a place in which the wicked thrive and dominate.

The reason that the wicked dominate is because G-d is concealed and undetected in our world. As a result, it's possible to feel as if there is no G-d at all, G-d forbid. People come to believe that there is no justice and no Judge, and naturally it's acceptable to take care of my needs even at another's expense. Sometimes this is subtle: choosing to benefit myself and not others where they aren't hurt by my actions. Sometimes it's more blatant-such as when a person is ready to hurt others to fulfill his own selfish desires.

G-d created a system in which the world appears to be independent so that we could have free choice. If G-d's presence were revealed and known to all, we would undoubtedly nullify ourselves before Him and constantly fulfill His will (as will happen in the future *geulah*, with the coming of Mashiach). However, in this event, we would be lacking the quality of free choice-of actions performed out of our own conscious decision-making.

For this reason, G-d created a world that conceals His presence. We then have the free choice to decide to serve G-d or rebel against Him, and be rewarded accordingly.

In Conclusion

After learning about the G-dly Soul, we began to learn about the Animal Soul. We discussed its essential nature (ego and the importance of its nullification), its attributes (intellect and emotion), and its garments (thoughts, speech, and deeds that can oppose G-d's will).

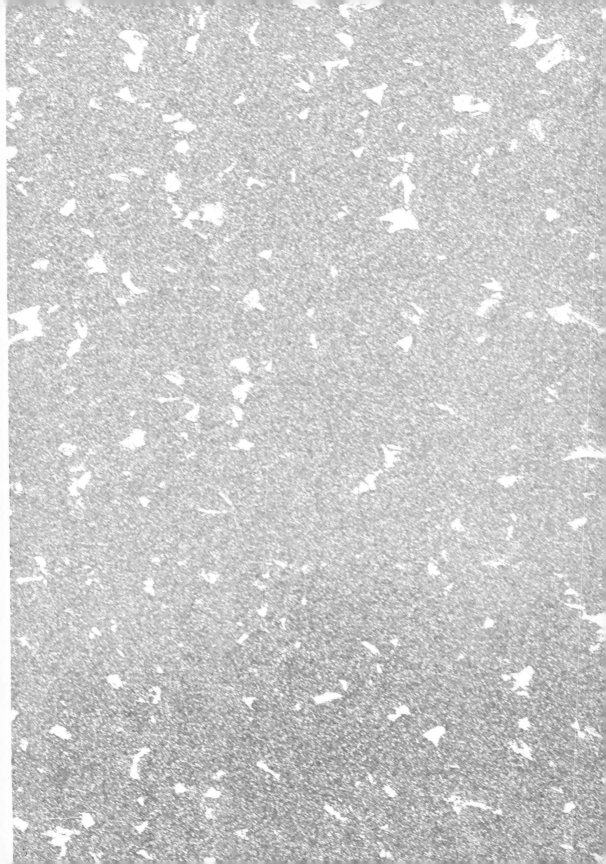

Chapter Seven

Forbidden or Permitted?

Kedushah, kelipat nogah, three impure *kelipot:* how things are elevated to the realm of *kedushah.*

(Tanya, chaps. 7–8)

Is Judaism a religion or a tradition?

Neither.

The Creator of the world gave us-His creations-a way to connect to Him, unite with the truth, rise above the material world, and be freed from the limitations of daily life. This path contains 613 channels, called *mitzvot*, and we try to fulfill as many of them as possible.

In order to connect with these channels properly and to understand what each one accomplishes, we learn about the Torah's inner dimension by studying the secrets of the Torah. On this level of study, the inner dimension of creation is revealed, identified, and discussed.

In this chapter, we will not only explore how a person can connect with G-d through the *mitzvot*, but even through the mundane activities of daily life.

Values: An Objective View

Generally speaking, our sense of good and bad is based on our world perspective, which is influenced by our education, the values we learned from parents and friends, the culture we live in, and our nature. In other words, our sense of good and bad is highly subjective.

It is likely (and quite probable) that if we were born in a different country with a different mentality, we would have different values. How then can we acquire an objective view, where our view of good is truly good and what we think is bad is objectively bad?

In the previous chapter, we presented an interesting tool for distinguishing between good and evil. We began discussing a way in which we could see the world objectively, as the Creator of the world sees it.

Let's develop this idea further.

The View from on High

When the Creator created the world, He infused everything with energy and Divine light. This light is what gives creation its life force and strength.

However, not all created beings are the same-they differ in the quantity and quality of light they contain. In some, the light is more revealed and perceptible, while in others it is so intensely hidden that it seems to be nonexistent. Sometimes the concealment is so great that a person could think that the world has no G-dly light, that the world functions according to nature, isn't being guided, and didn't need to be created since it always existed.

Kedushah and *Kelipah*

This state of concealment, where the G-dly light and life force is hidden and disguised deep within each creation, is called *"kelipah"* (literally, "peel") in the teachings of *Kabbalah*. Just as a fruit is comprised of the fruit itself and the skin or peel that covers it, so does the world contain Divine light and the material world that obscures it.

The question is, how intense and strong is the concealment, and is it possible to reveal the light?

There is no concealment in things that are holy (i.e., *mitzvot*) since they are the direct will of G-d. The physical objects that we use in order to perform a *mitzvah* get their vitality directly from G-d. Similarly, the energy we use to perform a *mitzvah* also comes directly from G-d.

This is why (as explained in chapter 4) a direct connection is formed with G-d while we are doing a *mitzvah*. We don't always immediately feel this connection, since the world is, after all, full of concealment, but this is what is happening. The more we can tune in to this, the more we become refined and spiritually sensitive.

On the other hand, objects used in doing a sin-such as non-kosher foods and prohibited acts (i.e., when transgressing negative commandments)-receive their vitality through *kelipah*. And since the inner vitality of *kelipah* energy is totally and completely concealed, it can't be used to connect to G-d. Not only are transgressions unable to connect us to G-d, they actually sever the connection-as discussed in the previous chapter.

What about Everything In-Between?

What about something that isn't a *mitzvah* or an *aveirah* (sin), such as going to work to make a living, studying secular subjects, traveling, sleeping, or just relaxing. Ordinary life. Most of the time, in fact, it seems that we aren't directly involved in doing *mitzvot* or committing sins. What happens then?

To answer this, we need to broaden our explanation of *kelipah*.

Four Kinds of Peel

From a verse in *Yechezkel* 1:4-"And I looked and behold, a stormy wind came out of the north, a great cloud, a burst of flame, and a glistening around it"-we learn that there are four kinds of *kelipah*: "a stormy wind," "a great cloud," "a burst of flame," and "a glistening."

These four *kelipot* subdivide into two main groups: a lower level and a higher level. The lower level of *kelipah* (which are referred to as "a stormy wind," "a great cloud," and "a burst of flame") is called "the three impure *kelipot*," and they are responsible for infusing vitality into all forbidden things.

The remaining *kelipah* ("a glistening") is called "*kelipat nogah*," and it is responsible for infusing vitality into all permitted things-meaning, anything that isn't forbidden or a *mitzvah*.

The Choice Is in Our Hands

When we use a "neutral" item in an elevated way-meaning *lishmah*, "for the sake of Heaven"-we have discovered its inner goodness and potential to be used in our service of G-d. We have then extracted it from the *kelipah* and elevated it to *kedushah*. Examples include eating in order to have the strength to pray, sleeping or relaxing in order to concentrate better when learning Torah, and exercising to have increased stamina for doing *mitzvot*.

On the other hand, if we use neutral, permitted activities only for our personal pleasure-even for something as necessary as health, yet with no higher purpose in mind-then not only is the item not elevated to *kedushah*, but we lower it and ourselves into *kelipah*.

In other words, both the permitted object that was not used for the sake of Heaven and our own soul that performed the action are lowered into *kelipah*. Instead of the soul becoming a vehicle of G-dly connectivity, it disconnects from Him and is bound with the Other Side.

Back to Values

Based on the above-mentioned concept, we can now better understand the difference between objective and subjective values.

There is the way *we* see the world and the way *G-d* sees the world. There are things that appear to us as very proper and beautiful, but from G-d's point of view they get their vitality from *kelipah* and are devoid of good. Of course, we don't mean that they completely lack good, but rather that the good they possess, their G-dly spark, is tremendously concealed. And, as we will soon explain, this is why they are called "*asur*" (forbidden), a word that also means "bound" or "tied up" since there is no way to access and release the spark of good it possesses.

Judaism, Torah, and *Kabbalah* all provide us with the tools to identify which things receive their vitality from *kedushah* and which from *kelipah*. Based on that information, we can know how to interact with various aspects and elements in the world. The Torah gives us an objective view of the world-life from G-d's perspective.

Two Ways of Looking at It

You can look at this reality in a negative light: "Really? No more freedom and relaxation? I can't do anything for me or just for fun anymore, only *mitzvot* all day?"

Or, you can see it positively: "G-d is everywhere and always with us, and life is completely infused with meaning and spiritual significance. Everything we do throughout the day offers us an amazing opportunity to connect to the ultimate reality-G-d."

With holy things (i.e., *mitzvot*), the connection is direct. For things associated with *kelipat nogah* (i.e., permitted things), the connection depends on whether the action being done is "for the sake of Heaven"-for some holy and higher purpose. And those things that are connected with the three impure *kelipot* (i.e., forbidden things), they connect us to G-d when we *abstain* from them.

Practical Examples

Kosher food comes from *kelipat nogah*. When I eat for a holy purpose and "for the sake of Heaven"-to use the strength derived from the food in order to serve G-d-the food moves into the realm of *kedushah*. But if I eat for my own personal pleasure, without any thought of using it for some holy purpose, then the food and I both go down into *kelipah*.

This applies to any of our mundane activities-work, daily chores, relationships, parenting. Whatever we do, the question to be asked is the same: how can I infuse this activity with a higher purpose? Am I doing this act due to selfish, pleasure-seeking ego or out of service to others, humility, and a desire to draw closer to G-d?

Repair Service

Is it possible to fix mistakes when we miss the opportunity to elevate a mundane activity (*kelipat nogah*), when we did things out of self-serving ego desires? Does the activity fall into *kelipah* forever or is it redeemable?

Yes! Never give up! The minute you regret what happened and firmly decide to never repeat it, both you and the behavior you did come out of *kelipah*. This is called *teshuvah*.

But what happens when you try to extract the G-dly spark that's locked into a forbidden thing from the three impure *kelipot*? For example, is it possible to elevate non-kosher meat by reciting a blessing and eating it with the intention of using the energy in order to pray and study Torah? And then you even follow through and pray and study. Does this elevate it or not?

No. Such natural, basic methods are unable to extract and elevate these sparks because the G-dly spark within an item whose vitality comes from the three impure *kelipot* is inaccessible-even if you practice all the holy intentions in the world.

It could even be that the spark within a forbidden item is greater than the spark in a permitted item. Nevertheless, it is *asur*-"tied down" so strongly that it cannot be released. On the other hand, in permitted things the spark is *mutar*- unbound from restraints. As a result, it can be elevated to *kedushah* with properly intended usage. And, as mentioned, even improper intentions when using permitted things are fixable.

This is the natural order of things. However, Jews transcend nature and they can even mend things from the three impure *kelipot*. How? Through *teshuvah me'ahavah*-repentance motivated by great love for G-d.

When we come to deeply and sincerely regret our misdeed as a result of sincere introspection, a true understanding of the severity of our transgression, and a sincere desire to improve and change, our transgressions are transformed into merits.

This is a very lofty level that is difficult to achieve. In the vast majority of cases, the *teshuvah* a person does is not of such a lofty nature. Rather, it's regular *teshuvah* whose main accomplishment is disconnection from the sinful deeds and a firm resolution to never repeat them again.

Regarding the loftier level of *teshuvah*, the *Talmud* tells us, "*Ba'alei teshuvah* (repentant returnees) are on a higher level than the righteous." The righteous can't elevate Divine sparks from the three impure *kelipot,* because they never engaged with such things. *Ba'alei teshuvah,* on the other hand, can even extract a spark from the three impure *kelipot.*

How Can a Negative Deed Become Positive?

How does a sin transform into a merit? To explain as simply as possible, it is the distress caused by the sin that motivated the person to do *teshuvah* that brings this about.

If he never did the sin, then he never would have felt distant from G-d and would have nothing to regret or feel pained about. The very fact that he transgressed is what caused him to feel deeply broken and sorrowful over what he did. This is the reason he now has a much stronger desire to come closer to G-d.

However, it's very important to clarify that *this does not at all grant permission or justification to go and transgress in order to elevate sparks in the three impure kelipot.* The only reason the sparks can rise to *kedushah* is because of the deep and sincere regret the person feels. Obviously a person who deliberately sins will not feel true remorse. This is why our Sages said, "He who says, I will sin and then repent' cannot do *teshuvah.*" Meaning, one can't "plan ahead" to repent for a sin he is planning to commit.

On the other hand, if a sin was already committed, then now, through deep, heartfelt *teshuvah,* he can extract the spark out of the forbidden and turn sin into merit.

To put it in more modern terms, this approach is like "leveraging" our sins. Instead of allowing them to drag us down and make us feel sad and down about ourselves, we use them to arouse our deepest, innermost spiritual strength to return to G-d with all our might—transforming the negative into something eternally positive.

Gaining by Missing Yom Kippur

A young woman visited a Chabad center in the evening after the conclusion of Yom Kippur. "I'm here to spend Yom Kippur with you," she stated.

"I'm not religious," she continued, "but I've never missed fasting on Yom Kippur. It's very important to me."

The rabbi didn't know how to tell her the truth. She was traveling, and she'd obviously miscalculated. The fast was over. She had just missed Yom Kippur!

He had no choice. The rabbi informed her that Yom Kippur had just ended and she no longer needed to fast.

The young woman was totally shocked. Deeply pained by her mistake, she experienced such utter remorse, more than she'd ever felt on any Yom Kippur when she'd fasted and regretted her deeds from the previous year.

Motivated specifically from this deep sorrow, she committed herself to learn, mend her ways, and come closer to G-d.

Missing one Yom Kippur was the impetus that caused her to do complete teshuvah.

In Conclusion

The awareness that G-d is constantly with us wherever we go should fill our lives with joy. We are not alone. He is accompanying us, looking out for us at every moment, and loving us without limit.

He created a spiritual reality that follows certain spiritual rules for life, enabling us at every moment to draw closer to Him. When we learn the revealed dimension of the Torah (*Chumash, Talmud, Mishnah, halachah*), we gain an understanding of what is forbidden and what is permitted, but not the deeper meaning of why.

By learning the Torah's inner dimension of *Kabbalah* and *Chassidut*-especially the *Tanya*-a person can begin to understand some of what happens in the world "behind the scenes": why some things are forbidden and other things are permitted and what are the consequences, the impact, of a *mitzvah* or a transgression.

Exploring some of the differences between *kedushah* and *kelipah* helps us gain a deeper understanding of how G-d sees the world. And then we can begin to make G-d's perspective a part of our life.

Chapter Eight

The Battle

The goal and desire of each soul is to win the battle;
the question is, What is considered a victory?

(Tanya, chap. 9)

Disguises

Until now, our discussion has focused on helping us learn how to navigate our internal spiritual system by gaining an understanding of the ways in which our two souls function and interact.

In addition, knowledge and awareness of this spiritual system increases our ability to identify the two souls and recognize their voices within us. This enables us to more easily identify which thoughts, words, and actions come from which soul.

However, one of the Animal Soul's tactics is to dress up like the G-dly Soul and try to persuade us to follow him. He knows that we won't listen if he presents himself as an animal. So he puts on a big black hat and a serious rabbinical suit in an effort to get our attention.

As such, it's vital that we be more clever than him and hone our ability to "sniff out" such tricks and disguises by discovering who is *really* speaking.

Let's take a look at the battle between the two souls-what they both want to achieve and what they each consider a victory.

Locations

The Animal Soul is located in the left chamber of the heart, and from there it spreads throughout the entire body. Our unrefined, negative traits like anger, lust, and pride are housed there before they rise up to the brain for consideration. Then from there, they are dispersed throughout the body.

The G-dly Soul is located within our brain, and from there it spreads throughout the body, including the right chamber of the heart.

The Animal Soul's efforts therefore start in the heart, with cravings and a strong desire to obtain what it wants. Then it tries to influence our mind, trying to convince us that it's worthwhile to pursue what it desires.

For example, you pass by a bakery and smell the baked goods. Your heart longs for them and persuades the mind that the most logical thing right now is to go inside and buy something delicious. The Animal Soul insists, "I haven't eaten in two hours," and "Who knows when I will pass another bakery?"

The Animal Soul wants *now*.

The opposite occurs with the G-dly Soul: the process starts in the mind. Our contemplation of G-d's greatness and glory arouses within the heart strong feelings of love and great joy over our merit to be connected to Him.

Battle for Control

The body is called a small city. A city can have only one ruler, leader, or king. If there is more than one, they fight with each other until one conquers the city and becomes its sole ruler. Then the ruler gets what he wants: all the city's inhabitants listen and obey only him.

This illustrates what happens with the two souls. They are in battle with each other for control over the body. Each one wants to be the sole ruler.

The G-dly Soul wants to be the sole ruler. Its desire is for all the limbs of the body to fulfill its wishes alone, to be its chariot. What exactly is this "chariot"?

Using more modern imagery, we would compare the chariot to a car. When you drive a car you completely control it. It goes wherever you decide, having no will of its own. The G-dly Soul wants the same: the body moving in accordance with its wishes, totally subservient, like a chariot controlled by the driver.

Besides this level of dedication, the G-dly Soul also wants the body to serve as a garment for its ten attributes and its thoughts, words, and actions. Then the G-dly Soul fills the body with everything it experiences-with all its attributes and garments. This way there's no room for anything else, and foreign attributes and garments are unable to enter the city.

How Does This Happen Practically?

Through contemplation of G-d's greatness, the mind (*Chochmah* and *Binah*) is full of G-dly wisdom and understanding. Further contemplation forges a bond with the conceptual attribute of *Da'at*, which generates the emotions of love and awe in the heart. If done successfully, such contemplation will produce a love like fiery flames-feelings of longing and yearning so intense that one is ready to forgo everything for the Creator.

A love that powerful overflows the heart's right chamber, home of the G-dly Soul, and spreads into the left side, where the Animal Soul resides.

Turn On the Air Conditioning

A simple man was driving an old jalopy on a sweltering hot day. Despite having all the windows open, the driver was still sweating profusely. Then he noticed a new Volvo passing by with all its windows closed.

He wondered, How can it be that the driver isn't hot? Maybe the heat doesn't enter the car if the windows are closed!

So he closed all the windows and naturally it became even hotter.

At the next traffic light, he pulled up to the Volvo and signaled for the driver to open the window.

"Aren't you hot with all the windows closed?" he asked.

"What do you mean? I have the air conditioning on!"

In Hebrew, the word "*avir*," air, is an acronym for *ahavah v'yirah*, love and awe.

Like the driver of the jalopy, we may think that "closing all the windows" will keep the heat out-that we won't have temptations, lusts, or cravings. But it doesn't work. The heat is coming from inside us! Instead, we need to turn on the "air"-*ahavah v'yirah*.

If the right chamber of our heart is full of love and awe, it will spill over into the left chamber and keep the desires and cravings of the Animal Soul in check. Then we can more effectively subdue the Animal Soul's claims for attention. We won't banish darkness by beating it with sticks, but by illuminating it with tons of light-the light of clarity that we shine on the situation with our feelings of love and awe for G-d.

Changing Our Attributes

When the love in the heart's right chamber is very intense, it completely fills the area and spreads automatically to the left chamber. There it encounters lusts and negative character traits and begins transforming them into positive attributes. Love for the world's pleasures becomes transformed into love for G-d.

This is the deeper meaning of the verse "And you shall love the Lord, your G-d, with all your heart," which we say every morning and evening in the *Shema* prayer. It is instructing us that our love of G-d should be "*bechol levavcha*-with all your heart." But the spelling of the word "heart," instead of the grammatically correct "*libcha*" with one letter *bet*, is spelled with two *bets*-"*levavcha*."

In the light of our discussion, the reason for this spelling is clear. The *Shema* is telling us to love G-d with *both* sides of the heart-the G-dly Soul and the Animal Soul. It's not enough that the G-dly Soul, who loves G-d naturally and automatically, has a love of G-d. Our inner Animal Soul should join together with the G-dly Soul, despite its natural inclination toward pleasure seeking, independence, separation, and distance from G-d.

The goal of our struggle is to have both souls "fall in love" with G-d, by investing all our energy and attributes into our relationship with G-d and thereby elevating everything to *kedushah*.

The Nature of Love

The first level of love is compared to fire that continually burns and wishes to grow ever stronger. The next stage of love is loftier: it's compared to water because it indicates pleasure and enjoyment in G-d, studying His Torah, and performing His *mitzvot*.

When I am in one place but wish to go to another, my desire to move is like a burning fire that longs to reach ever higher, lapping at the sky. But when I arrive in that new location, my movements are more like tranquil, cool water as I feel the pleasure of having achieved what I wanted.

This is a much higher level of victory-when the G-dly Soul experiences delight and pleasure from G-dliness. This level of Divine service is more common among the *Tzaddikim* whose joy is continuously in G-d and G-dliness. Nevertheless, even if we have yet to reach such levels, it's still important that we learn to experience pleasure and enjoyment directly from holiness.

Spiritual Pleasure

Achieving this spiritual pleasure is extremely important in striving to develop our service to G-d, because everyone has a natural capacity and desire for experiencing pleasure in life. Although we learned previously that delight from worldly things puts distance between us and the Creator, it's impossible not to express our G-d-given capacity for pleasure.

G-d gave is the desire for pleasure so that we can channel it for G-dly purposes. If we try to forgo all material pleasures cold turkey without replacing them with holy pleasure, we will be left without a way to experience pleasure. Then it's only a matter of time before we fall back into the pursuit of worldly pleasures to satisfy this basic human need.

Therefore, it's essential for everyone to find a way to experience pleasure in the realm of holiness. We can learn to truly enjoy the *mitzvot* we do and the Torah we study, and not just do these things from habit, because we are obligated to do so.

Furthermore, we can take a "neutral" pleasure, like enjoying a spectacular sunset, and use it as an opportunity to thank G-d for the beauty He created. We can say a *brachah* on an apple, and truly thank G-d for all the vitality and sweetness that He implanted in the fruit.

When we succeed at this, our Animal Soul is subjugated to the G-dly Soul, and all of our emotional attributes are directed toward G-d alone. They completely permeate our thoughts, speech, and actions and lead us to learn Torah, perform *mitzvot*, and be involved in good and holy things all the time.

The Animal Soul's Aspirations

The Animal Soul wants the exact opposite.

It also seeks complete control over every part of the body. It also wants its attributes to be invested in the body. And it also wants to have the body as its exclusive chariot. There is no need to go into more detail about this since each of us knows our Animal Soul very well...

But the truth is that deep down the Animal Soul doesn't really want to win. In fact, it's secretly hoping to lose the battle!

The *Zohar* compares this to an old story about a king who had only one son whom he loved very much. Because of his great love, the king commanded his son to stay away from strange women. At some point, though, the king decided to test his son, to see if he was able to obey his command. So he hired a beautiful woman to tempt his son.

Though she understood that the task she was hired for was a test for the king's son, she was secretly hoping that she would fail in her mission. Then the king would be pleased that the prince had succeeded as the king had hoped, resisting temptation and proving he was worthy.

It's important to mention here that this challenge was not just to test the prince, but also to *elevate* him. When we overcome our tests, we rise to higher levels. When we handle life's ups and downs, the very challenges themselves are what propel us to greater heights and levels.

The same thing is true about the Animal Soul. Externally, it appears to be against us, trying to bring us down and take us to unhealthy places. But deep inside, it's on our side. It wants us to say no! It wants us to withstand its temptation. Like the woman hired by the king, the Animal Soul was sent by G-d and knows that his Employer is hoping he fails.

The same thing applies to all worldly matters that seem to oppose us and interfere with our lives. We have to keep in mind that they are *actually in our favor*, rooting for us to withstand the temptation and ignore them.

Even when the other nations of the world seem to be against us, they are actually helping us. Their threats and challenges bring the unity of the Jewish people to greater levels. Their oppression of us brings out more of our inner strength.

Of course, the nations themselves may be unaware of how G-d is using them to fulfill His purpose, and if you ask them why they are inflicting us, they'll offer a different answer. They are unable to sense their inner dimension and truth. They see themselves as "hating" the Jews unequivocally.

Imagine a twist in the aforementioned story of the king: the woman hired to tempt the prince sends someone else in her place, but doesn't reveal the secret. This second servant has no idea that she is acting as an emissary of the king, even though the first woman knows.

The same thing applies to our Animal Soul. On the surface, it appears that the Animal Soul is our enemy and, in fact, in some areas of life it truly feels that way. But in its inner essence, it knows its real mission.

Even the Animal Soul Wants Us to Withstand Its Temptation

A European Jew who started growing in his Judaism, becoming more Torah observant, became a regular visitor at a local Chabad center. But despite the fact that he was keeping Shabbat and putting on tefillin regularly, he was still planning to marry his non-Jewish girlfriend.

The rabbi and congregants at the Chabad center were at a loss over what to say to him. They were reluctant to challenge him directly since he had only just begun to be more observant and did not understand what was at stake. They were unsure of how he would react and didn't want to alienate him.

When he heard that the rabbi would soon be leaving to visit the Lubavitcher Rebbe in Brooklyn, he said, "I'd like to come with you and ask the Rebbe for a blessing for my marriage."

They arrived on a Sunday, when the Rebbe was distributing dollars for charity. When he finally reached his turn in line, he told the Rebbe of his plans to marry his non-Jewish girlfriend.

To his shock, the Rebbe said, "I envy you."

He hadn't expected such a response and didn't know how to react. He had thought the Rebbe would try to convince him not to intermarry, lecturing him on the importance of being Jewish and preserving his heritage.

Instead, the Rebbe had said that he envied him!

The Rebbe went on to explain that coming closer to G-d is like climbing a ladder, and every test in our lives is like another rung on the way up. The greater the test, the higher the rung-and to face a test as great as this, with such incredible potential to bring him closer to G-d, was enviable.

The Rebbe was showing this man that he was facing a difficult choice. G-d had orchestrated his entire situation as a test so that he would withstand it and ascend far higher.

We have to look at our Animal Soul's purpose in the world in the same way. It was given to us for a reason: to give us challenges that we will need to overcome so we can ascend higher.

In Conclusion

Each of our souls wants total and complete control. Neither is willing to settle for anything less, and a 50-50 split is out of the question. We have to get to know each of our team players very well to ensure that the G-dly Soul is always victorious.

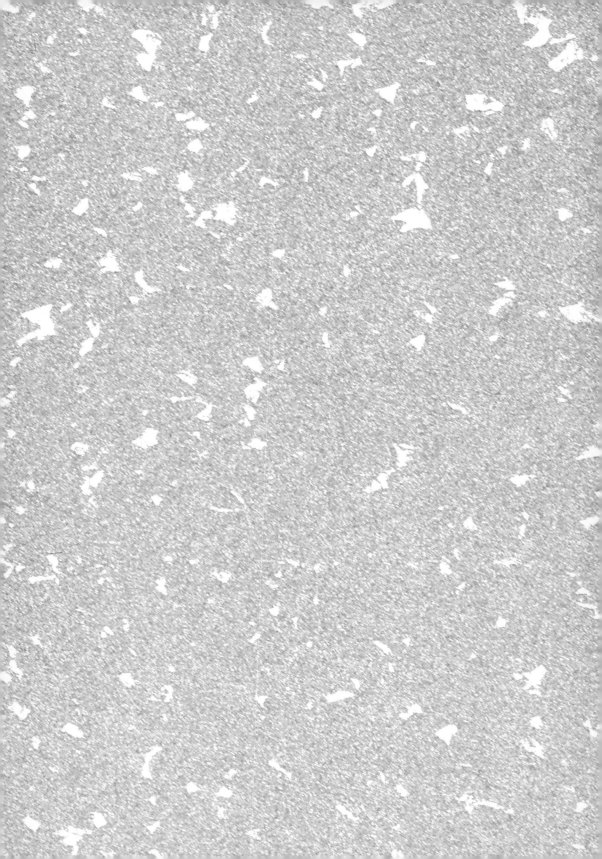

Chapter Nine

The Tzaddik

A Tzaddik is one who has mastered his inner world
by eradicating his personal evil inclination.

(Tanya, chap. 10)

Eliezer was a Torah scholar who studied day and night. Once, he met a Chassid of the Alter Rebbe and they began studying Chassidut together. He was so impressed by what he learned that he decided to devote his life to learning Chassidut.

"Where can I study this?" he asked. The Chassid told him he could go to the Alter Rebbe and learn with him.

The Chassid went to devote his life to studying Chassidut and following the lifestyle it prescribes. He was willing to forego everything for this.

After a few years of learning Chassidut with the Alter Rebbe, he was asked, "What answers do you find here that you never found before? What was it that attracted you so much?"

Eliezer replied, "I used to study Torah day and night, and I would say to myself, 'Reb Leizer! You are a great Tzaddik and scholar, always involved in Torah and mitzvot. How can G-d make a Heaven big enough for you?' And I would tell myself, 'G-d is infinite and surely He can make it happen.'

"Now, after studying the inner dimension of Torah, learning about my inner spiritual attributes and my G-dly and Animal Souls, I ask myself a different question: 'Reb Leizer! You are so self-centered and egotistical. Your Torah study is for your own honor and self-aggrandizement. You are far from being selfless. In prayer you constantly think only about yourself-how can G-d even stand you?'

"My question changed, but the answer is the same: 'Since G-d is infinite, surely He can put up with someone like me."

Are there selfless *Tzaddikim*-people who have achieved such high levels of serving G-d? And, a person might wonder, what does this have to do with me?

The answer is that it's very inspiring to see to what levels a human being can rise. By seeing their example, there are certain areas of our lives where we *can* conduct ourselves like a *Tzaddik*, and even more so, we benefit by knowing where we truly stand in the scheme of things-what my true level is and how much greater I can strive to be. Our *Tzaddikim* whom G-d gives us in every generation serve as exceptional role models to inspire us to grow.

A *Tzaddik* Who Suffers, a *Tzaddik* Who Prospers

Many people wonder why bad things happen to good people and why good things happen to "bad" people, also known as the concept of "a *Tzaddik* who suffers" and "a *rasha* who prospers."

But before we discuss this puzzling, important question, let's take a deeper look at the concept of "a *Tzaddik* who suffers" and "a *rasha* who prospers." Instead of examining the level of their actions and deeds, we'll analyze their innermost level, where the two souls engage in a power struggle.

We already explained that our world is one of concealment and *kelipah* that renders G-dliness so undetectable that a person could think there is no law and no Judge, and we can do as we please. The *Tanya* will discuss this issue in greater depth when he explains how darkness dominates the world so that we have the opportunity to turn it into light.

"TZiBuR"-Tzaddikim, Beinonim, and Resha'im

As we learned in chapter 1, the *Tanya* explains that the categories of *Tzaddik*, *beinoni*, and *rasha* can be understood on several different levels. The external level examines action: the *Tzaddik* has good deeds, the *rasha* has wicked deeds, and the *beinoni* has an equal balance of both. On the deeper, more inner level, the concept of *Tzaddik/rasha/beinoni* represents a person's inner world and the state of the struggle between the two souls.

Now that we have completed the *Tanya*'s first nine chapters and know about each of the souls, we can appreciate a deeper perspective on who is a *Tzaddik*, who is a *rasha*, and what's the difference between a *Tzaddik* who suffers and one who prospers.

After the Battle

For the *Tzaddik*, the battle between the two souls is over. The G-dly Soul has completely defeated the Animal Soul and enjoys complete dominion over the body-the "small city."

The right chamber of the *Tzaddik*'s heart has become so full of the G-dly Soul that it has spilled over into the left chamber, and the evil inclination has been evicted. The G-dly Soul has full control over the person, not just his garments of thought, speech, and action (as is the case with the *beinoni*), but even his emotional traits.

For the *beinoni*, the battle is not yet over. Evil is still present in his heart and undesirable thoughts can still show up. Of course, such thoughts are immediately banished; yet they could return. Not so for the *Tzaddik*. Since he has full control over his heart, there is no source from which undesirable thoughts can rise up, rendering impossible the possibility of undesirable words or deeds.

Such a state of affairs is difficult for us to describe, or even imagine, because we have rarely ever met people who have achieved this level. Nevertheless, this is the truth of their reality. Just like a normal, regular person would never think of hijacking a plane, for a *Tzaddik* the idea of violating G-d's will in even the smallest of ways is a completely foreign notion.

Complete *Tzaddik*, Incomplete *Tzaddik*

What is the difference between a *Tzaddik gamur*, a complete *Tzaddik*, and a *Tzaddik she'eino gamur*, an incomplete *Tzaddik*?

Just by looking at the two you can't tell the difference, since it's not something external that's reflected in their actions. Rather, the difference is internal, in their essence. In both of them, the G-dly Soul has defeated and banished the Animal Soul. The difference is, to what extent? Just how dominant is their good, how much of the evil was banished, and how much of the evil still remains buried deep down?

The incomplete *Tzaddik*-also known as the *Tzaddik* who suffers or "*Tzaddik vera lo*," the "*Tzaddik* to whom there is bad"-has banished his personal evil with the exception of a tiny portion that still remains in the left chamber of his heart. The remnant, however, is completely subjugated to the good, which is why he is called a *Tzaddik* who suffers-or, more accurately based on the Hebrew, a "*Tzaddik* to whom there is evil" (i.e., his evil is "to him" or subjugated to his good).

The obvious question here is, how can there be evil that's neither felt nor perceived? If it's right there-how could such a person not feel it and be influenced by it?

Let's take an example from the world of *halachah* (Jewish law) in order to answer this.

The Torah forbids us from eating or cooking milk and meat together. But what happens if you're cooking a large pot of meat and a few drops of milk accidentally spill into it? Is the entire pot now unfit for use?

It depends. You have to determine the proportion of volume between the meat and milk in the pot. If there is sixty times more meat than milk, the amount of milk is considered *batel beshishim* (literally, "nullified in sixty")-i.e., considered insignificant in comparison to the vastly larger amount of meat-and the mixture is permissible. If, however, the ratio is less-i.e., the quantity of milk is greater, and the volume of meat is not sixty times more than the milk-then the entire pot is forbidden.

This standard is not the same for all cases of prohibited items. Some only get canceled in a ratio of 1000 or even 10,000 times more kosher than non-kosher. And then there are some prohibitions that are never nullified (such as the smallest quantity of *chametz*, leaven, that falls into a pot on Passover).

Now, regarding our pot of meat into which fell a few drops of milk that are *batel beshishim*, the milk is still there. Being nullified doesn't mean it disappeared. The milk exists, but its volume is so small that it has no ability to exert any influence on the taste of the meat.

This example also applies to the difference between the "*Tzaddik* to whom there is good" (*Tzaddik vetov lo*) and the "*Tzaddik* to whom there is bad" (*Tzaddik vera lo*). The *Tzaddik vera lo* still has a few drops of evil (like the prohibited substance), but they are nullified by the overwhelming amount of good that he has. The only question is how negligible it is: 60–1, 1000–1, or 10,000–1. But whatever the amount is, it's unable to negatively impact on the good.

Love Good, Despise Evil

With people we see that the more they love something, the more they hate its opposite. For example, the more you love to sleep, the more you hate getting up in the morning.

Both types of *Tzaddik* hate evil and are repelled by *kelipot* since they conceal G-dliness. They differ in that the *Tzaddik vera lo*'s experience of revulsion is not total, complete, absolute, and part of his essence. He despises evil because he knows that G-d despises evil, but not because he truly feels that way in his essence. And this lack is because his love of G-d is not completely part of his essence. Thus, he still has a few drops of evil, and we call him a *Tzaddik she'eino gamur*-an incomplete *Tzaddik*.

The *Tzaddik vetov lo* has done more than *nullify* some remnants of evil to the good. He has actually *transformed* them into good. As a result, he's called a *Tzaddik gamur*, a complete *Tzaddik*, and he's completely free and clear of any evil.

He's also called a *Tzaddik vetov lo* because he is absolutely repulsed by evil. His love for G-d is so great and his unity with G-d is so powerful that he loathes evil because *he himself* feels that way-not just because that's what G-d wants.

This is not the case for the *Tzaddik she'eino gamur* who still has a supertiny, subtle feeling of ego and self-importance. Because he sees the world in one way and knows that G-d sees it differently, he puts on G-dly glasses and adopts G-d's perspective in his conduct and interactions. However, he himself is still not completely connected to this view.

Souls from the World of *Atzilut*

Kabbalah explains that there are four primary spiritual worlds-the highest is *Atzilut* (World of Emanation), then comes *Beriah* (World of Creation) and *Yetzirah* (World of Formation), and the lowest is *Asiyah* (World of Action). *Atzilut* is distinguished from the other three in that it is completely united with G-d. Separation and independence begin in *Beriah*. Nevertheless, despite *Beriah*'s awareness of itself, it is still completely nullified to G-d.

The souls of complete *Tzaddikim* come from *Atzilut*, while the souls of incomplete *Tzaddikim* come from *Beriah*, *Yetzirah*, and *Asiyah*.

Complete *Tzaddikim* bring their *Atzilut* reality with them into their life in the physical world and constantly feel connected to G-d. Incomplete *Tzaddikim*, on the other hand, despite the fact that their inner world is completely dominated by their goodness and holiness since their soul's source is from *Beriah*, *Yetzirah*, or *Asiyah*, they experience some amount of separation. And for this reason, deep inside them in a concealed form they have a remnant of evil that they are unable to completely and totally reject.

People of Ascent

Complete *Tzaddikim* are also called "*bnei aliyah*," people of ascent, because they elevate evil and transform it into good. They turn the darkness itself into light.

Furthermore, this name indicates that their Torah learning and performance of *mitzvot* are not for themselves, or for physical or spiritual gain and pleasure. Rather, it's all completely for G-d.

An incomplete *Tzaddik*'s service still contains a small, tiny measure of self-interest. *He* loves G-d, *he* wants to be one with G-d-yet this is still a personal desire. Granted, it's a holy desire, but his own will and self-interest are present.

The complete *Tzaddik*'s self-nullification to G-d is on a different level. The only thing driving his Divine service of Torah study, prayer, and the performance of *mitzvot* is the desire to do the will of G-d. He's not looking for unity with G-d or even to satiate his soul's thirst for G-d-just G-d's will. He's like a child who does things for his parents. He loves them more than he loves himself and is ready and willing to totally dedicate himself to them.

That's why the complete *Tzaddik*'s Divine service is free from personal interests, ego, or self-importance. He acts without any thought of what others will say about him or what he will gain by it. There's only the act itself. Thus, this is what his life is like consistently, in all areas, constantly and not only at times of prayer and study. His mind is filled with the greatness of G-d, his feelings are of awe and love for G-d, his thoughts, words, and deeds center only on matters of *kedushah*.

Even when he is engaged in mundane matters, it is all for the sake of G-d. He sees holiness in everything around him, in everything he does. His exclusive goal is G-dliness.

The Alter Rebbe was sometimes overheard addressing the Creator and saying, "I don't want Your Heaven. I don't want Your World to Come. I just want You alone." He wasn't looking for spiritual pleasures, gains, or rewards, just the essential connection with G-d.

Eating in Order to Bless

A Jew was once a guest in the home of a Tzaddik. This Jew happened to be very passionate and enthralled with blessings. Every time he recited a blessing, he spoke in a loud voice and with great conviction and concentration.

While he was in the Tzaddik's home, he observed the Tzaddik's conduct carefully and noticed that he made blessings quietly and apparently without much intention. He started to think that perhaps the Tzaddik lacked sufficient intention in his blessings.

Reading his thoughts, the Tzaddik said to him, "Do you know what the difference between us is when we say our blessings? You bless in order to eat, while I eat in order to bless."

For the *Tzaddik gamur*, his entire world revolves around *kedushah* and G-d, and his whole life is one long sequence of doing G-d's will.

In Conclusion

A *Tzaddik* is not merely someone who does a lot of good most of the time, but one whose inner essence has been changed by banishing all personal evil from within him. For the *Tzaddik*, the battle between the souls is over.

This is not the case for most of us, and it's likely that we will never reach such a level. In general, a *Tzaddik* is born with the potential to be a *Tzaddik*, and he receives special assistance and support from Above to achieve it. So why do we bother learning about it when our goal is to become a *beinoni* and not a *Tzaddik*?

The reason is that this helps us understand and appreciate what it means to be a *beinoni*. Moreover, understanding the *Tzaddik* helps us properly locate ourselves on the spectrum and avoid making mistakes about what level we truly are on.

It is written about the famous *Chassid*, Reb Hillel, that when he started learning *Tanya*, he said, "Until now I thought I was a *Tzaddik*. Now I only hope to someday be a *beinoni*."

Chapter Ten

The Rasha

The *rasha's* inner world is dominated by his
evil impulses, even when he isn't transgressing
in his thoughts, speech, or actions.

(Tanya, chap. 11)

A Jew who was not a Chabad Chassid once visited the Lubavitcher Rebbe for a personal meeting. Since he was a Chassid from a different Chassidic group, the Rebbe asked him to share a Torah teaching he had recently heard from his own Rebbe.

"My Rebbe," said the Jew, "discussed the passage in the Talmud that states, 'Every Jew-even a sinner-is full of mitzvot like a pomegranate is full of seeds.' And he asked, 'How can this be? How can a sinner be as full of mitzvot as a pomegranate is full of seeds?'"

"I also learned that Talmudic passage," said the Rebbe, "and I also had a question about it. If this Jew is really as full of mitzvot as a pomegranate, then why does the Talmud call him a 'sinner'?"

Our perspective influences everything. We surely want to judge others favorably. With the boundaries between a *rasha*, *beinoni*, and a *Tzaddik* well defined, we can judge anyone favorably.

Who Is a *Rasha*?

Understood simply, a *rasha* is someone who mostly sins and only does some *mitzvot*. But the *Tanya*'s definition is different: look past the deeds into the inner world. A *rasha* is a person whose G-dly Soul has not triumphed in its struggle against the Animal Soul.

Look into a *Tzaddik*'s heart and you'll see only a G-dly Soul. Look into a *rasha*'s heart and you'll see that his Animal Soul is predominantly overshadowing his G-dly Soul. It's possible that in his garments of thought, speech, and action, the *rasha* has control over himself part of the time, or perhaps even most of the time, and he doesn't sin. However, he is still considered a *rasha* because he *could* have moments of weakness when he commits a sin. For the *rasha*, sin is not completely out of the picture, and in certain situations, he succumbs.

This definition of *rasha* is very extreme. It means that a person could do good things most of the time and almost never commit sins, yet the *Tanya* defines him as a *rasha*. Why? Because there still remains the possibility that he will give in to his evil inclination.

Rasha Vetov Lo, Rasha Vera Lo

Just as there are two levels of *Tzaddik*, so there are two levels of *rasha*. The *rasha vetov lo*, the "*rasha* to whom there is good," is mostly evil, but within him is a bit of good, and therefore he still has the ability to defeat his evil inclination. And indeed he may defeat it most of the time. However, he lacks the spiritual sensitivity to realize that a sin is completely out of the question, and he has not completely nullified his will before G-d.

The *rasha vetov lo* hasn't made the firm resolution to take upon himself the yoke of Heaven and dedicate himself wholly to G-d. Thus his G-dly Soul is limited in its ability to have the upper hand. But once he sins (as a result of his inner evil inclination), he regrets it, makes amends, and tries to changes his ways.

It's a different story with the *rasha vera lo*, the "*rasha* to whom there is bad." He is completely unfazed by sin, doesn't feel it is wrong, and finds no reason to feel regret for his actions. In other words, there is no good in him (just like the *Tzaddik vetov lo* has no bad).

When we say, "There is no good in him," we mean that he doesn't feel or sense it. He still has a G-dly Soul, but he's not consciously aware of its presence. He is still considered a Jew despite the fact that he's a *rasha*, as our Sages have said, "A Jew, even though he sins, is still a Jew" (*Sanhedrin* 44a).

A Jew is always a Jew-he can still complete a *minyan*. Therefore, he should still do any *mitzvah* that he can, for each one counts significantly.

And he can still regret his misdeeds and improve his ways in order to connect with G-d on a deep, inner level. In other words, he can still do *teshuvah*.

We Have Sinned, We have Betrayed

One of the Alter Rebbe's Chassidim shared why he became a Chassid.

"When I was young, I learned in a yeshivah where the Torah's inner dimension was not studied. Every night, when I recited the bedtime Shema-the last prayer of the day when we make a spiritual accounting of what we did that day-and I reached the part where we say, 'We have sinned, we have betrayed...,' I would say to myself that since I hadn't truly 'sinned' or 'betrayed,' it must be referring to someone else who had done these things.

"But one day, I realized that this approach couldn't be correct. How could the prayer book say, 'We have sinned,' and be referring to someone else? This question was the catalyst that started me on my spiritual journey in search of an answer.

"I went to several yeshivot but could not find one.

"At one point in my travels, I arrived at a yeshivah that studied the teachings of the Baal Shem Tov. That's where I heard the teaching that the world is like a mirror that reflects our selves back to us. I learned that what we see in others is really a reflection of what is inside of us. When we see something bad in someone else, or someone sinning, it's a sign that this also exists within us.

"I immediately realized that by seeing others as sinners, it was really me who had sinned!

"But later on, when I was saying the bedtime Shema, I thought, What have I actually done that was wrong? I have not committed serious sins like murder or theft. There are just a few small things I've done that are far and few between.

"And so I began to say, 'We have sinned, we have betrayed...' while thinking, I have not sinned, and I have not betrayed...

"More time went by, and once again I came to the conclusion that my approach was incorrect. Again I started to search for the answer. My travels brought me to a different Chassidic group, and I learned from them that every sin, great or small, separates a person from G-d and transfers his vitality to the Other Side. Therefore, we need to repent equally for the smallest sin as we do for the greatest.

"After hearing this, I would say, 'We have sinned, we have betrayed...,' with all my heart, since it applied to both big and small sins.

"But with the passage of time I started to reconsider and wondered, What about tomorrow? Will I just do the same sins again that I am repenting for today? What is the point of feeling regret and doing teshuvah? I don't see how I can ever change.

"Finally, one of my travels brought me to the Alter Rebbe's court, where I began to study Tanya. Only then did I begin to understand and see the true meaning of teshuvah.

"I finally understood the incredible power I had to completely change. Teshuvah was more than just feeling regret over the past. It involved making solid resolutions that the future would be different."

In Conclusion

The *rasha* doesn't view sins and evil as completely forbidden territory, and he may occasionally transgress. The *rasha vetov lo* regrets his sins and does *teshuvah*, while the *rasha vera lo* has crossed the line to the Other Side and doesn't even feel regret. Still, a Jew is a Jew, and he can always do *teshuvah*.

Chapter Eleven

The Beinoni

The *beinoni* hasn't vanquished his inner evil
like the *Tzaddik*, but he wins every battle with
his Animal Soul and never surrenders.

(Tanya, chaps. 12–17)

The *beinoni* is situated between the *Tzaddik* and the *rasha*-as indicated by the name itself, which means "in-between." He is like a *Tzaddik* in that he *never* does a sin with his garments of thought, speech, and actions. But in his heart, with regard to the souls' attributes, he is like a *rasha* in that he still harbors evil.

The *Beinoni* vs. the *Tzaddik*

But why isn't the *beinoni* called a *Tzaddik* if he's learning Torah, doing *mitzvot* and good deeds, and never sins?

Because, based on what we've learned, the category of *Tzaddik* relates to the status of one's inner world-where only good and holiness are in one's heart. Not only does the *beinoni* still have an evil inclination in his heart, but also, the greater a person is, the greater are the urges with which he must contend. In practice, the *beinoni* is engaged in a constant battle.

The *Beinoni* vs. the *Rasha*

What, then, makes him different from the *rasha*? They both have evil in their hearts and are engrossed in a constant struggle. Even with respect to winning battles, the *rasha vetov lo* wins most of his battles. What inner difference is there between them that justifies elevating the *beinoni* to a completely different classification?

The *beinoni*'s superiority over the *rasha* lies in his *absolute* and *total* nullification before G-d and his acceptance of fully dedicating himself to serving Him (i.e., taking upon himself the yoke of Heaven). Transgressing is a foreign concept that is *completely out of the question*.

The *beinoni* has learned the *Tanya*'s initial chapters very well, perfectly grasping and internalizing the meaning of a *mitzvah* (connection to the Creator) and a sin (disconnection from the Creator). Just as we would never even consider eating poison because it's fatal, so it is clear to the *beinoni* that his soul is of primary importance, connection to G-d is his mission, and even the smallest transgression is intolerable.

A *beinoni* is not yet a *Tzaddik*, and thus he could be confronted by thoughts of cravings for foods or transgression of some kind. But because it is crystal clear to him that expressing such desires is unacceptable, he immediately rejects the thought. He absolutely refuses to continue considering such things for even a fraction of a second, and surely won't allow it access to his speech and action.

What about Thoughts?

We can't stop thinking or permanently stop the flow of our thoughts, but we can steer them in the right direction.

About sixty years ago, a Jew was riding on a train in Russia when a non-Jew sat next to him and began tormenting him. At one point, he threateningly held up a piece of non-kosher meat and demanded that the Jew eat it.

The Jew naturally refused. But the non-Jew countered by taking out a knife, holding it against the Jew's neck, and shouting, "Eat it or I'll kill you!"

The Jew knew that according to the halachah there are prohibitions for which we must die rather than violate them. But eating non-kosher meat was not one of them.

He gave in and agreed to take a bite. When the non-Jew threatened him again, the Jew took another bite.

The non-Jew was satisfied with the Jew's compliance. He stopped his threats and lowered his knife.

Then the Jew turned to him with a request: "Can you put the knife against my neck again? I want another bite."

The *beinoni* can have an inappropriate thought attack (like a knife held to his neck against his will). That's not a problem. The real question is: what happens in the very next moment after he realizes that it is a forbidden thought? The *beinoni* pushes it away immediately. It's clearly forbidden, and he flees from it like a person runs from danger.

The *rasha*, however, is likely to continue entertaining the thought. He might even move it from thoughts to words, and then on to action.

How Do You Do That?

As we explained, the concepts we have discussed here so far need to be thoroughly learned and internalized. It's a start, but it's not enough. Next, we have to get to the point where we make a firm, strong decision to actually do it-to actually put it into practice. Such resolution fills us with the energy, inspiration, and power to proceed and succeed.

This also applies to other areas of life. For example, to succeed at quitting smoking or to start a healthier diet, we have to understand *why* we are doing it-that is, we need the motivation to act. Then we have to make a firm decision to stick it out until the end.

If our resolution is not total, absolute, and unbending, our Animal Soul will always be able to find ways and means to attack and exploit this weak spot. In those areas in which we made a firm and final decision, the Animal Soul doesn't even start up with us. He knows he doesn't stand a chance and we'll never agree with him. Where, then, does he test us and how does he try to drag us down? He goes after those areas where our decision is *not* firm and final.

This also applies to our dealings with other people in our environment. When others see that we are firmly committed to the way we have chosen, they stop trying to persuade us to change.

A Day in the Life of a *Beinoni*

What does a *beinoni*'s day look like?

The *beinoni* is not necessarily a person who learns and prays all day long in the synagogue (although there are such *beinonim*). He could also be a businessperson whose daily routine includes a lot of Jewish content.

Let us see how a Jewish daily routine helps us live with the awareness that "there is nothing but G-d" and the resolution to not disconnect from G-d.

As soon as we wake up, even before we get out of bed, we recite the *"Modeh Ani"* prayer thanking G-d for restoring our souls to us and entrusting us to put it to good use. Then we ritually wash our hands as the *Kohanim* did in the *Beit Hamikdash*-the Holy Temple in Jerusalem-before starting their holy services. This reminds us that we woke up this morning in order to serve G-d (and also removes the spiritual impurity that settled on our hands while we were asleep).

Next, there are fifteen morning blessings in which we thank G-d not only for the soul He restored to us, but also for our body: our strength, our ability to open our eyes, stand up, walk, wear clothes and shoes, etc. If we truly think about what we are saying, and feel tremendous gratitude to G-d for supplying us with all of our needs, we have the gift of these daily reminders to fuel our day with joy.

Before the workday begins, there are morning *tefillot* and a Torah reading in synagogue twice a week. In order to prepare our hearts and minds for prayer, many people first study *Chassidut*-the inner dimension of the Torah. Studying *Chassidut* before prayer, when we stand before the Creator, helps us to recognize and know before Whom we stand.

During the actual prayers, the *beinoni* contemplates G-d's greatness, and this generates feelings of awe and love for Him (as explained in chapter 3). While reciting the *Shema*, we can sense how much we love G-d and want to devote ourselves to Him.

When the morning prayers are powerful and we feel connected to G-d, their potency can be a continual reminder as the day progresses that there is "nothing but G-d."

However, these inspired feelings of closeness can gradually weaken in the course of the day, and the *beinoni* benefits from several built-in "wake-up calls." Every time he sees a *mezuzah*, he recalls the *Shema* prayer, which is written on the parchment inside. This is a constant reminder that G-d's unity fills the universe.

Tzitzit also serve as a reminder, as it says, "And you will see them [the *tzitzit* fringes] and recall all of G-d's *mitzvot* and fulfill them" (*Bemidbar* 15:37). When the *beinoni* eats or drinks anything, saying the *brachot* before and after food can further permeate his awareness that G-d is with him at all times. There is also an inspiring *brachah* recited after using the bathroom, thanking G-d for the miraculous way our bodies function.

The *Beinoni* Harnesses the Power of *Kedushah*

The *beinoni* loves G-d and passionately wants to serve Him with his life, so even a small thought of doing something forbidden that crosses his mind gets immediately rejected. He also knows how to quickly steer his thoughts in the direction of *kedushah* in order to discourage thoughts that arise from his Animal Soul. The power of *kedushah* helps subdue undesirable thoughts, just like light drives away darkness.

This also applies to how he views others. When he realizes that negative thoughts, like hatred or jealousy toward another person, come directly from the Animal Soul, it's easier to banish them immediately.

In Conclusion

The *beinoni*, like the *rasha*, has an evil inclination in his heart. However, it is clear beyond any doubt to the *beinoni* that the evil is indeed evil, and he doesn't allow it to influence his thoughts, words, or actions. Prayer and awareness of G-d's continual presence are his constant companions.

The Second Gate
The Shorter Way
Tanya, Chapters 18-25

Chapter Twelve

The Inheritance

Since every Jew is like G-d's child, they naturally love Him, they are willing to be nullified before Him, and are ready to sacrifice themselves to sanctify His Name.

(Tanya, chaps. 18–19)

When the Alter Rebbe became a Chassidic leader, there was still strong opposition to Chassidut. Once, when he arrived in a city full of Torah scholars, he invited everyone to come to the main synagogue where he could address all their questions about G-d, Torah, and faith.

A large crowd gathered at the set time, and the Alter Rebbe asked everyone present to voice any arguments they had against him. He guaranteed that he would answer every question, and he promised that he wouldn't leave until everyone was satisfied.

And so ensued an evening of intense interaction as the crowd presented every possible question and complexity they had encountered about faith, spirituality, Kabbalah, and Chassidut.

When they finished presenting all their objections, it was time for the Alter Rebbe to respond. He silently ascended the Torah reading platform, gazed out at everyone gathered there, and instead of speaking he began to sing a niggun that came from the depths of his soul, a tune unlimited in its ability to soar heavenward nor bound by the confines of words.

The Alter Rebbe sang with great devotion, reaching a state of deveikut-Divine connection. Soon the entire crowd was singing along with him, each one experiencing the Alter Rebbe's fervor.

After several long minutes of transcendental singing, everyone opened their eyes.

"Do you still have questions?" the Alter Rebbe asked.

No, everything was clear, there were no more questions. Everyone was satisfied, their belief incredibly strengthened. The answers to the arguments seemed clearly in order. He was free to go.

Shortly afterward, as though awakening from a deep sleep, all their questions returned as they returned from their enraptured state. They ran after the Alter Rebbe to find him before he left their city.

"What have you done to us?" they cried. "All our questions have returned!"

The Alter Rebbe answered, "I only wanted to demonstrate to you that the intellect is not the highest part of the soul. There is a higher level. By singing the niggun we came to feel the soul, and when you feel the soul there are no questions."

Hidden Love

In the first section of the *Tanya*, we learned about the *beinoni*, appreciated how high a level this is, and discussed how this level can be reached. The path we mentioned requires intense intellectual effort-mental contemplation so deep that it produces heartfelt feelings that motivate and inspire us to practical action.

What do we do if we can't follow this intellectual path? Not everyone has the necessary skill and ability. Not everyone can intensely concentrate in meditative contemplation. Not everyone can learn and fully grasp the materials necessary for such contemplation. And even those who are able to meditate are not always able to inspire their hearts. If a person *can* do these things, this is the best possible path. But what about someone who can't? What options does he have?

Chapter 3 of the *Tanya* explains that the emotions of the heart are generated and birthed by one's intellectual comprehension-the mind knows, grasps, and understands, until love and awe for G-d are awakened and blossom in the heart.

As we will soon see, these emotions are already present in our soul. It's true that we usually don't feel them, which is why this kind of love for G-d is called *"ahavah mesuteret,"* hidden love, but it is definitely there within us. We need only to learn how to reveal this love without the constant help of contemplation.

A King's Son

Every Jew is G-d's child. Little children don't need to contemplate whether they love their parents. They just do. They don't need to deeply and intensely think about various concepts in order to conclude that it is worthwhile to love their parents. Rather, the love a child feels for his parents is natural. The love is always there. Yes, a child may swing through moods of different levels of intensity in their love, sometimes feeling it more and other times feeling it less, but it never changes the fact that he has this love for his parents at all times.

The same can be said about every Jew: we always have love for G-d. It doesn't have to be generated by contemplation; recalling it is enough. Take a moment to consider the fact that we are G-d's children, children of the King of kings, and the natural love that is always present within us will automatically reveal itself.

If we can find a way to reveal this hidden love, then we can bypass the need for intellectual contemplation, and then even those who are unable to produce contemplated love will experience love of G-d. And when revealed, this hidden love will motivate and inspire us to perform *mitzvot* and avoid transgression.

Unlimited *Chochmah*

We generally use the word *"Chochmah"* (wisdom) to describe intellect, understanding, and learning. But in truth, this is a better description of *Binah* (understanding). *Chochmah* is something different-it is the source of the intellect and therefore transcends conscious understanding, logic, and reasoning.

Our intellect is limited. No matter how much and how deeply we learn about G-d's greatness, it will always be limited. Our finite minds simply cannot grasp the infinite. *Chochmah* serves as our first point of contact with the infinite since *Chochmah* transcends our intellectual limitations, not being bound by these limits.

The Source of Simple Faith

There is a core point that exists in each and every Jew, from the greatest scholar to the simplest person, whether he grew up in an observant, religious home or whether he's never seen a Torah or heard about *mitzvot* before. This inner essence and core point inside every person is *Chochmah*.

Chochmah is the inherent faith and belief found in all of us. "All Jews are believers and the children of believers," the Sages tell us. Faith and belief in G-d are part of our inborn nature, our spiritual DNA.

How did it get there? We received it as an inheritance from our forefathers: Avraham, Yitzchak, and Yaakov. Our spiritual inheritance doesn't depend on our Divine service, labors, or efforts. Without exception, everyone has faith deep within him, just waiting to be revealed.

This core point of faith transcends our intellect. That's why most people can't tell you why or what exactly they believe. Something that's beyond our intellect can't be put into words. Moreover, we're talking about faith in G-d, Who is infinite and unlimited, a concept that's completely *impossible* for our limited minds to grasp.

Since faith transcends intellect, it can overrule and overpower the intellect. Meaning, even though our intellect sees reality in a certain way and that leads to certain conclusions, the core point of *Chochmah*-our reservoir of inner faith-is dominant and able to swing the final conclusions in line with its vision.

The most extreme example of this core point is *mesirut nefesh* (self-sacrifice)-total and complete devotion to G-d so that a Jew is literally willing to give up his life for G-d. As demonstrated throughout history, many Jews who were threatened with death if they did not reject their religion or bow down to idols chose to die.

Throughout history, these righteous Jews who chose to die rather than convert, who gave up their lives only because they were Jews, were not necessarily great, intellectual scholars with significant Torah knowledge and unswerving faith. Even the most ignorant Jews, some of whom did not even observe Torah and *mitzvot*, chose the path of *mesirut nefesh*. Some were even "anti-religious"!

Schneeweiss

Schneeweiss was a foreman in the Janowska concentration camp during the Holocaust. Though he was Jewish, he was particularly virulent against Judaism, and the inmates who valued their life stayed away from him.

As Yom Kippur neared, fear in the camp mounted. Everyone knew that the Germans especially liked to use Jewish holidays as days for inflicting terror and death.

On the eve of Yom Kippur, the tensions and fears were at their height. A few Chassidim came to the Bluzhever Rebbe, who was also incarcerated there. They begged him to approach Schneeweiss and request that on Yom Kippur they would not be assigned work that involved transgressing the holiness of the day.

Though he knew that Schneeweiss was a cruel man who knew no mercy, who had publicly violated the Jewish holidays and transgressed Jewish law even before the war broke out, the Rebbe was moved by the request of his Chassidim and agreed to try.

The Rebbe told Schneeweiss that it meant everything to these Jews not to transgress Yom Kippur, and strangely enough Schneeweiss agreed. That night the Jews were beaten mercilessly. And yet, they still gathered to sing Kol Nidrei.

In the morning, Schneeweiss summoned the Rebbe and told him, "I heard that you prayed last night. I don't believe in prayers, and on principle, I even oppose them. But I admire your courage."

Then he brought the Rebbe and the Chassidim to a building and told them to clean the windows with dry rags, so it would look like they were working. Later that day, two Nazi soldiers stormed into the room with a cart overflowing with food and announced that it was time to eat or they would immediately be shot. None of them moved.

The Nazis called in Schneeweiss. "If the dirty dogs refuse to eat," one of the soldiers screamed, "we will kill you along with them."

Schneeweiss stood up tall, looked the German directly in the eyes, and said quietly, "We Jews do not eat today. Today is Yom Kippur, our most holy day, the Day of Atonement."

"I command you in the name of the Fuhrer and the Third Reich, eat!"

Schneeweiss remained composed, held his head high, and repeated, "We Jews obey the law of our tradition. Today is Yom Kippur, a day of fasting."

A shot pierced the room, and Schneeweiss, the man who had publicly transgressed Jewish law in the past, died with mesirut nefesh, publicly sanctifying G-d's Name.

This core point that inspires such self-sacrifice transcends the intellect. According to logic and reasoning, it makes no sense to die for one's faith, and if he had asked his intellect why he was willing to do so, he would never have made such a decision.

In truth, "self-sacrifice" is not limited to a Jew being burned at the stake for his beliefs. There are smaller self-sacrifices that are considered *mesirut nefesh*. Anytime a Jew is willing to give up something, to forgo what he wants for the sake of a higher Torah ideal, it's a form of self-sacrifice.

This capacity for *mesirut nefesh* comes from the G-dly Soul's attribute of *Chochmah*. As a core point that transcends intellect, *Chochmah* is the meeting place for the Creator's infinite light and the human soul. This core point exists in every Jew and endows the hearts with "hidden love" for G-d.

If we can awaken and reveal the love we already have, then we can bypass the need for deep intellectual contemplation and have simple, pure faith.

"You Jewish, I Jewish"

Rabbi Mendel Futterfass was one of the great Chassidim of our generation and the previous one. He survived fourteen years of exile and imprisonment in Soviet Russia for the crime of teaching Judaism. When he would meet English-speaking Jewish men on the street, he would offer them a chance to put on tefillin by simply saying, "You Jewish, I Jewish. I tefillin, you tefillin."

Inevitably the people he met would choose to put on the tefillin. His approach revealed the inner core point of a Jew which transcends intellect. He did not try to explain intellectually why someone should put on tefillin; he only reminded the person that he was Jewish and therefore possessed love for G-d. He knew that the person's interest in putting on tefillin would naturally follow.

The Soul Is a G-dly Flame

Why won't the intellect agree to forgo its own existence and encourage us to surrender our lives, while our transcendent core point will do so?

It's a basic rule of life that every creation wants to strengthen its own existence. Self-preservation is the norm, not self-nullification. However, there are two exceptions: fire and the soul.

When a candle burns, the flame flickers constantly-as if trying to separate from the wick and unite with something greater. When we bring a candle close to a bonfire, we see how the flame bends toward the bonfire, attracted to the larger flame, ready to entirely unite with it.

Fire is naturally drawn to its source; it yearns to be unified, to become part of the greater fire, even if it means giving up its own existence. There's nothing else like this in nature.

The soul is similar. Within its nature is a willingness and readiness to part with its own existence and sense of self in order to become one with G-d. This is its desire, despite the fact that it's illogical and devoid of personal gain.

This characteristic is wired into the soul's attribute of *Chochmah*. Therefore, when a Jew's core point of *Chochmah* is revealed, he is willing to sacrifice himself and part with his own existence for the sake of the Creator.

In essence, this is the difference between *kedushah* and *kelipah*. Things that emanate from *kedushah* are willing to be nullified and ready to relinquish their existence for G-d, whereas *kelipah* is self-absorbed and constantly looking out for its own interests.

The Secret of *Galut*

If this is all true, and such a core point exists within us all, how can it be that we don't feel it?

The presence of this core point is hidden and obscured, imperceptible in our daily lives. It's possible to live an entire lifetime without knowing it's there. And yet, it is always a part of us, even though our involvement in worldly matters, our attraction to pleasures and physicality, block its revelation and obscure our perception of its existence.

The Pharmacist

There was a Jewish pharmacist in Russia during the early years of the communist revolution who was married to a non-Jew. He was completely nonreligious and he was so far from Torah observance that his pharmacy was open on Yom Kippur.

When a revolutionary group invaded the town, they rounded up the Jews and announced that they would kill all the bourgeois capitalists (i.e., Jews). All the non-Jewish townspeople were there, watching, including the pharmacist, and he suddenly stepped forward and announced that he too needed to be killed.

Everyone was shocked. No one realized he was a Jew.

"If he's a Jew, he should be killed like the rest of them!" some people shouted.

"No, we need him and his medicine!" others shouted. "He can't be killed."

Chaos erupted as the townspeople argued, and the revolutionaries feared for their own lives and fled. All the Jews were saved because of this Jew's sudden awakening that he wanted to die with his brethren.

When we face a test and have to decide, "Do I belong to G-d or not?"-when we encounter a moment of truth like this-our inner core point reveals itself.

The problem is that we only remember G-d when faced with an emergency. Once the crisis is over, we forget all about Him and return to our regular lives.

When the House Was Burning

A Jew was standing on the roof of his burning house. His only chance for survival was to jump off, but he was afraid. He looked up to Heaven and promised G-d that if he survived, he would put on tefillin, keep Shabbat, eat only kosher food, and on and on he went, making promises.

Then he gathered his courage and jumped off the roof. After landing safely and realizing he was alive and out of danger, he said to himself, Wow! When I'm under pressure, I say the silliest things...

We don't usually face emergency situations on a daily basis. As a result, we don't feel the need to call out to G-d to save us and discover our deepest connection to Him. We're generally not thinking about how dependent we are on G-d, and that transgressions will separate us from G-d, which we want to avoid at all costs. We run around thinking that we can live without learning Torah and doing *mitzvot*, that our connection with G-d is not that important and will remain unharmed.

Until we need Him. Then we start making promises.

If we could find a way to bring out our hidden love for G-d every day, we could use that power of connection to overcome our Animal Soul in our daily struggles and not just in times of dire emergency. In the coming chapters, we will explain why every day is an emergency, and how every transgression is as serious as idol worship.

In Conclusion

Every Jew is G-d's child and has a natural inborn love for Him. This love is typically revealed only at special times. However, if we could reveal it every day, we would not need intense intellectual contemplation to feel close to G-d. We would feel close to Him all the time.

Chapter Thirteen

Where Is G-d?

The Creator is everywhere; there is no place devoid of His presence.

(Tanya, chaps. 20–21)

Before the Jewish patriarch Yaakov passed away, he called for all his sons to come before him so that he could bless them. But before he began, he wanted to verify that they had not been negatively influenced by their time in Egypt. He wanted to hear that their faith in G-d, Creator of the world, was still strong.

In unison, his sons gathered around him and declared, "*Shema Yisrael*-Please listen to us, Yisrael [Yaakov's other name], the L-rd is our G-d, the L-rd is One."

This is the *Shema* that we say several times a day as part of our prayers: it expresses our faith and belief in the one G-d.

This declaration has deeper meaning beyond merely negating faith in idols or thinking that there are many gods capable of influencing the universe. "*Shema Yisrael*" is our foundational announcement to ourselves and to the worlds that there is *nothing else at all* but G-d.

Mesirut Nefesh

In the previous chapter, we explained that every Jew has hidden love (*ahavah mesuteret*) for G-d within him, which is derived from the G-dly Soul's attribute of *Chochmah*. It is the core point that transcends intellect and never leaves, gets tarnished, or changes. It can, however, be in a state of "sleep," from which it awakens in moments of truth when a Jew faces a test of faith and must decide if he belongs to G-d or not.

The classic example of this, as witnessed throughout Jewish history, is when Jews were willing to die rather than convert to other religions. For a Jew, being ordered to bow down to an idol and deny G-d is a crystal-clear redline not to be crossed, since he knows somehow, deep within him, that this will disconnect him from G-d. Even though this very same Jew may have willingly transgressed numerous Torah prohibitions in the past, that was only because he didn't sense just how serious were the consequences of his actions and figured his behavior wasn't "so bad."

We will now try to understand how even the smallest of transgressions causes separation from G-d-just like idol worship, which we would never agree to do. At the same time, even when we fulfill the smallest of *mitzvot*, this connects us to G-d with an everlasting bond.

But first, let's see if we can find where G-d is...

As a child, Rabbi Shmuel, the fourth Rebbe of Lubavitch, enjoyed carving wood with his pocketknife. One of the Chassidim of his father, the Tzemach Tzedek, the third Rebbe of Lubavitch, said to him, "If you can tell me where G-d is, I will give you my new whittling knife."

The young Shmuel replied, "If you can tell me where He is not, *I will give you mine!"*

Upon hearing the answer, the Chassid handed over his knife.

The Unity of G-d

G-d is everywhere. When we say in the *Shema* prayer, "The L-rd, our G-d, the L-rd is One," it means that not only is there no other power in the universe besides the Creator, there is nothing else but Him. There is no place in the universe where He is not found. How is this possible?

Let's try to explain the relationship between our infinite G-d and His finite creations. By examining the difference between creating something out of nothing (*yesh me'ayin*) and taking something and turning it into something else (*yesh meyesh*), we will be able to conclude that G-d is everywhere.

In our prayers, when we say to G-d, "You were [the same] before the world was created; You are [the same] since the world has been created," we mean that G-d before the Creation and after the Creation is exactly the same. G-d didn't change because He created the worlds.

Our experience of creating is quite different. Making something new impacts and changes us; after exerting so much effort, investing energy and skill, we are never the same.

Regarding G-d, however, we say that although He created the world (and by "world" we mean more than just planet Earth; we are including the millions of galaxies in the universe, as well as all the complex higher spiritual worlds and realms), it did not cause a change in Him. He remains precisely the same as He was before the Creation.

How Did He Create?

The explanation of this requires contemplation on the method by which G-d created the world.

But first, a general question: How do we as creations view the Creator? How do we measure our relationship with Him? Is G-d the biggest and greatest thing possible, or is He infinite?

If we view G-d as the "biggest and greatest," that means that we are the very smallest. Despite our smallness, we feel we can still be compared to Him. The only difference between us is that G-d is just a whole lot bigger.

What is the difference in relationship between something small and something bigger and greater, versus something small (or even large) and something *infinite*?

If someone has ten million dollars in the bank, this may sound like a lot of money. What's one dollar, or even a hundred dollars, in comparison to ten million dollars in the bank? But the fact is, it's still a limited, finite amount. As great a sum as it is, if the owner of the bank account buys something for a dollar, that's one less dollar in his account, and if he continues to buy more things, eventually he will spend all his money. It may take a long time, but it's a finite resource that will get depleted.

Or if we have a large reservoir of water, like the Kinneret , Israel's primary source of drinking water, and we use up bit by bit-well, we see just how dangerously low the level of the Kinneret can drop.

On the other hand, imagine having an infinite amount of money in the bank. Then it wouldn't matter if we spent one dollar after another, a million dollars or a billion dollars-the amount in the bank is infinite. In other words, the ratio of infinite to one, or infinite to a thousand, or infinite to a million is all the same.

Saying that G-d is the biggest thing we can possibly imagine, but not infinite, means that we believe that we can compare the world to G-d in some way. No matter how small the Earth is in the grand scheme, and how vast the universe and all its galaxies, we are still measuring G-d.

It also means that He had to invest time and effort into creating the world, implying that it would have taken more work to create the world with a thousand additional species of spiders or to make two hundred galaxies instead of a hundred.

However, viewing G-d as infinite means that we understand that we are not smaller than G-d, but rather insignificant and incomparable. Therefore, it takes the same amount of "effort" for G-d to create one stone or an entire continent, since both have the same value relative to the infinite (or, rather, they are both equally nothing in comparison to Him).

Creating a grain of sand or the Milky Way is all the same to G-d and requires no effort. G-d is infinite and unlimited; His creations are finite and limited, and therefore insignificant in comparison to Him. It does not take more effort for G-d to create small or large.

Something Out of Nothing

What is the difference between the things that we create and G-d creating the world?

When a craftsman takes a piece of wood and fashions it into a tool or vessel, he isn't creating something out of nothing. He is altering and rearranging existing material. And when he finishes, the tool no longer needs him in order to exist. What he created exists independently of him.

But with G-d, the situation is completely different. He created the world *yesh me'ayin*, ex nihilo-"something out of nothing," limited out of the unlimited.

The world's natural state is nonexistence. It can't function without G-d's ongoing involvement. The world didn't start as existing matter, which G-d then fashioned into a world. Rather, He started with nothingness and transformed it into something. Thus its nature is really nothingness, and it will revert back to that unless G-d continually intervenes and sustains every moment.

A Stone in the Air

Let's look at an analogy from our daily lives. A stone's natural state is to be under the influence of gravity, and it therefore rests on the ground. We don't see stones flying around in the air. That's impossible; it goes against their nature. We can, however, throw a stone into the air. The power in our arm propels the stone up, and it stays in the air until the power subsides. Then the stone begins falling back toward the ground, returning to its natural state.

The stone is unable to fly-that would go against its very nature. Even when it flew through the air, it was not due to its own ability. It was propelled by the power transferred into it by the one who threw it. When that power ran out, the stone stopped flying and fell back down.

Similarly, the world does not have the power to exist on its own.

Existence is the opposite of its natural state of nothingness. Thus, the world exists only because the Creator infuses it with life force and energy-"He commanded and it came to be." The world would "fall" into nothingness and cease to exist if G-d stopped willing it to be.

When we look around and see that the world exists, it's a mistake to think that it is happening on its own. In truth, it exists because G-d is continually infusing it with life force and energy. Despite what our eyes tell us, the world is really G-dliness-"there is nothing but G-d."

The World Was Created with Ten Statements

We find this idea expressed in the Torah's description of the creation of the world.

In the beginning of *sefer Bereshit*, we read about the creation of the world. For each creative act, it is written, "G-d said...and it was." This means that the world was created via G-dly speech-G-d spoke and the world came into being: plants and trees, flowers and grass, animals and fish, the sun and stars. He issued a command and they came into being.

What does it mean that the world was created through speech? Since G-d doesn't have a body or physical form, surely He has no mouth and G-d doesn't "talk." What does it mean when the Torah tells us, "G-d said"?

Why Is Creation Called Speech?

It's true that G-d does not have a body. He is beyond definition, boundary, limitation, or form, which is why it's so difficult for us to understand G-d's nature. The Torah uses analogy to help us gain a glimpse of Who G-d is.

The relationship between one spoken word and our faculty of speech is comparable to the relationship between limited and limitless that we discussed earlier. Just as one coin is insignificant when you have an unlimited pile of coins, so is one spoken word trivial in comparison to our entire ability to speak.

Our souls possess an infinite ability to produce spoken words. It is only our bodies that grow tired and limit our speech. Another way of saying this is that one word that I said a few years ago will have no impact on my ability to talk right now.

Take this a step further. One spoken word compared to the soul itself (which is the source of our faculty of speech) is surely insignificant and unimportant. It is an absolute certainty that our conversations do not in any way detract from the soul's ability to continue speaking.

For this reason, the Torah discusses creation in terms of speech, since the life force used to create the world is totally insignificant and incomparable to G-d. As such, it's obvious that we can understand that creating the world did not impact or change G-d in any way.

Eternal Speech

When we say that G-d spoke and the world came into existence, we don't mean that He spoke once over 5,774 years ago, created everything, and has been passively watching from the sidelines ever since. The very opposite is true. At each and every moment and every microfraction of a second, G-d "speaks" anew the ten utterances of creation ("Let there be light," etc.). And if He stopped speaking for even a moment, the world would cease to be. There would be no world.

Thus, G-d's "words" need to be spoken anew every moment for the world to continue to exist. And if the world is dependent on the word of G-d, than the true reality of the world is that very word of G-d.

On the last day of his life, the Alter Rebbe lay in bed with his grandson sitting beside him. At one point, the Rebbe turned to his grandson and said, "Do you see that beam in the ceiling? Know that I do not see it. I see only the Divine vitality, the word of G-d that gives the beam its existence..."

Hashgachah Pratit

Up to this point we have explained one aspect of the analogy of speaking: the words we say are insignificant in comparison to our potential for speaking. In a manner of speaking, the word of G-d that sustains all of existence is of no significance in comparison to G-d and obviously has no impact on Him. Just as our speaking is external and does not change us, so is G-d unaffected by the creation of the world He spoke into being.

There are more dimensions to this, which we will soon discuss further. But it is already possible to see a completely new way of looking at the relationship between the Creator and His creations: G-d spoke and created the world out of nothing. Creation does not exist independently. It is constantly dependent on G-d, Who recreates it anew every moment.

This is the idea behind the concept of *hashgachah pratit*-Divine providence. G-d is everywhere, since in truth the entire world is only G-d's word. As such, it's "easy" for Him to keep tabs on every single detail and "simple" to make miracles when necessary.

He is always with us, during what we perceive as good times and otherwise. Just as He gives life and sustenance to us in ways that we perceive as good, so He is responsible for everything that happens, including what we call "bad."

When His House Burned Down

The home of Rabbi Shmuel Monkes, a student of the Alter Rebbe, once went up in flames. The Chassidim knew his high level of G-dly trust and joy, and wondered how he would respond to this event, which they perceived as a tragedy.

Then they saw him dancing for joy, as though to answer their question.

"How can you be happy while your house is burning down?" they asked him.

"I am happy," he replied, "because it is clear to me that if I weren't a Jew, then my physical gods of idolatry would also have been destroyed in the fire. But because I know there is a supernal G-d Who controls everything, even if my physical house burns down, the most important thing remains-my connection with Him."

In Conclusion

In a moment of truth, a Jew is willing to sacrifice himself in order to remain a Jew. To prove that every moment is such a moment of truth, and that every sin can separate us from G-d, we remember the concept of G-d's unity and the idea that He is found everywhere. Creation is a process of something from nothing, and therefore has to be created anew every moment and in every place. If there was a corner of the universe that G-d did not will it to be, it would simply cease to exist as if it had never been there.

Chapter Fourteen
Why We Don't See G-d

G-d is everywhere, but we do not
see Him. He's hiding.

(Tanya, chap. 22)

The Maggid of Mezeritch, the student and successor of the Baal Shem Tov, once saw a little child crying. He asked him why he was crying, and the child replied that he had been playing hide-and-seek with his friends, and they had stopped looking for him.

"Don't cry. G-d has the same problem," the Maggid told the boy. "He is hiding from us, and we have stopped looking for Him."

If G-d is everywhere, the natural question is, Why can't we see G-d?

Our Speech vs. G-d's Speech

We explained that the world was created by the "word of G-d." "He said," and as a result, "it was"-the world was created. We emphasized the fact that something created out of nothing remains constantly dependent on its source for life and renewal. In the natural order of things, the tendency of the world is to return to its natural state of being-nothingness-unless it is created anew at every moment. G-d is therefore found everywhere since He is the life force and energy that all of creation is depending on for existence.

In addition, we used the analogy of speech to emphasize the relationship between the Creator and His creations: we are insignificant in comparison to Him. With or without us, He is the same. Creating the world made no change in G-d, just as our human conversations with friends do not reduce or detract from our souls.

But there is a quality that exists in human speech that is not found in G-dly speech.

When we speak, our words become separated from our souls (the source of speech) and are no longer found inside us. That's why we can't take back words after they are spoken.

For G-d, however, there is no place that is "outside" of Him. He's found everywhere. As such, we can't say that His speech has left and gone outside of Him. So when G-d created the world via speech, it didn't become separate from Him like our conversations become-it's all still contained within G-d.

We Are Never Really Separated from G-d

The fact that we seem to exist independently is a product of our own perspective. From G-d's viewpoint, nothing is ever apart from Him. We are still part of G-d and inside G-d as we were before the world was created.

This understanding of the world's unity with G-d is deeper than the explanation we gave before. The previous discussion pointed out that the Creator is everywhere and that He constantly renews our vitality and existence. But once created, one might think that the world is separate from G-d and that He sends life force and energy "from afar."

According to this new explanation-that we remain contained within Him-the meaning is much deeper. Even if we feel separate from G-d, we are still united with Him just as we were before the Creation!

But if this is indeed so, why don't we feel it? The reason is because this is the reality from *G-d's perspective*. From His viewpoint, this is truly how things are. From our viewpoint, we see only contraction-*tzimtzum*-and the concealment of His G-dliness.

This fact is no coincidence. G-d wanted the world to be created this way and that this should be our perspective. If there was no concealment in the world, and we could feel how we are constantly connected to and enveloped in G-d at all times, life and existence would be very different from the way we currently experience it.

The Ability to Choose

The world we live in conceals G-d. Our physical eyes simply don't recognize His presence all around us.

If we *could* see His oneness all the time, or sense and know that our lives are completely dependent upon Him at every moment, or be constantly aware of our connection to Him and what deepens or weakens this bond, we would lose our free choice.

Freedom of choice is a product of the fact that our eyes can't perceive the truth of our reality. Because we understand that the truth is there and we learn about it, we get an opportunity to make a choice: follow what our eyes see or what our intellect and faith know to be true. But if our faith and belief were as tangible as physical sight, we would live a completely different existence. We would not and could not have free choice.

G-d wanted a material world where He is hidden and undetected-a world with freedom of choice that tests us. This is why the creation of the world included an element of concealment-He is present everywhere, yet under the radar.

If We Only Saw...

Rabbi Levi Yitzchak was called the "Defender of Israel" because he always found a way to find merit for the Jewish people. He was an expert in judging people favorably.

There once was a Jew who was in the middle of his morning prayers. While he was still wearing his tallit and tefillin, he went out to his wagon and began fixing the wheels. People came over to Rabbi Levi Yitzchak and complained, "Look at this disgraceful conduct! He is fixing his wagon wheels while he's supposed to be praying!"

Rabbi Levi Yitzchak, however, turned toward Heaven and said, "Master of the universe! Look at your child. Even when he is busy fixing his wagon he finds time to pray!"

On another occasion, Rabbi Levi Yitzchak raised his voice in prayer on behalf of the Jewish people and cried, "Master of the universe! What do You expect from Your children? You put all the temptations of the world in front of their eyes, while they learn about Heaven by studying books. I promise You that if You placed Heaven in front of their eyes, and all the temptations of the world were in books, they would act very differently!"

The Home of the Turtle

Though G-d is truly found everywhere in every moment, we aren't able to clearly see His reality because He is concealed and G-d wants this concealment to be part of our reality.

True "concealment" means that one entity obscures another. But if G-d is everything, then surely He can't truly conceal Himself. It's like hiding my face behind my hands and thinking that no one can see me. My hands are no less me than my face.

The same can be said of a turtle when his head is tucked back into his shell. He thinks he's hiding, but he's only inside his shell.

When confronted with things that seem to conceal G-d's presence, we have to remember that those very things are part of Him.

The whole system of *tzimtzum* and concealment was created for our benefit so that we can experience free choice. Hiding His presence creates a situation in which we aren't aware that He is constantly with us. Part of this system includes a *tzimtzum* so powerful and intense that some creations have absolutely no knowledge or sense of their source. Nevertheless, they also receive their vitality from G-d-but it comes in a more external, backhanded packaging. Other creations receive their vitality in a more internal, face-to-face way.

Front and Back

When we give a gift to a beloved friend, we want to give the gift with a full heart, while looking our friend directly in the eye and saying words of endearment.

But if we have to give something to a person we dislike, we do so in a detached way, tossing it over our shoulder and avoiding any eye contact. Similarly, impurity and *kelipah* get their vitality from G-d, but in an indirect, detached way.

As a result, they receive a more detached, distant version of vitality from G-d, not an inner form. This kind of vitality does not deeply penetrate to the core of the *kelipah*'s being and consciousness. Instead it receives vitality, but in a distant, detached way.

This Is *Galut*

Because the vitality that the *kelipah* receives from G-d does not penetrate into its inner self, it feels a sense of separation and detachment from G-d-a *galut*, a form of exile.

And not only does the *kelipah* not feel obligated to nullify and dedicate itself to G-d, it even feels more exalted than Him. If interviewed, the *kelipah* would say, "I don't need G-d. I'm fully capable of getting along without Him."

In fact, from the *kelipah*'s perspective, the question is the exact opposite: "How can G-d manage without me?"

Arrogance and Idolatry

Idolatry comes in different flavors. Some claim that the world has no Creator, that there are only powerful forces of nature, like the idol worshippers of the past who claimed it was these powers that must be served.

Others claim that the world has a Creator, but He gave the "keys" to His servants, the forces of nature, such as the sun, moon, stars, wind, and laws of nature that rule the world. Since He isn't managing things, it is unnecessary to address Him directly. These forces have freedom of choice and an independent existence and can determine what happens in the world. Those who claim this reality feel it's better to speak directly with His servants, bow down, and worship them.

Clearly a person doesn't have to literally bow down to statues and practice idolatry in order to make such mistaken claims. Even someone who says, "There is a Creator, but I don't need Him or I can get along fine without Him," or "My own strength and power have brought me success," *in a certain sense is considered an idolater.* They are all essentially making the same claim: G-d is not the sole boss; other factors are exerting an influence in the universe.

Ofer was an Israeli who was interested in spirituality. He had studied a many different systems of meditation and ultimately decided he wanted to go to India, separate himself from the world by living in a monastery, and practice meditation there.

Before he left Israel, Ofer went to see his grandfather. His grandfather gave him a pair of tefillin and a sefer Tehillim-a book of Psalms. He told Ofer, "I know you don't feel much connection to these right now, but I'm asking you to take them and keep them with you."

After a long journey, Ofer arrived at a monastery where they practiced intensive meditation day and night. He enrolled as a regular student.

One of their rules was that all students had to separate themselves from their past. To comply, Ofer put his bag with all his clothes and personal belongings in the cellar. He changed into the robe of the monastery and joined the group.

For several months, he sat and practiced meditation like the others, but did not succeed in feeling "connected." He felt that something was missing. But despite the fact that he had not found what he was searching for, he remained in the monastery and assumed that eventually he would.

One day, in the beginning of autumn, Ofer realized that he could no longer stay in the monastery. Not only could he no longer concentrate, but he also began having very strange flashbacks, remembering Bible stories that he had learned as a child.

This was too much for him, and he approached his guru and told him of his struggles.

The guru told him that the problem was that he had not succeeded in letting go of his past. The guru asked him where his personal belongings were stored. Ofer told him they were in the cellar, and together they began walking in that direction.

When they found his bag, the guru commanded Ofer to throw his things into the fire burning in the fireplace.

Immediately Ofer remembered the tefillin and the sefer Tehillim from his grandfather. He froze, not knowing what to do. He didn't want to throw them into the fire, but the guru was pressuring him to toss them in. Slowly Ofer began to take things out, one by one, and throw them into the fire.

Finally, he was left with the last two items: the tefillin and the Tehillim. Ofer lifted the Tehillim in response to the guru's urging. He approached the fire and tried to throw the book in, but couldn't. The guru continued pressuring him until he finally threw the book into the fire.

A moment later Ofer put his hand into the fire, pulled out the Tehillim, and opened it to the first page. He read, "Blessed is the man who walks not in the counsel of the wicked, nor stands in the way of sinners, nor sits in the seat of scoffers. But his delight is in G-d's Torah, and he meditates on the Torah day and night...." (Tehillim 1:1).

A few minutes later he was standing outside the monastery's gates.

Several days later, Ofer arrived in a city where he met other Israelis. When he spoke to them about his recent experience in the monastery, they all realized that at the exact moment that he was rescuing the

Tehillim from the fire, Jews in that part of the world were praying Ne'ilah-the highest, holiest prayer of Yom Kippur.

There is a Jewish spark in all of us that transcends intellect. We don't understand it, and most of the time we can't feel it. But like Ofer, when our faith is put to the test, when we have to decide if we are Jews or not, if we belong to G-d or not, even when we have no clue that this spark is within us-it is revealed.

And when this Jewish spark is aroused, we can discover the deepest parts of ourselves and access spiritual powers and attributes we had no clue were there, to the point that we are willing to sacrifice ourselves.

In Conclusion

Even though we experience the concealment of G-dliness in the world, He is everywhere. G-d is the engine behind all of creation-sustaining life at all moments. When we live with the awareness that G-d is everywhere, we uphold the unity of our Creator. When we behave in ways that contradict it, we are actually furthering the concealment of the unity and oneness of the Creator.

Chapter Fifteen
The Inner Will

Since G-d is hidden in the world but
revealed in the Torah, the way to connect
to Him is through Torah and *mitzvot*.

(Tanya, chap. 23)

The Baal Shem Tov once asked one of his Chassidim to visit a particular village and bring greetings to one of his students by the name of Dov (later know as the Maggid of Mezeritch, the Baal Shem Tov's successor). The Chassid was happy to take on the task, and when he arrived in the village he immediately went looking for Rabbi Dov. He was sure that everyone would know this student of the Baal Shem Tov.

But when he asked for him, no one knew who he was talking about!

Finally, someone mentioned that there was someone named Dov who taught young children to read and write. He lived at the edge of the village. The Chassid found it hard to believe that such a man would merit special greetings from the Baal Shem Tov, but he had promised that he would find him, and so he headed for the other side of the village.

The Chassid came to an old dilapidated house. After knocking on the door and being let in, he saw that things were even worse inside. Nevertheless, the Chassid joyously told Rabbi Dov that he had brought greetings from the Baal Shem Tov.

When he felt more comfortable, the Chassid did not hide his astonishment about the poor condition of Rabbi Dov's home. "Tell me, how can you live in a house like this?"

Rabbi Dov did not answer. Instead, he changed the subject.

When it was time to leave, Rabbi Dov accompanied the Chassid to his carriage. After the Chassid was seated, Rabbi Dov peered inside and asked, "How can you live in such a small carriage? What kind of life is that?"

The Chassid replied that he did not live in the carriage; it was only used for traveling. "Come to my real home in the village where I am from, and you will see what a house I have."

Rabbi Dov then replied to the Chassid's earlier, unanswered question.

"This world is only part of our travels. Come to my real home, my spiritual home, and see what a house I have."

The Innermost Will

Not everything we do is what we really want to do.

There are two dimensions of will: inner and external. Our inner will is the goal, outcome, or consequence that we truly desire. It's the answer we give when people ask, "What are our goals, your aspirations? What are you hoping to achieve?"

But in order to achieve this goal, there are several steps we have to take along the way, things that have to get done first. We have to ask ourselves, Do we want to do these things or not?

Here's an example: A man from Tel Aviv decides he wants to go pray at the Kotel in Jerusalem. Prayer at the Kotel is his inner will.

Achieving this means taking the time, traveling by car, dealing with traffic, finding parking, and walking until he reaches the holy place. None of these activities directly interest him, but they are the necessary steps he must take in order to reach his goal and serve his inner will. And so he does them.

Inner will is the goal, and outer will is the means. And even prayer at the Kotel could be considered outer will: the true inner will is connecting to G-d.

Inner and Outer Will

What gives others a truer sense of who we really are, what we really want to do, and what is really our inner essence?

Without a doubt, it's our inner will. Our more external desires are not an expression and indication of our true inner essence. It's the path we have to take in order to achieve our true goal. Even though the world was designed in such a way that most of our time is spent dealing with external desires, these aren't our innermost desires.

In other words, you won't see the real me while I'm sitting in traffic or on the way to my goal, but rather when I'm at the Kotel involved with my innermost desire. "On the way" is not truly me-it's only the "me" that is hidden within the daily tasks of my life. At the Kotel, however, you can see and truly connect with the real me.

Let's apply this to G-d, Who also has an innermost and outermost desire. He has a goal and deep, inner desire-and He has an external desire that will lead to the goal.

Where do we truly encounter, recognize, and connect to G-d? When we meet Him in His innermost will.

G-d's Will and Wisdom

We explained at length how there can exist the paradoxical situation of G-d being everywhere and yet undetectable. However, when we mentioned that G-d is found everywhere, we were referring to G-d's light and G-dliness-the level that created the world through speech. And although speech is part of Him and always contained within Him (even after spoken), it's not G-d Himself.

The creation of the world is still only a reflection of G-d's more external dimension, His external will. It isn't the goal itself, but rather the means to attain that goal.

If we want to meet with G-d Himself, without any concealment, then we have to encounter Him as He's revealed in His innermost will: the Torah.

The Torah is G-d's innermost will, and He is found there in all His glory. There is no concealment in the Torah. Therefore, the Torah is our pathway to meet, connect, and unite with G-d.

There are several levels to this connection that we make with G-d through the Torah:

"Mitzvah" and "Tzavta"

The simple meaning of the word "mitzvah" is "commandment." G-d gave commandments and we fulfill them. But the deeper meaning of the word comes from its similarity to the word "tzavta," bond. Doing a mitzvah connects and unites us with G-d.

We can view this connection on two levels:

Chariot and rider: As we mentioned in an earlier chapter, when the Torah speaks of chariots, today's equivalent would be a car and the driver is the rider. A car doesn't have an independent will. It can't choose or influence the driver where to go. Rather, it is completely subservient to him and carries out his orders. And although it is in a sense completely dedicated and committed, its obedience still doesn't occur automatically. The driver has to actively drive the car. Furthermore, the driver is not united with the car. They remain separate entities.

Body and soul: The highest level of unity is the kind found between body and soul. The soul is invested in the body and completely fills it. If there were a part of the body in which the soul did not reside, that part would "wilt" and lose its vitality. This is actually one of the great mystical principles used by the Tzaddikim to heal sick people; they see the spiritual problem that is generating the physical illness. They are then able to treat the root cause of the illness-which is spiritual-with prayer, study, and spiritual methods.

The fact that the soul infuses the body means that the body does not have a will of its own. It follows the desires of the soul. And the soul doesn't have to convince or force the body to move-it happens automatically. The bond between the two is so total and complete that the soul's will has replaced the body's will, and the body's limbs are obedient to the soul.

Uniting with the Creator

In the moment that we perform a *mitzvah*, such as giving a coin to *tzedakah*, our hand becomes a chariot for G-d-completely nullified to perform His will. Its movements are not an expression of what it wants, but rather what He wants (as detailed in the Torah). And because a *mitzvah* is the goal of His innermost will, His will is revealed and known in the moment that we are doing the *mitzvah*, and it connects us directly to the Creator with a deep, inner bond.

Since we are speaking of a physical act-the movement of a hand-the connection formed is likened to the relationship between a chariot and its rider, the driver and the car. Although the car is totally and completely nullified and subservient, it still isn't fully united-car and driver remain two independent entities that have joined together.

In the same way, the hand itself is a physical limb, and therefore it can't form a perfect unity by surrendering its independent identity. However, the life force and energy powering the hand and enabling it to move and do the *mitzvah* (referred to as the garment of action in chapter 4) *is* uniting in an even deeper way.

The power to move is spiritual. It is the energy that moves the hand in its performance of a *mitzvah* such as *tzedakah*, and its unity with the Creator is loftier than the unity of rider and chariot. The energy powering the movement unites with G-d on the level of body-and-soul unity, becoming literally one with G-d and without a will of its own. And just as the body becomes an extension of the soul when it is performing a *mitzvah*, so is our power to act a manifestation of G-d the entire time we are doing a *mitzvah*.

A Higher Connection

What could be higher than the body's subservient nullification to the soul and the union then forged between body and soul?

Based on what we explained until now, it seems that our unity with

G-d stems from our self-nullification before Him, and the deeper and loftier the nullification, the deeper and loftier the bond that is formed. In other words, the more we put our own existence and sense of self on the side, the more united we are with G-d.

When Moshe descended from Mount Sinai, he said to the people, "I stand between G-d and you" (*Devarim* 5:5). Beyond the simple interpretation that Moshe connects us with G-d, there is a deeper meaning. The "I"-ego and selfishness-gets in-between us and G-d, separating us from Him. The more we think about ourselves and seek ways to increase our own personal greatness, the more distant G-d becomes.

But what does this mean? How can we nullify our "I" and make room for G-d to be close to us?

We need to use all of our abilities, gifts, and attributes in a holy way. We don't want to increase the glory and arrogance of the Animal soul's "I." Rather, we want to channel everything we are and all of our potential into our service to G-d.

G-d and the Torah: One Entity

The *mitzvot* are called the "limbs of the King." That means that the fulfillment of a *mitzvah* unites our body with G-d, like the unity of a chariot and rider and the unity of our power of action with the soul.

The connection made by Torah is even deeper.

While the body is completely unified with its limbs and organs, they still remain two entities: the limbs and organs and the body. Regarding Torah, however, we are told, "The Torah and G-d are completely one."

G-d is revealed in the Torah even more than He is in the *mitzvot*. Torah study therefore enables us to achieve a loftier union-both for us and for G-d. Torah is studied with the soul's innermost garments of speech and thought. And during study, they unite with the Creator like the soul is united with its garment of thought.

Previously we explained that the garments of the soul-thought, speech, and action-are not the soul itself. Rather, they add to the soul; it invests and enmeshes itself in them. And the soul's level of unity with its spiritual garments of thought and speech is deeper and loftier than its unity with the more physical garment of action.

The difference between Torah and *mitzvot* is similar to a king who orders that a new house be built for him. Before building, the king captures his vision in a set of plans and blueprints, which he submits to his engineers. No doubt, the builders, with every stone they lay, are connected to him and are directly fulfilling his will. But the engineers who study the king's plan itself-i.e., the pure "will" of the king-achieve an even deeper connection with him.

The Torah Is Dressed Up in Physical Things

The Torah is G-d's will and wisdom, so how can it be possible to grasp or understand anything within it, since the Torah is unlimited infinity?

Here is a wondrous thing: G-d compressed and packed Himself into the words of the Torah-its stories, homilies, and laws as we have them. He is right now found and present in the Torah in the same way He is found and present on High. And there in the Torah He is not concealed. G-d is everywhere in the world, yet He is concealed. But the Torah doesn't hide G-d. The very same wisdom that existed in the lofty high spiritual levels is the same wisdom that is found in the Torah-it's only "dressed up" in material matters.

To study Torah is to encounter G-d Himself. All the topics that deal with how to relate to our physical world that are discussed in the Torah, such as agricultural laws, the ruling to build a fence around one's roof, helping widows and orphans, paying workers on time, returning lost items, or what to do with a goring ox, all contain G-d's infinite Light.

As we explained in chapter 4, it doesn't matter how many garments a person is wearing when we hug them. When we embrace their garments, we embrace the person himself.

The same applies to G-dly wisdom that's dressed up in material matters-He is there inside. By grasping and understanding the material concepts in the Torah, we grasp G-d Himself.

So Why Don't We Feel It?

It's a good thing we don't!

The story is told of a king's servant who was assigned the task of preparing a new crown for the king. He toiled with devotion until he reached the point when the most beautiful and precious jewel needed to be placed in the head of the crown.

Suddenly he found himself unable to continue. He was too overwhelmed by his great awareness and deep understanding of the awesomeness of his privileged responsibility. Every time he tried to set the jewel in its place, his entire body trembled; he could not complete the task.

But the crown had to be completed! So he hired a simple citizen, a person who had no comprehension of the king's greatness, nor an appreciation of the value and meaning of the crown and its jewels. The craftsman asked the man to complete the task and he easily succeeded.

Our soul feels the importance and great merit of studying Torah and performing *mitzvot*, even though we consciously don't. And if we felt what the soul feels, we would be overwhelmed with awe, and unable to move, just like the king's craftsman.

Just knowing this-that we would be too overcome if we *really knew* how great G-d is-can help us reach a higher level of awe of G-d. And if we contemplate this concept while we are studying Torah, we will surely be inspired to improve our behavior.

In Conclusion

G-d is everywhere, but His presence in the world is hidden. However, we have access to G-d when we study the Torah, where He is openly revealed and free from concealment. This is why specifically studying Torah enables us to form a deeper, closer, inner bond with G-d.

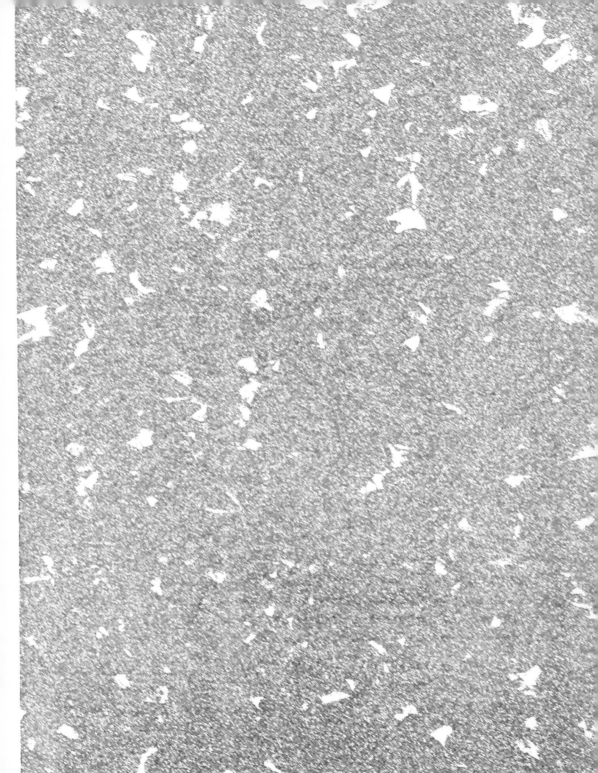

Chapter Sixteen

No Choice

Transgressing G-d's will separates us from Him. This awareness can activate our capacity for self-sacrifice for all *mitzvot*-from the lightest to the most severe.

(Tanya, chaps. 24–25)

Even though Rabbi Yaakov was an elderly Chassid in his nineties, he fulfilled mitzvot with the vivaciousness and enthusiasm of a youth, smiling, dancing, and rejoicing with each new opportunity to fulfill a command. Younger Chassidim, amazed at his vigor, asked him, "How do you have so much strength for such an energetic level of devoted mitzvah observance?"

"How could I not be excited each time our infinite G-d gives me an opportunity to connect with Him?"

How We View the *Mitzvot*

Some people see the *mitzvot* as a list of directions dispensed from Heaven to test us. When we pass the test we get a check, and when we don't we get an *X*.

They don't understand that there is intrinsic meaning to the *mitzvot* themselves, and in the actions performed to fulfill them. They think that we have *mitzvot* only to test our obedience and discipline.

But there is another approach. The *mitzvot* are more than a test-fulfilling the *mitzvot* has a spiritual impact on us and the world. As explained previously, the physical action that comprises each *mitzvah* connects and unites us with the Creator of the world in an everlasting way. Omitting a *mitzvah* is more than just getting an *X*-it's a missed opportunity to draw into the world the light uniquely connected to that particular *mitzvah*.

Prohibitions Connect Us Too

Just as the positive *mitzvot* are more than just "exercises in discipline," and they themselves forge a connection between us and G-d (remember, "*mitzvah*" comes from the word "*tzavta*," bond)-so are the negative *mitzvot* (prohibitions) more than mere tests of obedience. The physical act itself, the transgression itself, separates us from G-d. And there's no difference between "small" and "large" transgressions.

Not only does a sin disconnect a Jew from his life source, the Creator of the world, but in the very moment of transgression, he also becomes connected to the other side-the realm of *kelipah* and concealment.

Moreover, to a certain extent, a person who sins reaches an even lower level than the *kelipot* themselves. This is because the *kelipot* hide G-d's light as part of fulfilling the mission they were given directly by G-d to do (as explained in previous chapters). But a person who causes concealment of G-d's light by sinning is going against the will of G-d. Thus he denies G-d's oneness more than the *kelipah* itself.

This is why even the smallest of sins can totally and completely separate a person from G-d's oneness.

Based on this, we can try to understand how every sin is like idol worship. An idolater is someone who acknowledges G-d's existence, but refuses to nullify himself before G-d and His will. One who transgresses is doing the same: he knows that G-d exists, but denies His oneness. He does not accept that G-d is everywhere at all times, or that G-d actually cares about what he's doing at that moment. Naturally he feels free do to what he wants at the expense of what G-d wants.

It is clear to us that idol worship crosses a redline. Jews throughout history chose death over idolatry because they could fully sense that the act of bowing down to an idol would certainly cut them off from G-d and His Torah.

Now we see that the same separation from G-d caused by idolatry also occurs with *every little sin*. Please note that sinning doesn't cause us to lose our soul. Rather, it pushes the soul into a form of exile within our bodies, and thus it accompanies the body into *kelipah* during the sin. This means that a sin takes not only the Animal Soul but also the G-dly Soul down into *kelipah*, and what could be worse than sticking the king's son (along with the king himself) into a place of degradation?

Deep Sleep

Our soul is sleeping.

Our soul doesn't feel things because it is asleep. It doesn't feel the disconnection from G-d that occurs when we do even the slightest of sins-just like what happened when people used to worship idols.

Most of our life is so consumed by trivialities that we don't tune in to the wishes of our soul.

The soul wakes up when it feels itself drawing near the redline-an action that will cut it off from G-d. Typically, this happens only in an emergency.

Nevertheless, different individuals have different ideas of what constitutes an emergency. Different things wake up different people. Some are shocked to the depths of their soul at the suggestion of doing even a "small" sin, and they're ready to resist to the point of self-sacrifice. Others awaken only when their life is really on the line.

But that same core point, the inner Jewish spark, exists in *all of us*.

The Tablets of the Ten Commandments

There was once a Chassid who was involved in outreach work, trying to strengthen the faith of every Jew he met. In one such meeting, the Jew he was talking with accused him of meddling in his affairs.

"Why are you trying to inspire me to be more Jewish?" the man fumed. "Can't you mind your own business?"

"The entire Jewish people are like a Torah scroll," answered the Chassid. "And just like a Torah scroll is not valid if even only one letter is flawed or missing, so too we need all the Jewish people. If even one

Jew is missing, it's like ink missing from the Torah scroll. When one Jew is repaired, the wholeness of the entire Jewish people is restored."

Sometime later, when the Chassid was visiting his Rebbe, he asked if the analogy he had given was appropriate.

The Rebbe's face grew stern. "No, I am sorry, but it's incorrect to tell a Jew that he's like ink on parchment that could fade or get erased. That's like saying his soul is lacking something. Rather, every Jew can be compared to the tablets of the Ten Commandments. Each letter is engraved in the stone and an integral part of them.

"The tablets may get dusty and need to be cleaned in order to reveal the letters. But such concealment is merely superficial. The same idea applies to a Jew. His inner soul is clean and perfect and contains a unique Jewish spark.

"All that's necessary is to clean off the dust to reveal it."

A New Perspective

The previous chapters explained a process of contemplation that gave us a new perspective on the world in general and on the *mitzvot* in particular.

According to this deeper view of the world, G-d is everywhere and He gives everything in creation its existence and vitality, but His deep, internal will (what He really does and doesn't want) is written explicitly in the Torah-and not in all the details of creation. We connect to G-d through His guidance and instructions-the positive and negative *mitzvot* whose details are in the Torah that He gave us.

Fulfilling a positive commandment unites us with G-d in an eternal bond. Violating a prohibition (doing what He said not to do) cuts us off from Him and harms our relationship.

Most of the situations we encounter do not require the power of *mesirut mefesh* (self-sacrifice). If we are not faced with the need to clearly demonstrate if we belong to G-d or not, then our hidden powers and inner Jewish spark remain concealed deep within us. But now that we understand how every *mitzvah* connects us to G-d and even the slightest transgression separates us from Him, we can arouse the Jewish spark in our souls not only during emergencies, but also in everyday life.

We Awaken When We Face a Crisis

The *Tanya* helps us realize that we are actually in a state of emergency all the time. Internalizing this point will give us the ability to reveal our hidden powers and strength even in everyday life.

The *Tanya* also demonstrates how the level of *beinoni* is attainable for each of us. Everyone can practice restraint and avoid violating G-d's will in thought, speech, and action.

We know this is an attainable level because we have seen throughout history that everyone, even the simplest of Jews, is able to be *moser nefesh*-to be self-sacrificing in a crisis situation. When there is no other option, we rise to the occasion.

This applies to all of us all the time, now that we know that we're always in a state of emergency-that even the slightest sin threatens to separate us from the Creator as much as idol worship. Any time that we are able to withstand our tests, even without the need for contemplation and meditation, we are *moser nefesh*. All we have to do is recall who and what we are, and activate the spiritual emergency response measures in order to avoid sins in thought, speech, and action.

The same applies to fulfilling positive commandments. If I'm willing to undergo suffering for G-d's sake, then surely I'm willing to enthusiastically serve G-d, get up extra early to learn Torah with dedication and consistency, invest great energy in prayer, and push myself to give extra *tzedakah*.

Here's the punch line: If I'm willing to sacrifice myself to sanctify His Name, forgoing my life and even going through suffering for it, surely I can resist my urges and unhealthy desires and *live* a life that sanctifies His Name.

There Is No Choice

In the 1970s, a Chassidic family who had succeeded in maintaining their Jewish observance while living under the religious oppression of Communist Russia came to the U.S. and visited the famous Rabbi Moshe Feinstein.

He asked them how they were able to keep the Torah during such a difficult period.

The father answered, "Was there any other choice?"

This father had internalized the fact that Torah and *mitzvot* unite us with G-d, while the opposite separates us. He couldn't imagine life without Torah and *mitzvot*. From his perspective, there was no other option. There was no other choice.

Shema Yisrael

This helps us understand why the Jewish people are commanded to recite the *Shema* prayer twice a day, declaring G-d's unity. It's timeless, invaluable message puts us in touch with who and what we are, and helps us access our inner strength to serve G-d with self-sacrifice. This is the foundation of fulfilling Torah and *mitzvot*.

When we recall the fact that we have the power of complete devotion and self-sacrifice within us, the capability of foregoing everything for G-d's sake, there is no doubt that we are capable of overcoming our Animal Soul when it comes to the smaller issues of daily life.

In Conclusion

G-d is found everywhere at all times, but we don't see Him because He concealed Himself. To find G-d without any concealment we have to look in the Torah. And by connecting to the Torah we can "grasp" G-d.

Every *mitzvah* connects us to G-d, and every transgression separates us from G-d. We don't have to wait for an emergency situation in which our faith is tested in order to tap in to our soul. Any instance of not being connected to G-d is a crisis moment. Contemplating this will help us reveal our capacity for *mesirut nefesh* even in our regular daily experiences.

The Third Gate

Being Joyful

Tanya, Chapters 26-34

Chapter Seventeen

We Must be Happy

Achieving joy and overcoming depression are
vital for the G-dly Soul in its battle to overcome
the Animal Soul. Everything is for the good...
why get depressed over material matters?

(Tanya, chap. 26)

Happiness: A Means, Not an End

Our goal, as we have explained thus far, is to help our G-dly Soul be victorious in its battle against the Animal Soul. *Simchah* (joy) is one of the essential keys to winning the inner battle we encounter each day in this spiritual struggle. *Simchah* infuses us with tremendous *ko'ach* (strength), more than we can imagine we possess.

In the arena of sports, a person enlivened with energy and enthusiasm easily overcomes his opponent. Our spiritual victory in our daily battle is almost guaranteed when we feel energetic and exhilarated.

Why? Because joy frees our heart from worries and troubles that threaten to overwhelm us. It's not that the challenges disappear, but we have a greater ability to cope. Joy gives us the freedom to accomplish almost anything quickly and easily.

On the other hand, if our heart is heavy with worries that sadden us, it's as though our hearts are sealed shut. We become apathetic and lethargic and lose all our strength. Victory is impossible in such a state.

For this reason, Judaism views joy as a fundamental part of our daily spiritual work and service of G-d: *"Ivdu et H-shem besimchah!-* Serve G-d with joy!" (*Tehillim* 100:2). This is not just another thing that's important to do, like you have to pray, keep kosher, *and also* be joyful. Rather, it is a crucial element that must be present throughout the day. We need to pray with joy, give *tzedakah* with joy, keep kosher with joy-everything must be infused with joy!

(The fundamental importance of being joyous can be seen in the Hebrew language, which contains many words for different types of joy: *gilah, rinah, alizah, ditzah, me'ushar, chedvah, sasson,* and *simchah,* for example.)

Only Be Depressed If You Get Something Out of It

Feeling depressed creates an opening for the Animal Soul to

dominate us. It knows that depression makes us feel heavy, lethargic, and apathetic, and therefore much easier to defeat. There's nothing more powerful and effective in his service to G-d than a Jew who is happy!

That's why the Animal Soul invests a ton of effort into getting us depressed.

Sadness, though, can have a positive dimension, as long as it comes at an appropriate time, so that the great descent it puts us through can lead to an even greater elevation. For example, sometimes when we feel a little "stuck," it's the pain and anguish we experience and the tears we cry freely that enable us to find our way back to the right track. This is the sadness that *leads* us to *simchah* and is thus beneficial.

Such an emotion is called "bitterness," not "depression." Whereas depression weakens a person, causes him to despair, and makes him apathetic and even reclusive, *bitterness* or *remorse* is what we feel from contemplating our poor state of affairs. This generates a desire to change, progress, and actively climb up and out of the pit. It's popularly known as "hitting rock-bottom." And there's no place to go but *up*.

We're not talking about the kind of bitterness that's caused by resentment and self-pity, but rather the soulful introspection that inspires a decision to act for change.

How Do We Achieve Joy?

Thus far we've explained the importance of *simchah*, but how do we handle the fact that it's difficult to achieve and we aren't always successful?

In the coming chapters, we'll explore the things that interfere with joy, how to overcome our challenges, and how to deal with a closed, congested heart. Then we will explain what it means to truly be joyful with G-d.

To explain all this, we first need to discuss the things that prevent us from feeling *simchah*, and what it is that makes us constantly worry.

There are two primary causes: material worries and spiritual worries.

It's not uncommon for people to experience depression as a result of things that happen in life. But such feelings are obstacles that prevent us from being joyful. So what can we actually do when there are circumstances that seem to provide a legitimate reason to worry? Sudden illness, pain, chronic poor health, tragic accidents, being unable to find a soul mate, lack of marital harmony, difficulties in conceiving children, lack of finances, cruelty, injustice, and violence: the list goes on and on. Don't we *deserve* to be sad?

The First Step Toward Joy

To rid ourselves of sorrow and worries, we first have to *want* to be happy. It sounds too simple, almost strange, since who wouldn't want to be happy? But many people simply do not want to be happy-preferring instead to sit helplessly and bemoan their fate. And most people certainly don't realize that they have a *choice*. There is actually a tendency in Western culture to view happy people as shallow and depressed people as deep. So it's easier to remain unhappy; it fits in with one's self-image.

Therefore, the first step is to understand that we *need* to be happy-we are *obligated* to be happy. Happy people are healthier, more productive, enthusiastic, successful and motivated, full of a zest for life, and much more willing and able to help others. Our feelings of *simchah* has an impact on everyone and everything around us throughout the day. And, most important, we can easily defeat our Animal Soul when we are energized with joyous enthusiasm.

Now that we understand the value of being *besimchah*, and we at least *want* to be happy, how do we deal with all the reasons there are for being depressed?

The *Rosh Yeshivah*

About two hundred years ago, there lived a wealthy European rosh yeshivah (dean of a Torah academy), whose made his livelihood by transporting and selling timber down the river. One day a rumor reached the yeshivah that the river had overflowed. He had lost his entire investment-a huge amount of lumber.

The students were unsure how to tell the rosh yeshivah this devastating news, until one brave student volunteered.

Quietly entering the rabbi's room, he shared that he had just learned the Talmudic teaching that "just as a person blesses G-d for the good, so he should bless G-d for the bad."

"I heard the following explanation for this teaching," he added. "It's not that we should say the same blessing on both the good and the bad, since there are two different blessings for good and bad news. Rather, we should feel the same feeling of gratitude to G-d in either situation.

"But I don't understand this section of Talmud," said the student. "How can we be grateful to G-d for bad things that happen?"

The rabbi answered, "Everything G-d does is for the good. We may not immediately see this, but ultimately it is for the good. For example, when a person loses his job, and then he finds even better work elsewhere, or when a person is forced to move and many good things happen in his new location."

The student was not satisfied with this answer and told the rabbi that he still did not understand it. "If something is bad right now, what does it matter that it will later transform into good?"

"You have to know that everything happens with hashgachah pratit-Divine providence," the rabbi continued. "Nothing occurs in the world unless G-d wants it to happen. And since He wants what's good for us, then all that happens is undoubtedly for the good-even if we don't see at that moment how this can be."

The student was still dissatisfied and protested again. "This doesn't make sense to me. Even if I know something will eventually be revealed as being good, it still feels bad now."

So the rabbi tried to offer an even deeper explanation.

"The things in life that seem bad to us are really loftier and spiritually higher than the good things. Nothing bad comes down from Above, but sometimes the good that rains down on us is so great and intense that it seems bad. For example, a very strong light that shines on us is blinding and prevents us from seeing anything-not due to a lack of light, but rather from too much light. Sometimes the light is so great that it exceeds what we can handle and winds up blinding us temporarily. Yet the truth is that the suffering and tests we encounter actually demonstrate G-d's great love for us."

"Rabbi, do you mean to say that if we hear bad news we should begin to dance with joy?" the student responded.

The rabbi nodded in agreement.

"And if someone were to tell you now that your ship has sunk and all your property is gone, would you dance?" the student conintued.

Again, the rabbi nodded in agreement.

"If that's the case, esteemed Rabbi, then you can start dancing."

The rabbi immediately understood what his student was implying and he fainted.

When he recovered a few moments later, he turned to his student and said, "I also don't understand this piece of Talmud."

There are no worries when we are cognizant that our livelihood comes exclusively from G-d, because He can shower us with infinite blessings. The more we strengthen our awareness that our livelihood flows directly, abundantly, and unceasingly from G-d-the Source of all good-the easier it will be to deal with financial challenges. The same is true regarding other tribulations in life.

All for the Good

In previous chapters we explained that G-d is everywhere; He is with us constantly and continually sustaining the world. Everything that happens is under His supervision, with His approval, and exactly what He wants to happen. And even though it may not always appear as such, G-d wants what's best for us. Therefore, when bad things happen, we can keep in mind that it will lead to a good outcome.

The challenge is that we don't always grasp this. It's like a small child whose parents take something dangerous away from him. He cries because he doesn't understand that it's for his own good. He doesn't know that they will bring him another, safer, better toy.

We often feel the same way when something happens to us that is very painful, whether it's getting fired from our job or discovering we have a serious health problem. We are human and our first reaction is to cry. In that moment, it's easy to forget that everything is from G-d, that everything is part of G-d's plan, and that "this, too, is for the good."

Let's review the Torah's account of Yosef. After many long years of separation, Yosef is reunited with his brothers in Egypt. It was their jealousy and hatred toward him that led to their selling him into slavery, which brought him to Egypt. Now they are afraid that he will take revenge on them. Instead, Yosef tells his brothers that it was all for the good. As a result of what they had done to him, he is now the second-in-command in Egypt, almost as powerful as Pharaoh, and responsible for a plan for how to survive during the seven years of famine. G-d prepared the way for Yosef so he would be able to support his family in the years of famine.

The Donkey, the Rooster, and the Candle

The famous Rabbi Akiva was once on a trip visiting several villages. He had with him a donkey to carry his equipment, a rooster to awaken him in the morning, and a candle by which to learn Torah at night.

One night he arrived in a village where no one was able to host him. "It's all for the best," he said to himself and took his belongings and went to sleep in the forest.

In the middle of the night, a lion came and devoured his donkey. "It's all for the best," he said.

Then a fox came and ate his rooster. "It's all for the best," he said again.

Later, a wind blew out the candle. "It's all for the best," he repeated.

In the morning, Rabbi Akiva went into the village and discovered that robbers had entered the town during the night and abducted all the inhabitants. If any of them had agreed to host him, he would have been taken as well. Had the donkey or rooster made a noise, or the candle been shining, he would have been captured. Indeed, everything that had occurred was all for the best.

Accepting Suffering with Joy

Here's a deeper understanding of what happens to us: the greatest good is *specifically* the thing that appears to us as bad. When a sick child is given bitter medicine, he cries, certain that his parents hate him or even worse. He already starts to cry when he sees his parents approach the medicine cabinet.

He doesn't understand that it's for his good and they want to help cure him.

But what's harder for a parent to do-give a free gift or give lifesaving medicine to their child? Which act requires deeper soul powers from the parents? And which act best demonstrates the parents' love for their child?

The deepest bond and the strongest, most powerful love is revealed specifically when the parents are causing their child discomfort in order to heal him. The same applies in our relationship with G-d, our Father in Heaven. His greatest love for us is revealed when He causes us suffering that is meant to help heal us. It demonstrates that our bond with Him is very deep-as the verse states, "G-d rebukes the one He *loves*" (*Mishlei* 3:12).

When a stranger's child misbehaves, does it bother us enough to rebuke him? Usually not. But when there is a deep, loving relationship between a parent and child, when it's our own child, whom we deeply love, who needs rebuking, we will reprimand him.

However, let's be clear: this doesn't mean that we instantly feel like it is love when we are being reprimanded. Emotionally it may still hurt. But the more we are able to internalize this primary concept-that everything that happens to us is under direct *hashgachah pratit* from G-d, Who loves us with an unfathomable love-the easier it will be for us to accept suffering with joy.

This doesn't mean that we should *desire and seek out* suffering. We only want "good things" from our human perspective. But if we're already experiencing suffering, then understanding and accepting that it comes from G-d's love for us gives us the ability to feel joy in every situation.

What Suffering?

Rabbi Zusia, a student of the Maggid of Mezeritch, was known as a person who accepted suffering with joy. A Chassid once visited him in his decrepit hovel. The Chassid said that he had been sent by the Maggid in order to learn how to accept suffering with joy.

"I don't understand why you were sent to me," said Rabbi Zusia. "I have never experienced suffering."

Rabbi Zusia's perspective was so deeply internalized that he had reached a level where he no longer experienced his trials as suffering, but rather as the deep good that it really was. He so profoundly understood this concept that everything is for the good that it transformed his experience of life.

Nothing Is Ever Bad

To take this concept even deeper, not only is everything that happens for the good, and not only will we *eventually* see how it is good, but everything that happens is good right now already. It doesn't appear that way only because it's a level of good that's so powerful and lofty that it transcends our comprehension.

We can compare this to a rabbi teaching his students. If he taught them the material in all its intricate depth, understood from his level, they wouldn't grasp a thing and only get confused. At the very same moment that he's giving them the greatest of wisdom, his lofty level prevents his students from absorbing anything, and they perceive the experience negatively.

What would a caveman think if he entered a modern hospital and saw his father lying on an operating table surrounded by four people wearing robes and masks and holding up knives? Surely he would conclude that they're trying to kill his father, when in fact they are performing a lifesaving procedure.

Rabbi Nachum Ish Gamzu

Rabbi Nachum Ish Gamzu received his unique name because he was constantly saying, "Gam zu letovah-This, too, is for the good." He knew that it wasn't only that things would eventually *reveal how they are for the good, but that even* at the very moment *when they looked bad he could say it was good.*

The story is told that Nachum Ish Gamzu was once selected as the Jews' emissary for delivering a chest of jewels to the king, in the hope that this gesture would encourage the king to cancel a harsh decree against the Jews. On the way, Nachum Ish Gamzu stopped overnight at an inn. He awoke to discover that the innkeeper had stolen all the jewels and refilled the chest with sand. But, as usual, he said, "This, too, is for the best."

When the king opened the chest and found it full of sand, he was enraged. But G-d performed a miracle and sent Eliyahu the Prophet, disguised as one of the king's ministers, to suggest that this was the same miraculous sand that Avraham had used to win his battles.

The king immediately sent soldiers to test the sand.

When they verified that it was true, the king was thrilled. Completely appeased, he canceled the harsh decree against the Jews, ordered the chest refilled with jewels, and gave this gift to Nachum Ish Gamzu.

Changing Our Perspective

Often, people tend to feel estranged from G-d when bad things happen because they think G-d doesn't like them, that their suffering is a punishment being inflicted because they were so bad. But the truth is the opposite. "Punishment" from G-d comes from deep love, and G-d is very close to those who call upon Him in truth (*Tehillim* 145:18).

And there is nothing more truthful than the prayer of a person who calls out to G-d from the depths of his suffering.

When we change the glasses with which we look at the world, we see that G-d is absolutely everywhere, everything is for the good, G-d doesn't send us anything bad, and the suffering we experience is for our benefit. The whole picture begins to change, our hearts separate from pain and suffering, and our joy becomes more internalized. We can feel closer to G-d than ever before.

The challenge is what we will allow to determine our mood: that which our eyes see and our body feels, or what we know to be the truth-that even our suffering is for the good and is part of G-d's love for us.

In Conclusion

Overcoming our Animal Soul requires a state of joy. Sadness and depression are only beneficial when they become the catalyst for inner growth that can propel us to even higher levels of joy. Internalizing the truth of G-d's unfathomable love for us, and that everything He does is truly for our good, will help us remain joyful even when facing any issues that threaten to drag us down.

Chapter Eighteen

Spiritual Concerns

Never despair over your spiritual state. Depression over spiritual matters should be set aside and addressed only at preset times by doing *teshuvah*.

(Tanya, chaps. 27–28)

In the previous chapter, we explained that feeling sad and depressed over material matters is incorrect and unhealthy. Instead, we need to work on internalizing that absolutely everything is for the good. If we are always aware that even what seems bad is only for our good, we can always be happy.

But what if we are depressed over spiritual matters?

A person could reach a level where he no longer worries about his bank account or political issues, since he's internalized the fact that all is for the good. Now, however, he has concerns from a different source: spiritual matters, such as the state of his Divine service and past sins he committed. He's troubled because he appreciates the negative spiritual impact his transgressions cause, damaging his connection with G-d, and is depressed that only he is to blame. These thoughts can also bring him down, but they seem to be for a more "worthy cause."

Dealing with Spiritual Concerns

In the beginning of the *Tanya*, we learned about our two souls and the constant battle between them. We realized that for our G-dly Soul to be victorious, we need to get to know both souls very well.

Here is another thing that's important to know: depression is one of the most powerful weapons employed by the Animal Soul. He invests tremendous effort into this, since he knows that it's much easier to get us to follow him when we are down and broken. A depressed person is weak and lacks the strength to deal with the world. It's easier to bully a depressed person into acting against his will.

Therefore, bear this in mind: if you are in the middle of praying or learning Torah, and you get hit with a wave of depression over sins you've committed, it's clearly coming from the Animal Soul, which wants you to give up.

You are in the middle of serving G-d and he wants to stop you.

But he knows that you are too spiritually inspired by your prayers or studies to be dragged into a discussion about material worries. That's why the Animal Soul is trying to disturb you with your spiritual state. That's something you might heed.

You can handle this by completely ignoring this wave of troublesome thoughts coming from the Animal Soul, recognizing that he is the source. You can train yourself to switch gears and get your mind occupied with other subjects.

It's impossible not to think-our thoughts flow constantly. But we can steer our thoughts in a more positive, holy direction. This is possible because aspects of *kedushah* possess an inherent advantage over elements that oppose *kedushah*. It's like the superiority of light over darkness, where lighting even one small match instantly illuminates a darkened room. The same effect happens when you choose to entertain only positive, holy thoughts-the bad thoughts simply disappear.

"Healthy" Spiritual Worries

When the body is not well, it notifies us through the sensation of pain. We get the message that something is wrong and consult a doctor for diagnosis and treatment. Our soul does the same thing. When our soul has a problem, it also signals us with pains and worries.

If that's true, then why did we just suggest ignoring thoughts and worries about our spirituality?

The answer is that both are true. There are times that are appropriate for addressing distressing thoughts about our spiritual state. How else can we grow if we completely ignore them? The most favorable time built into the fabric of our lives is at the end of the day, when we recite the bedtime *Shema*. This is an auspicious time for introspection and contemplation of the day that just passed-what could have been done differently, how we can improve our behavior and make tomorrow more successful.

Throughout the day, when thoughts about our negative spiritual condition threaten to distract us while we are in the midst of serving G-d, we can tell them to "come back later." Then, when we will be reflecting on our spiritual state and resolving to make improvements, we can revisit them and let them through.

This is a healthy, positive process that can bring us great joy. It stems from being truly bothered by our shortcomings, being very committed to making changes, knowing that G-d grants forgiveness, and being aware of how the entire process has brought us even closer to G-d.

This is true G-dly joy inspired by the sadness felt during introspection. Negative thoughts that originate from a place of truth will return at the appropriate time when we can properly process them.

And if the thoughts that attacked us midday do not return, it is a sign that they were not coming from a place of *kedushah*, but rather from the Animal Soul who was trying to interfere with our spiritual efforts.

The Analogy of the Long Beard

Soul-searching is often compared to the inventory check conducted by a business owner. At the end of the day, month, or year, he assesses the amount of money earned and spent and uses his findings to determine what adjustments need to be made. Just as a businessman can't do inventory in the middle of the busy workday and waits instead for specially allotted times, so it is with spiritual accounting.

A person was walking down the street and saw a Jew with a long beard.

"Excuse me, Rabbi," said the man. "When you go to sleep at night, is your beard under the blanket or over it?"

The Jew stood in silence, unable to answer. For the next two weeks he couldn't sleep-plagued by thoughts about whether his beard was under or over the blanket while he slept.

Did it matter where his beard was? Certainly not! This Jew was plagued with worries about something trivial. In the same way, the Animal Soul loves to have us worry or obsess about something ridiculous so that we'll be unable to focus on what really matters. He especially wants us to assess our spiritual state throughout a busy day, when we can't really properly focus on this important task.

This is why true soul-searching about who we really are and how we can improve and become kinder, more considerate of others, more consistent in our Torah learning, more careful with our speech, etc., is done during preset times. This way we can truly focus on our introspection and assessment.

Spiritual Worries While Doing Mundane Tasks

What about negative thoughts that plague us during work and other mundane tasks and not when we are in the middle of our prayers or Torah study?

These can also be thoughts from the Animal Soul and not from a source of *kedushah*. Once again, our Animal Soul's approach is to get us to feel sad and down about our misdeeds, because then it's easier to sway us to transgress. The Animal Soul knows that once we feel sad, we'll start looking for ways to feel happy and up, and that's when the Animal Soul floods us with unhealthy suggestions for feeling better.

It's a one-two punch: first the Animal Soul "attacks" with negative thoughts and reminders of our lowly spiritual condition; then it tries to lure us into unhealthy pleasures and sins that will confirm in our minds that we really are hopeless and make us feel even lower. It's like the person who is dieting and knows he shouldn't eat that piece of cake. And once he breaks down and eats it, the Animal Soul rushes in to say, "See you can't keep a diet-just eat the whole cake!"

Thoughts about Our Present Spiritual Condition

We said that feelings of depression about transgressions we have done in the past must be pushed off to be dealt with at a prearranged time. But what can we do about negative thoughts that aren't about material matters or transgressions we committed in the past, but about where we are currently holding in life?

Once again, it may be the Animal Soul on the attack. In this case, he's trying to convince us that *at present* our condition is not good and we should feel depressed about that!

In other words, until now we were talking about getting bombarded by troublesome thoughts that claim that we are bad because of things we did in the past. The current case is a different story. The Animal Soul now knows that we'll ignore thoughts about how bad we are because of sins we did in the past. We have a strategy and we know it's better to deal with this at a later time. That's why he's using a different tactic: troubling us about our present state.

The Animal Soul fully concedes that either we haven't committed sins or we already did *teshuvah* and repented for them. Nevertheless-sins aside-he argues that our current spiritual standing is clearly poor. And his proof? The fact that we constantly encounter bad thoughts in the here and now: doubting our faith in G-d, denial of the Torah's truth, thinking of all kinds of inappropriate behavior, etc.

"Despite all your efforts," rages our Animal Soul, "you are still the same-full of arrogance, ego, and corruption! And not only is it not receding, it's actually growing and getting worse!"

The Solution: Joy

It seems that there's nothing to be happy about in this situation.

We are being dragged down, feeling despondent that there is any hope of overcoming all the internal negativity and baseness inside us.

Nevertheless, there is a reason to be joyful. We can feel happy that there is a Torah *mitzvah* that we can now fulfill: "Do not follow after your heart and after your eyes, by which you go astray" (*Bemidbar* 15:39). Every victory we achieve by ignoring these negative Animal Soul thoughts constitutes fulfillment of this *mitzvah*.

This joy is not about the distressing thoughts themselves, but rather that they provide us with an opportunity to perform another *mitzvah*, which strengthens our connection with G-d.

Also Know Where You Stand

In truth, there is a deeper dimension here. Another reason we feel depressed about having base thoughts is because we aren't properly aware of our true spiritual position. It's egotistical and arrogant to be depressed because we still have an active evil inclination within us that's generating bad thoughts. We can delude ourselves into thinking that we are *Tzaddikim* who have nullified all our evil inclination. But the appearance of negative thoughts forces us to face the truth, and we get depressed.

None of this would bother us if we were clear about our true spiritual level. Even the *beinoni* who never sins (as explained at length in the first section) has yet to completely vanquish his Animal Soul. Not only does he have to contend with it, but it's actually grown stronger over time to maintain balance with his G-dly Soul-"the greater the person, the stronger the evil inclination."

"Itkafya"-Subjugating Evil

The main focus of the *beinoni*'s spiritual efforts is *itkafya*-subjugating the *yetzer hara*, the evil inclination, and not allowing it to express itself. This involves rejecting, countering, and pushing aside the evil inclination at every opportunity that arises in our daily lives. On the other hand, *ithapcha*-Aramaic for "transformation"-which involves transforming bad into good, is mainly the job of the *Tzaddikim*.

Despite the fact that the *beinoni* doesn't transform his evil inclination into good like the *Tzaddik*, every act of *itkafya,* of subjugating evil-every triumph over his *yetzer hara*-has a huge impact that gives G-d tremendous pleasure. As it says in the *Zohar*, one small act of *itkafya* does more to increase the honor of G-d than any other deed.

G-d's pleasure from our acts of *itkafya* can be compared to a naturally sharp, inedible food that a cook works to make tasty. The *beinoni* still possesses spiritual evil, but it has become "sweetened" after being subjugated so many times. Instead of transforming it, he channels it into good acts. On the other hand, G-d's pleasure from acts of *ithapcha* is compared to a food that is naturally sweet-just like the *Tzaddik* who is completely good and sweet.

The work of *itkafya*-of repressing the *yetzer hara*'s urges to violate prohibitions and overcoming cravings for overindulgence in permissible things-is one of the most fundamental parts of the *beinoni*'s life. And every act of *itkafya*, no matter how small, gives G-d great satisfaction.

For example, even when we eat kosher food, we can give G-d pleasure by choosing to eat foods because they are healthy and not just because they are tasty. And then, when we stop before we are completely full, it ensures that our eating was for the needs of the body and not just to satisfy lusts and cravings.

This also applies when we hold back from saying everything that's on our mind, when we hold back from listening to everything we wanted to hear, when we resist looking at something inappropriate, and of course pushing away negativity and inappropriate thoughts like judging people unfavorably.

To a certain extent, there is an advantage to *itkafya* over *ithapcha*-the *beinoni*'s role over the *Tzaddik*'s. It's not a surprise when a *Tzaddik* does G-d's will, since he has no struggle and nothing opposing him. But it's a big deal when the *beinoni* does G-d's will, since it means that he succeeded in overcoming his evil inclination and Animal Soul. And it makes no difference how mild (such as putting off a meal for a few minutes) or intense (such as avoiding gossip) the struggle was, because the *beinoni*, unlike the *Tzaddik*, has to overpower the desires of his Animal Soul in everything he does.

The Parrot Analogy

The incredible quality of the *beinoni*'s *itkafya*, even when applied to the smallest of things, is similar to the way we feel when watching a parrot speak. We are amazed at the feat, even if the parrot repeats one simple word. But it's not the parrot's great wisdom that amazes us-it's the simple fact that a bird can talk! It defies what we know of the laws of nature, where humans talk and animals don't. Similarly, when the *beinoni* goes against his nature and represses his Animal Soul's urges, it is an amazing feat!

According to the *Talmud*, even the smallest efforts that we make to act in a holy way has a big impact on High and results in great holiness descending upon us-i.e., each *mitzvah* we do results in an opportunity to do another one.

So, too, every small act of *itkafya* that we do here in the physical world has a massive effect on the spiritual realms. And as a result we receive tremendous power to progress even further in our spiritual work. In other words, the merit of our acts of *itkafya* helps us obtain greater G-dly assistance in our Divine service. This is no small matter.

To Be Holy

It's important to point out that the idea of *itkafya* is not a novel concept found only in the *Tanya* or the teachings of *Chassidut*. It's a positive *mitzvah* from the Torah. As the commentaries discuss on the verse "You shall be holy" (*Vayikra* 20:26), this means that we are obligated to sanctify ourselves even in permitted activities. Even with things that are permitted, we are required to try to control our *yetzer hara*'s urges. For example, eating is permitted-but we can stop before we become over-satiated. Ideally, our involvement with all things that are permitted can be for a holy purpose.

This is how the *beinoni* fulfills the commandment "You shall be holy." He's not a *Tzaddik* and will always have an inner struggle with his Animal Soul. By becoming accustomed to practicing *itkafya*, he will slowly progress and be sanctified, and he will see positive changes in his struggle with the Animal Soul.

Gradually, the battles will change and become more subtle. The war is not yet over, but the battles are significantly easier-no more sieges and nonstop attacks, for the *beinoni* has now reached a higher level. What was once a major battle will no longer be an issue.

Being aware of the work ahead, our work of *itkafya*, will help us face the Animal Soul when it tries to convince us that we have failed in our spiritual efforts. We are not *Tzaddikim*-of course we are going to have spiritual struggles! And the more we struggle and prevail over the Animal Soul, the more we strengthen our connection with G-d. What greater joy can there be than this?

Foreign Thoughts during Prayer

Until now we explained how to handle various worries:

Dealing with aggravating thoughts about material matters by knowing that everything is for the good

Dealing with troublesome thoughts about past sins only during the introspective bedtime *Shema*

Dealing with distressing thoughts about our present spiritual condition by being joyful that we can now fulfill the *mitzvah* of "Do not stray after your heart"

But what should the *beinoni* do about disturbing thoughts that attack him during prayer, even when he's praying with great *kavanah*? What approach should he take then?

In this situation, unlike annoying thoughts that pop up in the middle of the day, which give us an opportunity to be joyful when pushing them away, these should be completely ignored! As we are taught, "Struggling with a filthy person will make you filthy as well." The smallest fraction of a second in which we consider the source and cause for such thoughts is already a defeat. These are thoughts that should be banished completely.

Pushing Away Thoughts

One of the Baal Shem Tov's Chassidim asked for advice about overcoming improper thoughts. The Baal Shem Tov sent him to find the answer by visiting another Chassid in a particular village.

It was late at night when the Chassid arrived at the village, but he noticed that a light was still on in the house. He knocked on the door, but there was no answer. He knocked again, only louder. Still no answer. He tried again and again and again, yet no one opened the door. Eventually he gave up and went to find somewhere else to spend the night.

In the morning he returned and was welcomed warmly. The other Chassid happily hosted his guest for several days. Although the Chassid observed his host very carefully, he could not pick up any clues of advice for his struggle.

Just before he left, he revealed to the host that he had been sent by the Baal Shem Tov to learn how to deal with improper thoughts, yet he still didn't know what to do.

"But I already showed you when you first arrived," said his host. "I didn't open the door and welcome you in when you knocked. Ignore those thoughts!"

Opening the door to confront the person knocking is already a level of interaction. Any attention paid to foreign thoughts is an achievement of their goal.

If a temperamental person enters the synagogue and brazenly approaches you during prayer for the sole purpose of annoying and confusing you, you'd certainly ignore him and put even more effort into concentrating on your prayers. This is how you need to perceive any foreign thoughts that want to disturb your praying.

And If You Need to, Seek Help

Just because we have such thoughts doesn't mean we have to be sad and fall into despair, G-d forbid. On the contrary, they should make us happy. The fact that these troubling thoughts are attacking us in the midst of prayer is *the best proof that we are praying properly.*

The *Zohar* calls prayer a "time of war," since the main battle between the souls is waged during the process of prayer. The Animal Soul knows that prayer has an impact on our entire day. And if during that time of prayer we get a taste of holiness by tuning in to He before Whom we are standing, what our job is, and what our goal in life is- then the rest of the day will be similarly influenced and inspired.

Such a possibility worries the Animal Soul, so it exerts great energy to oppose the G-dly Soul especially during prayer. When threatened, the Animal Soul is motivated to attack the G-dly Soul and interfere with its efforts. Therefore, the Animal Soul launches extra, more intense attacks specifically because the G-dly Soul is praying so well. We can feel encouraged by viewing this opposition as a compliment.

We sometimes find that the negative, Animal Soul–based thoughts that are plaguing us disappear the moment we finish praying. This is further proof that they were coming from an impure source.

If you are unable to ignore these disturbing thoughts during prayer, here is a very effective strategy: pray directly and sincerely to G-d to have compassion and help you by removing the distracting thoughts. Because of the incredible impact our prayers have on the higher realms, G-d is very aware of the importance of our struggles, and as such, it's no longer just a private, personal appeal for help. We say in prayer, "Act for Your sake and deliver us" (*Yirmiyahu* 14:7). It's time to stop viewing the world from our self-centered perspective that sees the struggle as our personal problem.

Since we each have a G-dly soul that is "truly a part of G-d Above," the battle involves Him as well. This perspective is enough to weaken the *kelipah*'s hold over us and elevate the struggle from a personal, ego battle to a G-dly war. From here, with the realization, that what we do and think matters so significantly, the path to the soul's victory is much easier.

G-d Wants Your Bothersome Thoughts

Rebbe Menachem Mendel of Kotzk once turned to one of his Chassidim and said, "I know what you were thinking during the Yom Kippur prayers this year.

"At first you asked G-d to help you find work so that you would have enough income to be able to study Torah and pray in peace. But then you thought about it further and realized that having too much money would also burden you with worries, so you asked for less."

The Chassid stood there in shocked silence.

"But perhaps G-d wants you to have burdens that you nevertheless overcome and then you can successfully pray and study Torah," the Rebbe concluded.

In Conclusion

Distracting thoughts about past sins should only be dealt with at set times. Distressing thoughts about our present poor spiritual condition stem from an incorrect self-assessment. When worrisome thoughts attack us during the day, be happy about the opportunity to fulfill the *mitzvah* of "Do not stray after your heart and eyes." When these disturbing thoughts appear during prayer, they are a sign that our prayer is good. Ignored them completely and put even more effort into your prayers.

	Depressed about your material situation (health, family, livelihood)	Depressed that you sinned in the past	Depressed that you have sinful thoughts during the day	Depressed that you have sinful thoughts during prayer or Torah study
Incorrect perception	See your material struggles as bad while ignoring their Source and the ultimate intention behind them.	I have to deal with these thoughts about my previous sins right now.	Someone on my level should not be having such thoughts.	These thoughts prove that my prayers are no good.
Correct perception	"Everything is for the good"-suffering is an expression of G-d's love for us and is really all good.	When such a thought attacks in the middle of the day, it's a sign that it's coming from the Animal Soul to knock me down. I will tell the thought to go away now; I'll pay attention to it later during the bedtime Shema. Then I'll be able to do teshuvah and feel happy because G-d is forgiving.	Only a Tzaddik is free from such thoughts. I should be happy since these thoughts give me an opportunity to fulfill the mitzvah of "Do not stray after your heart."	The G-dly Soul's prayers are so powerful that the Animal Soul feels threatened and is trying to slow it down. I'm going to ignore these thoughts and pray even more intensely. And if I fail to ignore them, I'll beg G-d for His merciful assistance.

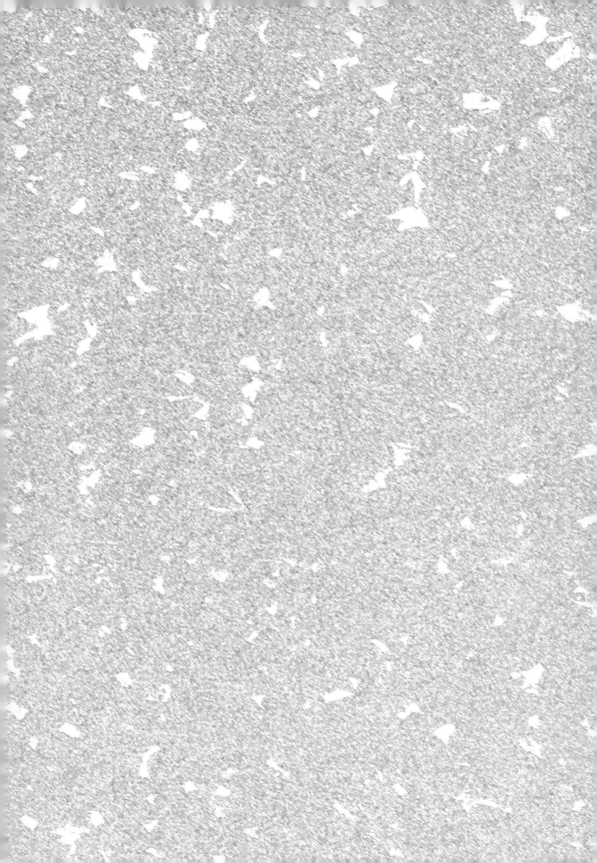

Chapter Nineteen

A Broken Heart Is a Whole Heart

When the problem is not with cognitive understanding
but with emotional perception, it is a problem
of too much self-satisfaction. One must do true
and fundamental soul-searching and arrive at the
conclusion that one should not be so satisfied.

(Tanya, chaps. 29–30)

We've been speaking about different kinds of intrusive thoughts that block us from being happy and techniques for overcoming them.

But what happens if we are succeeding at overcoming our negative thoughts, yet we still don't feel joy because our heart is congested and closed, hard as a rock, unable to feel?

Such a state is called *"timtum halev"* (related to the word *"atimut"*- impenetrable, dull) and requires a different kind of treatment.

A Heart Problem

In previous chapters, we discussed the *intellectual* approach to treating depression- our incorrect reading of the facts can make us depressed. When we understand that there is a Creator of the world Who controls everything and does what's in our best interests, we will naturally be happy.

Now we are talking about a different situation: intellectually we see the picture correctly, and intellectually we know that everything is for the good, but we don't connect emotionally with what we know. Our feelings don't follow and we remain sad. The problem is not with our comprehension, but rather with our ability to internalize what we know and translate that into how we feel.

With a blocked heart, we are unable to pray or access our emotions, and so we continue to feel depressed and weighed down. Here it doesn't help to *know* that everything is for the good since it's a heart problem, not a mind problem.

Spiritual heart congestion is primarily caused by too much self-satisfaction. We are so content with ourselves that we fail to notice our shortcomings, lose touch with our surroundings, and are completely numb. As a result of our overconfidence about being totally fine, we become arrogant and our hearts are blocked. This causes emotional issues whose symptoms include anger, bitterness, and a lack of joy.

In such a state, logic, reasoning, and explanations are ineffective, and a different approach is necessary.

The recommended treatment is offered in the *Zohar*: "A [thick] log that doesn't catch fire should be splintered." The same strategy can be applied to the soul. A clogged heart leads to spiritual insensitivity; and without the ability to feel, the "fire" of the soul can't catch and ignite the heart. The treatment: "break" the heart, and it will ignite with the soul's fiery love.

Crushed in Order to Be Whole

This "breaking" is done with thorough introspection-deep inspection of one's soul and self. When we take an objective look at ourselves without any sugarcoating, our self-examination reaches our very core and reveals that the Animal Soul is still the major player in our inner world (even in the *beinoni*). We are still full of cravings and negative thoughts that alienate us from G-d.

Or perhaps we already passed this stage and are currently free from sin. In such a case, our introspection can focus on our history of sinning and help us understand that we are still imperfect.

Sometimes we may find that we are praying properly and feel love for G-d, but the feelings vanish soon afterward. We conduct an accounting of the soul but fail to find any blemish. In this case, the approach is to think about the content of our dreams and how they demonstrate where we are truly holding in our spiritual efforts.

Either way, our efforts to shatter the heart, feel pained over our state, and confront our evil urges are specifically what will enable us to overcome the Animal Soul.

Imagine a person who angers easily and struggles to bring it under control, or maybe he is sad and depressed and can't seem to find joy. After learning the previous chapters, he already knows that it's wrong to feel this way-but it doesn't help to change the situation. His problem is not one of understanding, but rather that *he can't transform what he understands into feelings*.

Instead, he has to "break" his ego and dismantle the faulty image he has of himself being on a higher level than he truly is. By being angry at his anger or depressed about his depression, he'll be able to open up and free his heart so that everything he understands can translate into emotions.

Suffering: Motivated *Teshuvah*

When people see a friend of theirs turn to a life of Jewish observance after going through great suffering, like a divorce or bankruptcy, they assume that the experience left him feeling vulnerable and in need of comforting, and he found solace in religion.

That's not correct. While he was busy living his life, he never paid any attention to his soul. But the suffering he went through flattened his ego and enabled him to start to feel his spiritual side. This is what led to his *teshuvah*.

Darkness Is Nothingness

As mentioned, the problem we are currently addressing is different from the previous ones. It's not a lack of understanding, but rather a struggle to connect to the understanding and develop appropriate feelings.

This problem is caused by an overabundance of ego, which is compared to darkness. The soul, on the other hand, is compared to light. When we examine the difference between light and darkness, we must know that light is a true state of existence, while darkness is not, since it's actually just the absence of light.

This applies to us as well. The soul is the true reality. Ego and arrogance are nothing more than a lack of awareness within the soul.

This idea presents us with another method for stamping out arrogance and ego: strength and toughness. Sometimes it's necessary to speak aggressively to our Animal Soul. Since "darkness" has no true existence, our tough talk reveals its nothingness. In fact, the only reason that *kelipah* appears strong and powerful to us is to empower us to stand up to it.

The Ugly Jew

The Talmud tells a story about Rabbi Elazar ben Shimon, who once saw a particular Jew in the marketplace and called him ugly.

"If you have a problem with my appearance," said the Jew, "then go complain to the craftsman who created me" (i.e., the Creator of the World).

But Rabbi Elazar was not referring to a physical ugliness, but rather a spiritual lack of beauty. He only spoke harshly to the Jew in order to break the kelipah of arrogance enveloping him and help open a channel to his soul.

When the man himself, in his reply to Rabbi Elazar, mentioned his Creator, this awakened him to rediscover his faith and do teshuvah so that his soul was no longer "ugly."

This is also the way Moshe Rabbeinu spoke to the spies when he rebuked them for speaking poorly about the Land of Israel. He didn't try to convince them of Israel's goodness because he knew that buried inside them was the fact that they were "believers and sons of believers." Only, the *kelipah* had overcome them with its concealment. That's why he spoke to them aggressively, with anger-in order to nullify the *kelipah,* so they would regret their words and do *teshuvah* for speaking against the Land of Israel.

We should also use this approach when faced with doubts about our faith and belief in G-d. Such thoughts have no truth to them, and when we forcefully stand up to them, they are instantly nullified.

Judging Favorably

Crushing, brutally honest self-examination may indeed help a person feel less self-satisfied. However, he may still feel that his condition is much better than that of his friends and acquaintances. Instead of looking further into his own shortcomings, he turns and looks at others and figures, *I may not be perfect, but compared to everyone else, I'm not so bad!*

There is an additional contemplation to treat this, which incidentally can teach us an important lesson in judging others favorably.

We often look at others and judge them by *our* standards and morals, concluding that we're better than them. But the proper way to assess someone is according to his personal situation, as taught in *Pirkei Avot* (2:4): "Don't judge someone until you have stood in his place." The *Mishnah* is teaching us that it's entirely possible that if we were in his shoes, had his soul, grew up as he did, in his environment, and were currently confronted with the same situation-we would also sin, and perhaps even more.

The truth is, everyone is challenged on his individual level. One person's test is avoiding sins and conquering lusts, but overcoming his *yetzer hara*-the evil inclination of his Animal Soul-requires activating all of his inner powers. Another person needs those inner powers in order to pray with concentration, recite blessings with intent, or refrain from gossip and idle talk. Yet if the second person fails to trigger these inner powers and overcome his test, he's no better than the first person who commits a sin. Both failed to reveal their inner strengths and overcome their Animal Souls on their level. Both have failed their personal test.

The fact that one man's test is greater than another one's test is irrelevant, since each one of us faces situations that are highly individualized and tailor-made.

Assess Ourselves

Judging others favorably is the recommended approach to take... with regard to others. With respect to ourselves, however, we can't use this as an excuse for sinning. Thus, when judging favorably, we need to think only about all of the influential factors in *the other person's* life, appreciate just how difficult his test is, and then ask ourselves, *But am I withstanding my own tests, which are less difficult than his?*

In other words, our introspection needs to assess ourselves (not others) by two measures:

1. **Quantity**-how many good deeds have I actually done? With this measure, we can determine whether or not we can do more.

2. **Quality**-how hard have I worked to achieve my current level? How much effort did I have to invest to do all those good deeds? How hard did I have to work in order to overcome my evil inclination? In other words-how subservient to G-d have I become along the way?

These assessments are not visible to others. It's quite possible that we are much worse than the simpleton. He may be exerting himself and investing much more effort than we are, and possibly even vanquishing the urges of his Animal Soul much more successfully. But because our life circumstances are different, the quantity assessment is in our favor and we appear to be on a higher level.

By truly meditating on this, we can fulfill the teaching in the *Mishnah* "Be humble before everyone"-i.e., truly feeling that we aren't better than other people and respecting others accordingly. The awareness that we may even be lower than others can break through the hard covering around our sealed hearts caused by too much ego and self-satisfaction.

Because the aforementioned meditation is likely to cause a person to feel depressed about the state of his life and his spiritual level, it's important to learn how to have a balanced perspective that enables us to transform depression into joy. We'll be exploring this in the upcoming chapters.

In Conclusion

Besides depression that comes from negative thinking, a spiritually congested heart can also rob us of our joy. This sealed heart syndrome is caused by too much ego and self-satisfaction, and it's treated with deep contemplation and examination of one's true spiritual condition. Because the heart is sealed by *kelipah*-which lacks a true sense of reality, and whose entire purpose is only to conceal the truth-we can overcome it by aggressive assertion in words, thoughts, and deeds.

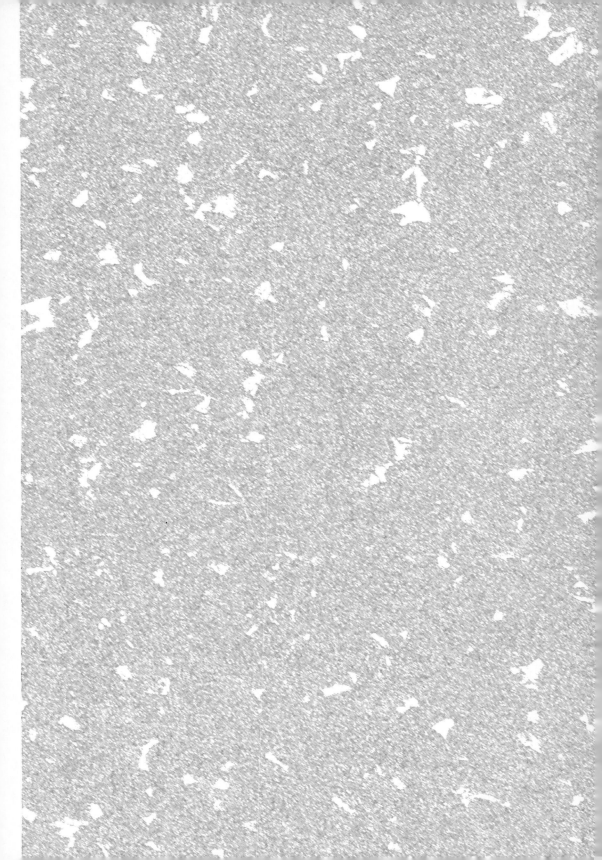

Chapter Twenty
True Joy

The joy that comes after soul-searching...

(Tanya, chap. 31)

When we are depressed because of too much self-involvement and ego, there is a simple solution: find someone more depressed than you and help them.

Why does this work?

We get depressed because we're too focused and stuck on ourselves. As soon as we help someone else, we get out of our self-centered focus. Then there's room for the joy to come back in...

Depression That Leads to Happiness

In the previous chapters, we explained that a lack of understanding prevents us from feeling happy. If our perspective on life is incorrect, narrow, and limited, it leads to depression. It's a mistake to look at the world around us and relate only to the physical reality while ignoring the deeper dimension.

A person who makes this mistake is unable to grasp that everything is for the good-and not just that it will *eventually be good*, but that it's *truly good* even right now as well. Without this perspective, many occurrences will knock us into depression.

Therefore, we discussed the fact that everything that happens is indeed for the good. From there we moved on and discussed what happens when a person understands that everything is for the good but is still depressed because his heart is spiritually congested, shut down, and unable to emotionally feel what his intellect knows.

We discussed how the problem is caused by ego and smug self-satisfaction, which can't be treated by deepening our understanding that everything is for the good. Our hearts don't feel what our minds understand. Instead, we need to deliver a crushing blow to the heart that deflates the ego. A congested heart conceals the soul, but a crushed and broken heart is unclogged and enables the soul's light to shine.

We explained how to crush the heart by subjecting it to a deep and truthful personal accounting that demonstrates how unjustified our feelings of self-satisfaction are. This intense introspective process leads us to cry and feel pained over how far we are from G-d compared to our initial false assessment.

There's only one problem: this solution doesn't seem to make sense. The original problem was depression, and here we see that the treatment causes depression! In other words, first we got advice on how to *prevent* depression and discussed how destructive depression is. But now we are offering an anti-depression treatment that involves feeling depressed?

The Ax and the Forest

There is a midrash that relates that when the metal blade of the ax was invented, the forest feared it as an enemy. The ax wisely pointed out, "I can't cut you down on my own. I have to be connected to a wooden handle. And since we have to work together, what are you worried about?"

In other words, it takes wood to chop down wood.

The same idea applies to the battle between *kedushah* and *kelipah*. *Kelipah* are elements in creation that conceal the *kedushah*, and the way to overcome *kelipah* is by using *kelipah* itself!

Depression comes from *kelipah* and is therefore forbidden. Yet there are situations in which the only way to overcome the *kelipah* and depression is by using the *kelipah* against itself.

It's the equivalent of "two negatives make a positive"-when two negative numbers are multiplied by each other, the answer is always a positive number. Being depressed about our depression gets us out of the depression. Feeling frustrated at our frustration gets us out of the frustration.

When we take a step back and review our situation, we realize that depression, frustration, anger, and a lack of joy all stem from the ego; by using it against itself, we can be free of it.

Thus, there's no reason to worry that the self-examination of the previous chapter will make us depressed. The opposite is likely to happen: feeling depressed will shake us up and deliver us from feeling depressed. However, the transition from depression to joy is not instant- an additional step is required: *merirut*, bitterness or ruefulness.

Bitter vs. Depressed

"Depression" means feeling weighed down, full of despair, and lacking the will to make changes in life. "Bitterness" is the feeling that despite how bad things seem, I want to change, improve, and advance my life.

On a deeper level, the pain felt in depression is about me: I am lacking, I am failing. The "I" is the main point. The pain felt in bitterness relates to the blemish in our relationship with G-d. Thus, depression brings us down, while bitterness leads us to change.

What You Are Needed For

A rich and generous Chassid of the Alter Rebbe lost everything and fell into heavy debt. He went to meet with the Alter Rebbe and tearfully shared his experiences. He sorrowfully mentioned that he didn't know what to do about the many tzedakah obligations he was committed to.

The Alter Rebbe replied, "Everything you told me thus far is about what you need. Have you given any thought to what you are needed for?"

With a shock, the Chassid heard his Rebbe's words and realized his mistake. His sorrow wasn't "for the sake of Heaven"-his tzedakah pledges were driven by his ego's need for honor. He was more bothered by his blemished reputation than what would happen to the poor people who needed the tzedekah.

When he realized this, he fainted on the spot.

When he came to, he resolved to make some changes and work hard to internalize this message. He stayed with the Alter Rebbe, spending time in deep contemplation and study that led to the joy of self-improvement.

After a few weeks, he received the Alter Rebbe's blessing to return to his trading business and soon regained his riches.

"Bitterness": When and How?

In previous chapters, we discussed dealing with depressing thoughts by pushing them off and confronting them at a later, prearranged time. In this case, the situation is different and there is no need to wait.

Pushing off depressing thoughts relates to depression over spiritual matters. However, when we feel depressed about material matters, and it's hard to internalize the fact that everything is for good, now is the time for a spiritual accounting that shakes our core and moves us to bitterness. In this way, the depression doesn't lead to despair. Instead, the depression can be a catalyst that motivates us into action.

Get Up and Do

A story is told about yeshivah students in Communist Russia who were secretly learning with their rabbi. They were discussing what needed improvement in their spiritual lives when the child on lookout duty suddenly signaled that the secret police were approaching. Instantly they all hid.

Once the danger had passed, the rabbi asked them, "Why did you flee so fast?"

They said they had been afraid for their lives.

"If you know how to flee when you think your lives are in danger, why did you just sit there and cry over your spiritual states instead of getting up and making a change?"

When something truly hurts or bothers us-and not just our ego-we spring into action and make changes.

When material things depress us, even though we know intellectually that it's all for the good, when we can't break free of depression's heaviness and find joy, it's time for self-assessment regarding the state of our spiritual lives. And once we see that our spiritual state is not as great as we imagined it to be, and perhaps even less healthy and worse off than our physical state, our material concerns suddenly seem far less relevant.

Imagine a person who is depressed because he owes a local store a thousand dollars. As soon as he remembers that he owes the bank a hundred thousand dollars, the debt to the store becomes a smaller issue and bothers him less. His real problem is the larger debt to the bank.

So too we can be "depressed" about our bigger problem-our spiritual state of affairs.

A true assessment of the state of our spiritual life and how far away we are from G-d (the emphasis is on the "far from G-d," not the "I") will pull us out of the mud and get us working on making changes in our life. After that, true joy is already on the way.

The fact that a person fell to the lowest levels doesn't have to hinder his happiness. We have two souls: the G-dly Soul and the Animal Soul. Our fall-regardless of how far or low we may have fallen, and what negative things we did-comes entirely from the Animal Soul.

Even at our lowest points we still have our G-dly Soul. Granted, it was in a state of exile when we sinned, but it was nevertheless always there. And now that we have "awakened" from our depression and are in the process of making changes that will lead to joy, we can free the G-dly Soul from its exile and enable it to serve G-d.

Thus, at this point there is no longer a need to feel depressed about being far from G-d. In fact the opposite is true: the farther away we were from G-d, and the "deeper" in exile that our G-dly Soul was-the greater our joy when the G-dly Soul is liberated from exile.

The Source of Joy

It seems that the reason for being happy is the fact that we have a G-dly Soul-"a real piece of G-d above"!

This is like a prince (the soul) who is in prison (the body). When he is freed and returns to his father's home, the joy is immense. And even though the body and the Animal Soul remain unchanged (and there is no guarantee that they will change any time soon), it doesn't interfere with our joy. Our happiness is due to the G-dly Soul's freedom from the prison and exile in which it was being held.

We can all reach such a level of clarity about how important and precious the G-dly Soul is to us, that only it is allowed to influence us.

This should be our attitude when we study Torah or perform any *mitzvah*: we can feel great joy over the fact that every *mitzvah* frees the G-dly Soul from its imprisonment.

And even though we know that the body and the Animal Soul are still there, and in which direction they wish to go, this doesn't need to depress us. After all, I didn't create myself! I didn't decide to have a body that's attracted to pleasures and negative things. It was G-d's idea, and part of G-d's plan.

This appreciation helps us transform our personal problem (the Animal Soul is always a solo performer) into a problem we share with the Creator, since He made the system. When our approach to problems ceases to come from a selfish, ego perspective, actualizing a solution is much easier.

When we see life tainted by our ego, we are always at risk of depression. When we put ourselves at the center of everything, then the constant feeling is, *I* lack and *I* am not close enough to G-d. But by approaching all of our problems and challenges collectively, with G-d as our partner, it is much easier to rise above depression.

G-d made things this way because he wanted the soul to experience *"yeridah letzorech aliyah,"* descent for the sake of a later ascent. As such, there's nothing to be depressed about, since this is how to play the game and we can't change the rules. What we can do is play by the rules that meet the soul's needs by letting it express itself physically via Torah and *mitzvot*.

In Conclusion

It's not enough to intellectually understand that everything is for the good. Sometimes our ego prevents us from experiencing the feelings that should accompany this understanding. By overcoming the ego we can turn depression into bitterness, which will lead us to action and repair.

This descent is for the sole purpose of ascent. And when we free ourselves from depression and restore our soul to its source-that is the greatest joy possible.

Chapter Twenty-One

The Joy of the Soul

G-d is cause for feeling true joy-
joy for the sake of joy.

(Tanya, chaps. 33–34)

In the previous chapters, we discussed how to deal with our problematic ego, the self-satisfaction that prevents us from being truly happy. By overcoming our ego, we can stop feeling depressed and achieve deep happiness.

In this chapter, we'll look at another method that everyone can use in order to feel joy at any moment. This method is called "warming" up. When a person feels that someone greater than him loves and cares for him, someone who gives him warmth and affection, it "melts" his arrogance.

The Joy of Relationship

There is a level of joy that isn't dependent on external factors, like money or health. Happiness that depends on outside factors does not last. As soon as those factors change or disappear, so does the joy.

True everlasting joy is based on *relationship,* not on the possession of things. Like the joy that a simple peasant felt when he was given the chance to sit next to the king, or, in our day, there is the joy of a youth who has the chance to talk to a person he totally admires.

If we truly understood that the King of kings, the Creator of the universe, cares so much about us and is right here with us *all the time,* our joy would be unlimited.

A Deeper Contemplation

Finding true joy in this way requires a deeper level of contemplation than the kinds described previously. It is based on the understanding of who G-d is and who we are.

When we keep in mind that G-d is infinite and we are finite, this helps us understand that there is absolutely no comparison between G-d and the world. Just as He was everywhere and filled every space *before* the creation of the world, so He is everywhere and fills the world right now. The world is nullified before Him, infinitely incomparable to Him, and *does not possess true existence* except by His will. So even though we can't see Him, He is actually everywhere at all times.

Thinking about this point should fill us with tremendous happiness. Especially if our depression was caused by arrogance and ego, which happens when we don't sense G-d's presence right next to us. If we are able to deeply contemplate and internalize the fact that G-d is always with us (through good and bad), we will be free to rejoice just from the fact that we are always together with Him.

How Fortunate We Are

Set aside a moment to contemplate this. Stop everything else, sit down, and meditate on our great privilege to be alive *now* and be close to the Creator of the world. As soon as we understand that G-d is exalted far beyond anything that could possibly block His light, our perspective is entirely altered.

A person who suddenly inherits a huge amount of money from a relative feels incredible joy. We have received a priceless inheritance from our forefathers, worth more than anything: faith that G-d is always here with us.

This is why the prophet Chavakuk wrote, "The righteous shall live by their faith" (*Chavakuk* 2:4). *Emunah*-faith-is the one *mitzvah* that serves as the foundation for all the other *mitzvot*. The joy we feel from our faith that G-d is with us inspires us to fulfill more *mitzvot*, which bring us more joy, as we will soon see.

How We Know that G-d Loves Us

Intellectually knowing and believing that G-d is with us in all places at all times is a tremendous reason to be happy. How can we prove to ourselves that G-d loves us and is with us every second?

One very effective technique is to make a list of everything we have that we can be grateful for. When the *yetzer hara* is attacking, trying to prove how far from G-d we are, we can counter by reviewing our list: G-d gave me eyes to see, ears to hear, legs to walk, hands that perform countless tasks. We can list every item we have that we benefit from every day: our shoes, clothes, home, furniture, food, water.

The more we elaborate, the more grateful we will feel. For example, instead of thinking how much we appreciate having food to eat, we can say thank You for each *type* of food: many kinds of fruit, many varieties of vegetables, how colorful and tasty each one is, etc.

A Bag of Diamonds

The great happiness we feel from our gratitude for G-d's abundant blessings fills us with incredible excitement and vitality. This inspires us to fulfill the *mitzvot,* not as a heavy obligation, but as a way of expressing our abundant gratitude to G-d Who gives us so much.

Our *mitzvot* are really a tremendous privilege, allowing us to serve G-d Who loves us!

If the *mitzvot* feel like a heavy sack of stones, we don't run to take on more *mitzvot*. But if they feel like a precious sack of diamonds, then we are happy and grateful to add more.

Double Joy

When a person does *mitzvot* with great joy, he brings G-d joy as well- including our work of *itkafya* and *ithapcha,* as explained in previous chapters. And then, in addition to that joy, we feel even more joy from knowing that our good deeds generate joy up above.

It's like a child who is happy because he can make his parents happy. And he's even happier when he *sees* just how happy he made his parents. So every Jew can feel abundant joy because:

1. G-d is with us, and
2. G-d delights in our efforts.

The Holy Brothers

Two holy brothers, Rabbi Elimelech of Lizhensk and Rabbi Zusia of Anipoli, were arrested by the Russian government and thrown into a small, crowded prison cell with one pail in the middle to be used as a toilet.

Elimelech was distraught. "With that pail here in our midst, we are forbidden to think about Torah!" he cried.

But his brother Zusia was full of joy.

"What is there to be happy about?" challenged Elimelech. "We are in a small crowded cell, the only Jews here, and we can't even think about Torah because of that pail!"

Zusia responded, "Usually I'm happy when I connect to G-d through Torah study. But that pail makes it impossible. So, instead I'm happy because I am a Jew."

When he heard this, Elimelech also became filled with joy, and the two brothers began to sing and dance.

When the guards came to see what the noise was all about and why the two Jews would dare to be so happy, all the prisoners pointed to the pail. The guards immediately removed it. Now Rabbi Elimelech and Rabbi Zusia could even study Torah!

Everyone has a "pail" in his soul that prevents him from being happy. In order to remove it, we have to tap into the source of true happiness, something that isn't dependent on external things. One internal factor that isn't dependent on any externalities is simply that you are a Jew and G-d loves you. With such joy, you can be assured of successfully getting rid of the pail.

"Make for Me a Sanctuary"

After we have done deep, incredible meditation about G-d's oneness and His presence that is always with us, how can we retain these powerful conclusions? How can we ensure that they stay with us and become a permanent part of our consciousness? How can we truly feel that G-d is right here with us at all times? How can we make this part of our daily physical lives without having to hide away from the world?

The answer is by living a life of Torah and *mitzvot*.

When the *Beit Hamikdash* (Holy Temple) stood in Jerusalem, a Jew could go there and "meet" G-d. The *Beit Hamikdash* was a place of tremendous holiness, where G-d's presence could always be felt and tangibly perceived. After the destruction of the *Beit Hamikdash*, G-d's presence was sent into exile, along with the Jewish people. "Meetings" with G-d could now happen only via Torah study.

G-d's presence is revealed when we learn Torah and fulfill *mitzvot*, making G-d always accessible. We have the ability to reveal G-d through the Torah and its *mitzvot* anytime!

Some people are able to learn Torah in *yeshivah* all day long. But setting aside special times for learning Torah regularly in the morning and at night (everyone according their level) is enough to make it happen. Going out into the world to work and do business according to the ethical guidelines of the Torah is also a meeting place for G-d. By conducting business with faith, giving *tzedakah* from our income, helping the poor, doing deeds of kindness-that is, by doing any Torah *mitzvah*-we are aware that we are with G-d all the time.

In Conclusion

True joy flows from the knowledge that G-d is always with us everywhere and delights in our efforts. Living a life of Torah and *mitzvot* enables this awareness to be absorbed and internalized deep inside our consciousness.

Chapter Twenty-Two
Loving Every Jew

In order to love every Jew, your soul has to be more important than your body-true love is soul to soul.

(Tanya, chap. 32)

The last few chapters dealt with negating depression and obtaining joy. First, we explained why it's so important to be happy. Joy gives us energy and fuels our inner strength so we can be victorious in our daily challenges.

Next, we explained that

• Depression about material matters is unnecessary (because everything is for the good, even suffering);

• Depression about our sins is unnecessary (we can deal with it later when we make a spiritual accounting at the end of the day; we are the boss of our thoughts);

• Depression about negative thoughts-desires, cravings, doubts in our belief in G-d-are unnecessary, and we should ignore them (only *Tzaddikim* are free from such thoughts; we aspire to be *beinonim*);

• And panicking because negative thoughts attack us in the middle of our prayers is unnecessary (on the contrary-it shows that we were praying properly, and our Animal Soul felt so threatened that it attacked us with all those thoughts to slow us down).

Then we addressed depression caused by a clogged-up, sealed heart. We discussed methods for crushing and breaking our heart that make it possible to feel five different types of joy:

1. Joy because we have a G-dly Soul, and every *mitzvah* we do frees it from its exile in the body and liberates it from the Animal Soul, which restricts and limits it.

2. Joy because the G-dly Soul can fulfill the principle of "descent for the sake of a later ascent," and express itself in the world through Torah and *mitzvot*.

3. Joy because G-d is everywhere and constantly gives us an opportunity to get closer to Him.

4. Joy because G-d is happy when we act properly.

5. Joy in the performance of Torah and *mitzvot*, through which we become a dwelling place for holiness.

In this chapter, we will see that one of the direct consequences of all of this, as well as a test of our joy, is fulfilling the *mitzvah* of *ahavat Yisrael*-loving our fellow Jew.

"Love Your Fellow as Yourself"

The Torah tells us to "love your fellow as yourself" (*Vayikra* 19:18). Is it really possible to love someone as much as we love ourselves? Can we care about someone else in the same way that we care about ourselves?

Can we see the positive in others the same way we see the positive in ourselves? Can we forgive others the same way we forgive ourselves? It seems like an impossible task!

Indeed, if we were just a body it *would* be impossible. But since we know that we are not just a body, that we also have a soul, true, unconditional love is possible.

One Soul

Our bodies are wholly self-focused, driven by the egotistical self-interest of the Animal Soul within us. The body sees the world through the ego's eyes, evaluating everything with one question: "What do *I* get out of it?" or "What's in it for *me*?" Wrapped up in ego and self-interest, the love that results is based on extrinsic factors, and this kind of love wanes as soon as those factors disappear.

When G-d created us, He placed within us a G-dly Soul that is literally a "part of G-d above"-a piece of G-d Himself that's implanted in each and every one of us. But because our souls are then sent into separate bodies in this world, this creates the illusion of distance and isolation from one another, when in fact all of our souls are part of one collective soul. The G-dly Soul feels deeply connected to the G-dly Soul within all other Jews. Knowing this truth helps us achieve real unity.

If we were capable of seeing each other the way we really are, from the perspective on High, we would see one large body comprised of all our souls together. Each of our souls is like a limb of this one body that contains all the souls.

Obviously we have never seen the limbs of our own body fight or feel disconnected from the other limbs. An arm doesn't fight with a leg; the ears do not feel estranged from the eyes. It is one working unit. In the same way, all souls feel united. Before the souls descended into the world to be divided into separate bodies, they were a single unit. Up in their spiritual source, the souls existed as one with no division among them. So controversy and arguments are impossible from the soul's perspective.

But because the soul is concealed in exile in a body, it is restricted from freely expressing its natural feeling of unity with all other souls. We can then get dragged into disagreements or become angry and judgmental toward one another.

As we learn how to be more than a body by discovering our soul, we become more elevated, and then we can start to feel what *ahavat Yisrael*-love for others-is truly about.

"That Is the Entire Torah"

When we choose spirituality over physicality and soul over body, we can begin to feel true love and connection. True love for a fellow Jew is possible only when we see that the soul is more important than the body. The goal of every *mitzvah* that G-d gave us is to help us learn how to give priority to our soul more than our body, so that we live our lives in harmony with the soul and we are not driven by the desires of the body.

The *Talmud* quotes Hillel the Elder as saying, "'Love your neighbor as yourself' is the entire Torah-all the rest is commentary."

When we learn Torah and fulfill G-d's *mitzvot,* we draw G-dly light down into the world. But the vessel for catching and absorbing this light is our unity. When *mitzvot* are performed without unity, the light is drawn down but there is no receptacle to contain it, like a pail full of holes that can't hold water. No matter how much liquid you add, the pail leaks. As such, our love and unity is the entire Torah, since this enables the G-dly light to come into the world and elevate all of us.

The greatest pleasure a parent has is when he sees all his children helping one another. When all of the family is sitting together around one table in love and unity, this gives the parents tremendous pleasure. Likewise, when the Jewish people get along, and there is unity among us, G-d's pleasure is even greater.

Joy: The Key to *Ahavat Yisrael*

As we learned earlier, joy enables us to be more sensitive to our soul than our body. Joy is a state in which our mood is determined by spiritual and not physical matters. When we are truly happy, the body and the material world become less significant. Physical differences between people also become less important, since our primary focus is on the common soul connection between us. If we are in touch with our souls, this enables us to see the souls of others. This emphasis on the soul more than the body fosters unity.

Though it's very popular to talk about unconditional love, unity, and equality, it's no simple matter. True love between us is only possible from the soul's perspective. When we reach the level where our soul is more important than our body, it becomes possible to love everyone.

We aren't implying that a person should neglecting his body-the Torah commands us to properly care for our bodies and guard our health. But this is a *mitzvah* we can fulfill without making our body the most important thing in our lives.

Since we naturally are very interested in our body, making the soul priority number one in our lives takes concerted effort. This effort is well worth it, as we will learn.

In essence, *ahavat Yisrael* is a reflection of how much emphasis we place on the spiritual versus the physical. When the root of our joy comes from the soul, we can love every Jew. But if our joy comes from our focus on bodily pleasures, it will be very difficult to love every Jew.

Love of a Fellow Jew and Love of G-d

Ahavat Yisrael is really an expression of one's love for G-d-when you love someone, you start to love what they love. And whom does G-d love? The Jewish people. Therefore, if we truly love G-d, then we naturally love our fellow Jew-our Beloved's child.

But what about a Jew who offended or hurt me? What about a Jew who stole something from me? What about a Jew who I see acting improperly? Just how much do we have to love every Jew?

We love another Jew because of his soul, not because of how he acts. A Jew may behave in a seriously offensive way and we may despise his conduct, but not the person himself. When we focus on his soul-which is really one with our own soul, like the limbs of one body-we can love him. Even if we have to take someone to a rabbinical court if necessary, we can still love *the person himself,* even while we dislike his behavior.

Put Your Spirituality on the Side

The Alter Rebbe was once seen leaving the synagogue in the middle of the Shabbat prayers. His congregants wondered why he had left and where he went. What could be so important to warrant leaving before the prayers were over?

Someone slipped out and followed him. He soon discovered that the Rebbe had gone to take care of an elderly widow who was sick in bed. He personally went to make sure she had warm food and a hot fire to save her from the icy cold. He put his own spirituality aside to help take care of another Jew's physical needs.

Ahavat Yisrael Is a *Mitzvah*

Loving other Jews is a *mitzvah*. G-d rewards us for loving our fellow Jew even if we don't see the results of our love affecting him. We need not worry that we may have somehow failed if we love others but we aren't loved back or we don't see whether or not we have an impact on him. Our obligation is to try to fulfill this vital *mitzvah*.

How can we possibly come to love every Jew?

Sometimes we claim to love everyone while at the same time we can't even love our next-door neighbor. It's true that the goal is to love everyone. But reaching that level starts with loving one person. Love just one Jew properly, and then move on toward loving everyone.

The ultimate goal, of course, is to love every Jew without limit-the impact on High will be immeasurable.

A Taste of the World to Come

Our prophets promise that in the future time of redemption, envy, hate, conflict, war, and competition will cease to exist as the world fills with the knowledge of G-d, and everyone will be conscious of our soul connection to one another.

We can live in this redemptive state even before Mashiach comes by tuning in to our souls more than our bodies. By being soul-focused, instead of body-focused, our sensitivity to the bond we all share will be heightened, and the things we think separate us will lessen in importance.

Though this may seem like no easy task, the path to reaching this elevated, joyous state is the same as the path to all true joy: changing our thought patterns, overcoming our animal ego and arrogance, and connecting to G-d through learning Torah and doing *mitzvot*.

As we learn to stop living in the world of the ego, and start living by the light of the soul, we will start seeing ourselves as G-d's servants, here to fulfill His will, not ours. And as we become closer to G-d, we will learn to be more like G-d, put on this earth to be givers, not receivers. This is the G-dly path to true satisfaction, to true joy.

What If We Don't Succeed?

What if we meet another Jew and find that we are unable to love him? What if we see only the bad in him; we can't seem to locate anything good about him?

If we are unable to overcome this perception, the best approach is to pity him. Feeling compassion for someone tempers our anger against them and encourages love. If we saw someone doing something very offensive, but we knew he had a terminal illness, our compassion would be aroused and overcome our anger and resentment.

We don't mean feeling compassionate out of arrogant feelings of superiority, thinking that we are better than the other person. Rather, we think about his situation and how far he is from G-d, and that's why he behaves this way. His soul is trapped and suffering, restricted from finding any means of expression in his life. It's the same as the pity we feel for our own soul when we are aware of our own lowly state.

In Conclusion

The souls of all the Jewish people are connected and united as one soul. To attain true *ahavat Yisrael,* we need to focus on our souls. We only fight and disagree when our bodies are more important to us than our souls. By focusing on the soul, we will discover an inner wellspring of love for every Jew, just as we love ourselves.

The Fourth Gate
It's All about Doing
Tanya, Chapters 35-37

Chapter Twenty-Three

Man's Soul Is a G-dly Candle

We achieve an even higher level of self-nullification,
and a natural unity with G-d, by doing *mitzvot*
than through our emotional experiences.

(Tanya, chap. 35)

In the first chapters, we had a lengthy discussion about the internal world of the *Tzaddik*, *rasha*, and *beinoni*.

The *Tzaddik*, we learned, is a person who has completely changed his essence. Not only are his thoughts, words, and deeds devoted to G-d, but he has also transformed his mind and emotions into pure good, completely focused on *kedushah*. He doesn't transgress, because even the *thought* of sinning never crosses his mind.

The *beinoni* is not on this level. He still possesses an evil inclination (i.e., ego, arrogance, concealment of G-dliness) in both his mind and heart, that is, his intellect and emotions, but it never gains access to his garments of expression (i.e., his thoughts, words, or actions). The *beinoni* constantly battles against his personal evil inclination in order to enable his G-dly Soul to dominate.

In the light of this description, we can see how hard and intense the *beinoni*'s life is, dominated by constant battles. And we may think (at least initially) that the struggle is in vain. No matter how hard and long he battles, the *beinoni* will always possess some evil and always be at war. He may win battles, but only a *Tzaddik* can win the war. So what's the point? If the only thing a *beinoni* accomplishes is victories in his garments (thoughts, words, and deeds), while his inner essence, intellect, and emotions remain unchanged, what has he accomplished?

We previously mentioned one possible answer when we learned that every small victory-pushing away a negative thought, holding back from speaking an unkind word, and so on-gives G-d great pleasure.

But this answer leads us to another question: why did the G-dly Soul have to be enwrapped in the Animal Soul and then the two of them put together in a physical body? If the whole purpose of our service is for the G-dly Soul to be victorious over the Animal Soul, then why stick the G-dly Soul inside the Animal Soul?

It would be enough to simply place them in the body and have each one "stay" on its own side. Why does the G-dly Soul have to work with the Animal Soul in order to keep the body alive, if it will never truly succeed in changing it through this venue?

The Purpose: Nullification

In order to answer this question, we need to examine the purpose of the creation of the world. Why was the world created? How do we benefit from it? And what does G-d get out of it?

Let's review and better understand how we connect with G-d.

We said that *kedushah* can reside only where we enable it to reside-where there is humility and nullification before G-d-because only someone who "makes space" for G-d in his life can receive His light. But regarding an arrogant, egotistical person, G-d says, "He and I can't reside in the same place."

Why is this true? Why does there have to be self-nullification? Is there no other way to make a vessel for G-d's light besides forgoing our pride, our sense of self-importance, and, it seems, our very being?

To truly grasp this, we have to think about the fact that G-d is infinite and unlimited while we are finite and limited. These thoughts can arouse a sense of humility in us.

Nullified before the Infinite

Let's try to imagine an elephant going through the eye of a needle. We can't picture this impossible feat because an elephant is enormous in relation to this tiny opening. How much more impossible is it for something that is completely unlimited and infinite to be found in a limited, finite place?

As explained in previous chapters, it is only by transcending our Animal Soul with its physically limiting body and concentrating on our G-dly Soul (the infinite within us) that we are able to begin to be a fitting dwelling place for G-d's presence, the *Shechinah*. Since we can't connect to something unlimited with limited tools, the only way to connect with the infinite, unlimited G-d is through our unlimited G-dly Soul.

On a deeper level: even revealing our G-dly Soul may not be enough nullification to house G-d's presence. The G-dly Soul, to a certain extent, has become a separate entity from the Creator-the feeling that "*I* love G-d" and "*I* serve G-d" demonstrates the soul's independent reality. As such, the soul still lacks the ability to house G-d's presence. It can connect, but only in a limited way.

Are You Truly Nullified?

Once, a Jew came to the Alter Rebbe and bragged that he had learned the entire Talmud. His arrogance was apparent; the Jew remained a non-nullified vessel that was incapable of housing G-d's presence.

"Yes, you may have studied the Talmud," the Rebbe responded, "but what has the Talmud taught you?"

Another Jew arrived to speak with the Alter Rebbe and said that he had studied the entire Tanya and was now in a state of nullification.

Obviously, he too still possessed pride and ego.

*"It's true that you studied Tanya," the Rebbe told him, "but **you** studied. You and the Tanya are still two separate entities."*

The *Shechinah* can be found in a place that understands and accepts the fact that "there is nothing but G-d." As soon as there is a sense of something other than G-d having true, independent existence, even if it's something holy-like the G-dly Soul-its ability to serve as a vessel for the *Shechinah* is lessened.

Nullification from Arrogance

Ofra was an Israeli young woman who went to India to participate in a ten-day silent retreat offered in a monastery. She wanted to "nullify" herself by using this time to examine her inner self. But after a few days, she began to feel uncomfortable with what she sensed was idol worship. When she had signed up for the retreat, she was led to believe that the monastery was a neutral center for meditation. She realized now that this was not quite true.

Even though she was disturbed by some of things she was seeing and hearing, she decided to complete the course in the hope that she would indeed achieve a deep level of inner nullification.

After the retreat was over, she regretted her exposure to idolatry and went to a Chabad center to find out how she could make amends.

The rabbi there suggested that she memorize a chapter of Tanya that deals with the prohibition of idol worship.

After a few hours of trying, she decided it was too hard for her and asked for something easier. The rabbi made another suggestion. "Don't do anything. Just don't ever tell anyone that you participated in that silent retreat."

She liked that idea. It sounded easy enough. Yet two hours later she came back to the Chabad center in tears.

"It's impossible!" she cried. "Sitting in silence didn't help me self-nullify anything!

"As soon as I met a group of people, I saw how much I wanted to tell everyone about my big accomplishment. I wanted them to know how self-nullified I had become after ten days of silence."

Overcome Your "I" with *Mitzvot*

What is the highest level of "nullification"?

A person is compared to a candle. The flame is the *Shechinah* that dwells upon us and the wick is the body. The wick is thick and coarse-like the body-and it holds the flame only because it is full of wax (or oil). Without the wax or oil, the wick would burn out quickly and produce a dim, sooty flame.

What is more like the wax? What is finer and more "nullified" before G-d-the soul or good deeds?

At first glance, it would seem to be the soul, but on deeper examination we realize that it is the *mitzvot*.

We might think that wax represents the soul-the wax is pure and fine, allowing the wick to glow with pure, shining light, just as the soul permeates the body and enables the body to contain the light of the *Shechinah*.

But this can't be enough. Just the soul alone is not enough to make this happen. It is specifically the *mitzvot* that enable the body to contain the light of G-d's presence.

As we said, even the soul of a complete *Tzaddik* who serves G-d with awe and love still has its own existence-there is *someone* who serves G-d and *someone* who loves G-d. This "someone" who loves G-d is still a "self," and, as we said, this contradicts the fact that "there is nothing but G-d" and naturally opposes the *Shechinah*'s dwelling there. The *mitzvot*, on the other hand, are absolutely nullified before G-d since they are His very will, as it is expressed in the Torah.

Inner and External Will

Why do the *mitzvot* help us achieve a higher level of nullification and thus a greater level of connection?

As we explained in earlier chapters, there are two levels of will.

The inner will is the true purpose and goal that we seek, while the external will is the "means," the necessary steps, on the way to the fulfillment of the inner will.

For example, a person wants to work. What he truly desires is the money he'll make, but in order bring in this income, he has to work. Thus, he wants both-but not on the same level. Going to work is his external will, and the money he earns is the inner will. Of course, there are even deeper levels where the money earned becomes the external will in comparison to the way the money will be used, which is the inner will.

These two levels are also found with regard to the Creator. He created the world and everything in it, but his inner will is for the existence of the Jewish people and their fulfillment of the Torah. In other words, the whole world is a means to obtain the ultimate goal: the Jewish people fulfilling the Torah. As such, what G-d truly wants is found in the Torah.

G-d's will is everywhere, but it's dressed up in garments that hide it. Only in the Torah can we find His inner will without concealment. Therefore, it is specifically the *mitzvot* that are nullified before G-d and thus able to serve as "oil" or "wax" (which is completely consumed) for the "wick" (the body) and enable the light of the *Shechinah* to shine on us.

The World of Falsehood

It's possible that the ideas presented until this point contradict your natural sense of things. It seems that standing on a mountaintop, looking at an incredible view and marveling at the beauty of creation, would be a more powerful way to feel connected to G-d than performing a practical *mitzvah* such as giving *tzedakah*, putting on *tefillin*, or lighting Shabbat candles.

Feelings, however, are misleading, even lofty ones that rise to a higher level than words and deeds. Feelings indicate our own sense of self and existence. People can be swayed in different directions by their feelings, causing them to connect less with the truth.

The path to finding the truth was given to us by G-d as a free gift when He gave us His Torah. For this reason, even the simplest of *mitzvot* connects us directly to G-d, because it's His inner will, free of concealment or obscurity.

So a person may be observing *Shabbat*, but then think that he can enhance his spiritual experience by turning on his MP3 player to hear music. He may *feel* a lofty spiritual experience, but in fact he has violated one of the *mitzvot* of Shabbat and missed a chance to connect to G-d. He accomplished the exact opposite of what he wanted to achieve by following his feelings.

Today's world is full of examples of such dangers. There are many "uplifting" experiences that don't lead to true spiritual advancement, while some "boring" and less flashy experiences have an unfathomable positive impact on our souls. The world of advertising works diligently to convince us that Coca-Cola is great for us, and that we'll have a better life if we drink it, when it actually contains ingredients that are unhealthy. Who advertises carrots?

Practical Mitzvot: The Ultimate Nullification

Earlier in this chapter we asked a question: why does the *beinoni*'s G-dly Soul need to be "enveloped" in the Animal Soul if it will never be able to transform and alter it like the *Tzaddik* does?

Remember, the *beinoni*'s life is a constant struggle against negative thoughts. His Animal Soul's emotional experience is translated into thoughts that then go up to the mind for our consideration and temptation. And while the *Beinoni* succeeds at pushing away these thoughts, the Animal Soul's essence remains unchanged-its intellectual and emotional attributes have not been transformed to goodness. Yet, at the moment that the *beinoni* performs a *mitzvah*, he is absolutely nullified before the Creator.

Now, this level of nullification is not a deeper, inner one. The *beinoni* has not truly changed his inner world, and it's even possible that he immediately returns to fighting off thoughts of sin the second after he finishes performing the *mitzvah* (which does not happen to the *Tzaddik*). However, *while* he is performing the *mitzvah*, his Animal Soul is also nullified before G-d.

This experience of nullification occurs primarily during the performance of practical, physical *mitzvot*. And even among the *mitzvot* themselves, there is an advantage to *mitzvot* performed with an action over those done with speech or thought (such as Torah study).

On its own, the G-dly Soul is incapable of moving and directing the body. It must work through the Animal Soul. As such, since the *mitzvot* that are performed with thoughts and speech don't involve moving the body, there is very little interaction between the G-dly Soul and the Animal Soul. Thus nearly no investment of the G-dly Soul has been put into the Animal Soul-at least not in a perceptible way.

On the other hand, the *mitzvot* performed with actions involve much more of the G-dly Soul's influence on the Animal Soul, and this leads it to a greater level of nullification.

Since the *mitzvot* of action (ideally when done with feeling, but even without feeling, this still happens) are G-d's will without concealment, the Animal Soul gets nullified and then even it can become absorbed within G-d's light. In other words, the light of the *Shechinah* can also rest upon the Animal Soul.

This answers why the G-dly Soul needs to be contained in the Animal Soul, and why the G-dly Soul needs to work through the Animal Soul in order to move the body. The mission and goal-as will be explained in detail in the upcoming chapters-is primarily to influence the Animal Soul, refining it and illuminating it with holiness. This is why such a great emphasis is placed on *mitzvot* in general and *mitzvot* of action in particular.

In Conclusion

Since the *beinoni* is unable to transform his Animal Soul like a *Tzaddik* does, we asked two questions:

1. Why does the *beinoni*'s G-dly Soul have to be enveloped in the Animal Soul instead of allowing each to occupy a different part of the body?

2. Why does the G-dly Soul have to work through the Animal Soul in order to get the body to move in accordance with its wishes?

We answered by explaining that true connection to G-d happens through nullifying one's ego and sense of self, and that this nullification comes through our deeds more than feelings-for feelings are a greater expression of one's "self." By doing *mitzvot*, even the *beinoni* is able to participate in the general purpose of creation by getting his Animal Soul absorbed in the world of *kedushah*.

Chapter Twenty-Four
The Purpose

The purpose of Creation is to transform darkness into light, bitter into sweet, and to discover the truth in our world.

(Tanya, chap. 36, part 1)

In the previous chapter, we explained that although the *beinoni* doesn't transform his Animal Soul like the *Tzaddik*, and "only" succeeds at controlling his thoughts, speech, and actions-nevertheless he achieves something tremendous. When he performs a *mitzvah*, and a physical action-oriented *mitzvah* in particular, his Animal Soul becomes absorbed in G-d's light at that moment.

We noted that the inclusion of the Animal Soul in G-dly light is part of fulfilling the purpose for which it was created. As such, to a certain extent, the *beinoni*'s accomplishment is just as lofty as the work of the *Tzaddik*. This chapter will expand on our discussion of the *beinoni*'s work and clarify how it fulfills its purpose.

Why Do We Need to Know the Purpose?

Forty years ago the first spaceship flew to the moon. It was carrying three carefully selected astronauts who underwent extensive training for many months. Living conditions in the spaceship were less than ideal: they had to eat strange food and wear bulky space suits and uncomfortable helmets.

During their journey, the astronauts were assigned tasks given by the control center back on Earth. Despite their difficulties, one can imagine the sense of duty and mission they carried with them, and the great satisfaction they felt after successfully performing even the smallest task on the spaceship. They knew the importance of their mission. All the people of Earth were watching this historical event, waiting to see them land on the moon, and every moment of their time in the spaceship was part of fulfilling the goals they were assigned.

Imagine the astronauts on that space mission receiving additional instructions in the middle of their journey and saying, "Leave me alone! I want some time off to enjoy the view and watch the stars. Stop driving me nuts with all these orders!"

The same thing happens with us. When we known the reason our souls descended into the world, it gives us a sense of purpose that makes us feel like emissaries. And then we feel great satisfaction and accomplishment in everything we do.

The Lowest World

Our world is the absolute lowest level in the whole system of worlds. Prior to the Creation, G-d's infinite light was everywhere, openly revealed, without any concealment. Yet His desire was to be revealed specifically in a place of concealment.

The word for "*olam*," world, is related to the word "*halam*," hidden. G-d created a system of worlds where some are more spiritual than others. Our physical world is at the very bottom; that is, it's the least spiritual. As G-d's creative light descends through the levels of worlds, each descent increases and deepens the amount of concealment.

The greatest level of concealment is the final stop, our world, where G-dliness is so hidden that there are some here who feel that there is a no Creator. A person can live his entire life in this world and be sure that there is no G-d, because it superficially appears that way to him. However, we have to be clear: G-d isn't less present in our world-He's just much more hidden.

The Four Worlds

The creation of the universe occurred in four stages, also known as the four worlds. But they aren't physical worlds that take up physical space or exist beyond the moon; rather they are spiritual worlds that exist in a spiritual dimension that parallels our world, existing right here with us. They are all called "*olamot*," worlds, because even the loftiest world is "*ma'alim*" (hides) G-d's light.

Asiyah, **the World of Action**-this is the lowest level. It has the greatest amount of concealment and is described as being a place of nearly complete concealment with only a fraction of revelation. In this lowest dimension-the physical World of Action-the concealment is absolute; G-d's light is not felt at all.

Yetzirah, **the World of Formation**-this world is half revelation and half concealment. The creations that inhabit this world can sense their independent existence, yet also know that G-d is their source, and therefore they willingly nullify themselves to Him.

Beriah, **the World of Creation**-this world is mostly revelation and only a fraction of concealment. The creations inhabiting it have no sense of independent existence at all and feel at one with G-d. However, the fact that they feel *something* is a level of separateness.

Atzilut, **the World of Emanation**-this world is totally and entirely revelation, a world of unity. The creations inhabiting this world don't even have a sense of their own reality. In this world dwell the ten *sefirot*, the ten G-dly powers with which G-d created the world.

The Worlds within the Soul

The soul also has these four dimensions or stages, and by way of comparison we can gain insight into the nature of these worlds.

The parallel to *Asiyah* is our actions and deeds. This aspect of life seems to be disconnected from the soul, since we see that a person's actions can contradict his words, thoughts, or beliefs. Moreover, after we accomplish some feat in the material world, our connection with it ends and our participation is undetectable. Similarly, the world of *Asiyah* gives no clues as to Who created and directs it.

The next level up, *Yetzirah*, corresponds to our speech. Here, we know who spoke the words, but they immediately lose their connection to the one who uttered them.

The next level, *Beriah*, corresponds to thought. Of all three garments of the soul (thought, speech, and action), thought is called the "united garment"-it is simultaneously "attached" to the soul and its "garment" of expression.

Just as our clothing enables us to represent ourselves to the world, so do the soul's garments: with action we communicate with the physical, material world; with speech we communicate with other humans (who speak our language); and with thought we communicate with ourselves. Thought is deep and internal, but still not the person himself.

Above the garments are the soul's attributes of intellect and emotions-parallel to *Atzilut*. They are much closer to a person than his garments, yet they also are still not the person himself. However, we don't call them "garments" because they are totally united with the soul.

Compressing the Soul into Its Attributes and Garments

The soul's attributes enable us to know and feel. But their extreme closeness to the soul conceals them, keeps them in our subconscious and prevents them from being expressed. In order to express them, we need *"tzimtzum"* (compression).

How does this work? The soul is a huge pool of knowledge, as almost everything we have ever experienced remains in our consciousness. In order to express myself, I have to compress my entire pool of consciousness down to one thought through which I can communicate with myself.

Nevertheless, the thought is abstract and without detail-as evidenced by the fact that five minutes of thought can produce an hour-long talk. Expressing the thought in speech form requires drawing it down and compressing the soul even further-i.e., making the thought more physical and further away from its source in the soul.

Next, the soul goes through further compression by transforming the speech into action. It is the greatest transitional jump, since an hour of discussion can generate two months of work.

For example, in our intellect is a clear picture of the kind of house we want. In our thoughts, we tell ourselves what the house looks like, and then in speech we share the details with the contractor. And while the speech stage could be over in a few hours, the actual building could take years.

Now, in the stage of speech, and certainly in those before it, it's clear that we are the source for the idea of building the house. In the action stage, however, its connection to us is less detectable.

In the spiritual realms, *Atzilut* is where G-d extended from Himself into existence His "intellect and emotions." *Beriah* would be akin to His "thought," since thought is constantly dependent on the soul's guidance. And while *Beriah* senses that G-d is the Creator, the very fact that it feels something demonstrates that it is already a "world" with *kelipah* that conceals G-dliness.

Yetzirah corresponds to G-d's "speech"-simultaneously united with Him and separate from Him. It has independently existing creations, but they understand the correctness of being nullified before G-d.

Asiyah represents G-d's "actions." It contains great, and sometimes even absolute, concealment. Its creations don't feel there is a Creator-just as our participation isn't clearly seen in the deeds we've done.

Let's deepen our understanding of this with an additional example.

When we see a fruit after it has been picked from a tree, we can't tell which tree it came from. Nevertheless, we know without a doubt that there must be a tree from which it came. This parallels *Asiyah*.

When the fruit is still on the tree, we know that it comes from that tree. At the same time, there is already a fruit-an entity ready to be separate from the tree. This is *Yetzirah*.

Before there was an actual fruit, it existed potentially within the tree. It was only a potential fruit of formless material, not existing in a form that we recognize. This corresponds to *Beriah*.

And before the tree grew, the seed from which it would later sprout was still part of another tree. Even there it also had the potential to produce the fruit-but it was still without matter, a state of nonexistence in comparison to the actual fruit that would later grow. This is *Atzilut*.

Atzilut is the first stage of the world's creation, where everything is still one with the Creator and, like the Creator, not an existing, independent reality. The next stage is *Beriah*, where there is already matter-a sense of independent existence, though it lacks form. *Yetzirah* is the stage where form is added to the matter, but it still knows that G-d is its source. In the final stage of *Asiyah*, the creation feels itself to be a separate, independent existence since it can't detect or feel the Creator.

As He is above and before all these stages, G-d is called *"Ohr Ein Sof"* – abstract, without form or boundaries.

The Purpose...Down Here

It would make sense to think that *Atzilut* is the purpose of Creation because it is the loftiest level. But actually it's not. If it were the purpose, there would be no need to create all the worlds that come after it.

Moreover, what's unique about *Atzilut* in comparison to the Creator Himself? Both of them are in a state of nonindependent, self-aware existence, except that *Atzilut* comes on the scene a little later.

The real novelty and innovation is in the lowest world of *Asiyah*.

One of the reasons the teachings of *Kabbalah* refer to our world as *"alma deshikra"*-a world of falsehood-is because it lies. Meaning, it conceals the truth that there is a Creator Who runs the world, and even attempts to claim the opposite: that there is no Creator and the world runs on its own. But G-d put us in the world to reveal the truth: there *is* a Creator and He constantly orchestrates every detail.

The Reason for Creation

At this point we need to ask, why was the world created and for what purpose? On the surface, it seems like one question, but it's really two separate questions.

Why was the world created? So we can peel away the concealment. So we can look past the surface to discover the truth.

But why did G-d create a world that conceals the truth instead of one in which the truth is always revealed?

We will get to this question shortly. But first, why did G-d even need or want all that He created? This is a more difficult question to answer.

Great Jewish Torah leaders have discussed this for generations and offered a variety of approaches:

G-d wanted to be a king. And since "there is no king without a people," He needed someone to rule over. Therefore, He made the world and us.

G-d is the essence of good and wanted creations to whom He could give. He created a world and people to whom He could show goodness.

According to the *Zohar*, G-d wanted us to know Him. By contemplating the world He created, we discover and learn about Him. Therefore, He created a world.

Each of the three responses answers the question, but they raise a new question: If G-d is infinite and can do anything, how can we say that He needed us so He could have someone to rule over, or so that we would come to know Him? Is He really lacking something that He needs us to provide it?

In the writings of the Arizal (Rabbi Yitzchak Luria, the famous kabbalist and Torah innovator who lived in Tzefat about 450 years ago), he teaches that G-d lacked nothing and didn't need us, but simply wanted to reveal the wholesome perfection of His powers. In other words, the world wasn't created for us, and we didn't provide something that G-d was missing.

Let's compare this approach to the *Zohar*'s answer that G-d wanted us to come to know Him. It's like two professors at a university-one publishes an article to display his wisdom for all to see, while the other publishes an article just to express his ideas. The second one isn't looking for fame or praise. He simply published it because the ideas were in his head, and he wanted to get them out and actualize that which was in potential.

While the *Arizal*'s approach is correct and answers our questions, it doesn't satisfy us (which is why the *Arizal* ultimately rejects it). G-d doesn't have unrealized potential-only we do. For G-d, whatever exists in potential automatically gets realized.

In addition, there is a common problem to all the above-mentioned answers (see the addendum at the end of this chapter, which addresses the correctness of each approach). Each answer provides a logical reason and explains G-d in a rational manner. It's hard for us to break free from our reasoning and understand that we are bound by our logic but G-d is not. After all, He Himself created the system of logic, just as He created the world. And if He had desired that things be different, He would have created other rules of logic and our minds would have come to different conclusions.

Because He created the rules of logic, and prior to that there were no such rules, He is not subject to the rules of logic in our world or even the higher worlds. Therefore, any explanation for why the world was created that starts with "because" is automatically an attempt to compress G-d into human logic. Yet, from G-d's perspective, human logic plays no role.

Beyond Intellect

Based on all this, it would make sense to simply say that there is a reason G-d created the world, but we are unable to understand it. Just as the main character in a computer game can't understand its programmer, so it is impossible for us to grasp our "Programmer."

But even this answer limits G-d. Essentially it's saying that we understand that *we* don't have the ability to comprehend G-d.

Which is, once again, we as rational and logical people "projecting" our perspective onto Him, humanizing Him, and concluding that He certainly would not do anything without a reason. And so we conclude that there has to be a logical reason that G-d created the world, but we just can't understand it.

By analyzing this more deeply, we will realize that this is also a mistaken approach. For we also possess a dimension that transcends intellect. It may be subconscious, but we know that it exists and even motivates and drives us.

In other words, we have inherent desires that aren't ruled by logic. This is actually the definition of desire: the soul's inclination toward a particular direction-not because it makes sense, but rather because it's so deeply wired into our being.

Take, for example, a person whose inclination is to help others and another person who is naturally a spiritual seeker. Either one could give an excellent explanation as to why his way is the most logical and correct. However, these are explanations that they developed after already experiencing the desire for these pursuits. The desire did not arise from the explanations.

That's why, if we investigated the person who likes to help others and asked him why he does it, we could challenge every answer he gives by continually asking why. Eventually, all he can say is, "Because"-since there is no reason. Ultimately the reason transcends logic and intellect.

Our desire to live works similarly. Ask someone what he lives for, and you can continually challenge his answers by asking, "But why?" Eventually he will be forced to say, "Because." That means he's reached a place where there is no logical answer.

Incidentally, the explanations offered by science for natural phenomena work the same way. Take any explanation that science gives for an aspect of nature, and you can continually ask, "But why?" After a few rounds of that, you arrive at the final answer: "Because!"

This is always the case with nature and science phenomena because ultimately you reach the foundation, which is *"yesh me'ayin"*-nature was created from nothing, which science can't explain intellectually.

G-d also works this way. There are dimensions of Him that are logical and graspable with our brains, and then there's the level that transcends reason and intellect-where the true answer is "Because," since there is no reason.

It's not unreasonable for us to seek intelligent, logical explanations, but if we don't or can't understand something, it's because G-d Himself doesn't necessarily have a logical reason or cause. Inherent in Him is that He decided it should be this way, without any logic that we can understand.

So, ultimately, when we ask why the world was created, the answer is, "Because."

As far as the purpose for which the world was created, and why it was specifically created in the way that it was, we will discuss this in the next chapter.

In Conclusion

G-d is most concealed in our world, and thus it is the hardest place in which to reveal Him. Nevertheless, working to reveal Him is how we fulfill the purpose of Creation.

Addendum:
Each of the Four Answers Is True...on Its Own Level

Each of the answers for why the world was created that we presented in this chapter is correct with respect to its own level, which corresponds to one of the four worlds.

On the level of *Asiyah*, the World of Action, which corresponds to the garment of deed, the world was created for actions and deeds-so that we would perform *mitzvot* and live a life that follows the *halachah*. Thus, the answer that relates to this level is "There is no king without a people"-He wanted to be our King and have us fulfill His commandments, and so He created us.

On the level of *Yetzirah*, the World of Formation, which corresponds to the emotional attributes (particularly *Chesed*, kindness), the world was created for doing kindness-so that the Creator could "show kindness to His creations." This relates to *mussar*, the Torah's ethical and moral dimension, which appeals to the emotions, teaching us how to behave in an ethical way and the system of reward and punishment based on our conduct.

On the level of *Beriah*, the World of Creation, which corresponds to the intellectual attributes, the world was created for us to know the Creator. This relates to *chakirah*, the Torah's logical, rational dimension, which appeals to man's intellect and suggests rational explanations for the Creator's existence.

On the level of *Atzilut*, the World of Emanation, which corresponds to the primary core point that precedes rational thought, the world was created "to reveal the perfection of His powers"-and not for us. This relates to the teachings of *Kabbalah*, which give spiritual explanations for performing *mitzvot*.

And on the level of G-d's infinite light, *Ohr Ein Sof*, which is above all definition (you can't even say that it's above intellect since that still shows a connection to intellect), the answer is, "Because." Even G-d Himself has no reason for creating the world-G-d simply craved a dwelling place in the lower worlds. This relates to the teachings of *Chassidut*, which contains all of the above explanations, but begins with a "craving"-i.e., a drive that transcends any explanation.

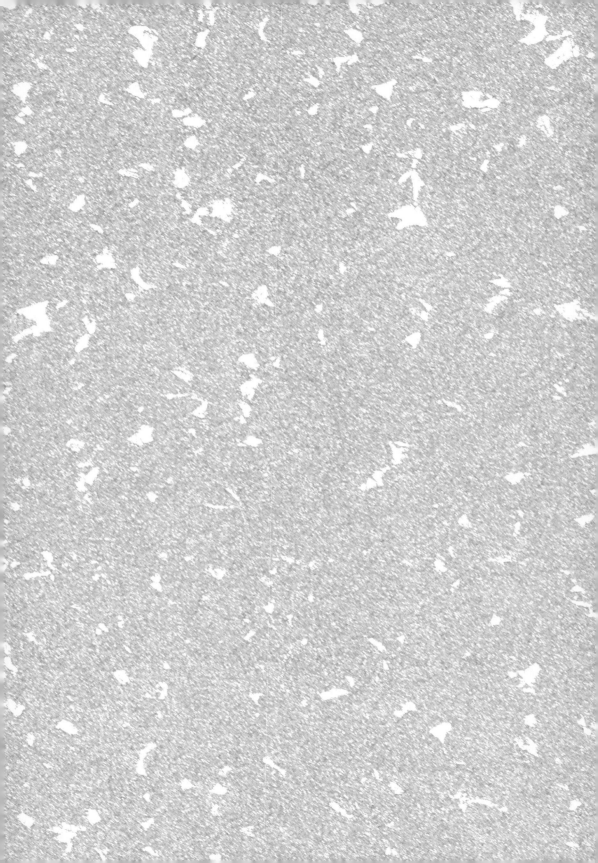

Chapter Twenty-Five

Revealing the Spark

Revealing the G-dly light that's in the world is
an essential stepping-stone for the great revelation
that will occur in the times of Mashiach.

(Tanya, chap. 36, part 2)

As we said previously, G-d created an entire system of worlds that obscure His great light. However, this concealment is only from our perspective-that is, *we* don't see G-d in this world. From G-d's perspective, He's everywhere equally.

This is what G-d desires: to be revealed specifically in the place of greatest concealment. As such, He first needed to conceal Himself.

Concealment and Revelation

What if G-d's presence were revealed everywhere, the truth was visible, and we could feel our souls?

The world would look entirely different. Instead, what we are most in touch with is our ego (the Animal Soul). Most of us are far less in touch with our G-dly Souls. We live with the world's false facade that there is no G-d. This influences us to grant ourselves permission to behave in a way that's inconsistent with G-d's will and vision for our world.

In other words, the reason there are thieves and murderers and evil in the world is because the Creator is hidden and undetected. If His existence were obvious to everyone, no one would be able to act against His will.

If the world didn't conceal the truth, we could see how G-d is the sole Sovereign over everything, and we would understand clearly what He wants from us. And then we would undoubtedly behave accordingly.

Moreover, if we could see the G-dly spark in everything and everyone around us, it would be totally clear to us that everything is completely under G-d's control and the world runs according to His will. We would understand that "nothing bad descends from Above" and "everything is for the good."

Sounds great. So why didn't G-d create the world this way? Why did He conceal Himself? Why didn't He put us directly into a world of revealed goodness from the start, a world where we feel our souls and not our egos?

And this question leads to a more pressing one, since such a world of revealed goodness is the ultimate destination of our goal in life. We all yearn for the final redemption, for a world where we see G-d everywhere, feel our souls, and no longer have the sensation of being separate, independent beings. We all yearn for the era when war and evil will disappear. So why does G-d keep us in suspense? Make the world this way from the beginning.

The Advantage of Light that Comes from Darkness

The higher spiritual worlds are full of revealed light. Our world, in contrast, is called a "world of darkness," since the light it contains is concealed.

It's not such a great feat for the light in the higher realms to be revealed. Even now they have light, each world according to its level. These worlds are similar to a candle that you light in the middle of the day-it doesn't have much of an effect.

On the other hand, it's a tremendous accomplishment when light is revealed in our dark world. And the impact is felt immediately, like the light of a single candle illuminating the night.

Because G-d wanted His light to specifically be revealed in a place of spiritual darkness, He created a world of concealment where the light could be revealed. Our effort to uncover G-d despite the concealment created by pain, tests, and difficulties transforms darkness into light and reveals true good.

On a personal level, this means that all of the hardships and challenges we experience are not meant to bring us down, but are designed to elevate us. Instead of running from the dark places in our spiritual lives, our job is to fill them with light. When we do so, we discover a superior kind of light-one that came from transforming our personal darkness.

The Way to Revealing the Light

G-d entrusted the Jewish people with the task of revealing the truth, and He endowed us with all the necessary tools for the job: a G-dly Soul that is formed from *kedushah*, an Animal Soul from *kelipat nogah* (partial concealment), and the Torah.

The Torah (which is related to the word *"hora'ah"*-teaching or instruction) is, among other things, a book that guides us in the process of discovering the truth in the world. Besides the handed-down traditions and customs, and a method for connecting to G-d, the *mitzvot* (*"mitzvah"* is related to the word *"tzavta"*-bond or connection), the Torah shows us how to reveal G-d's presence in the world.

Far from impossible, G-d's revelation in the world is actually something that already happened once before in history: when we received the Torah. All the Jewish people stood at the foot of Mount Sinai and heard G-d Himself as He spoke to us directly, without any intermediary, and said, "I am the L-rd, Your G-d..." (*Shemos* 20:2).

At that moment of intense Divine revelation, the entire world trembled in response. The Jewish people all *saw* what G-d was saying (an analogy for spirituality) and *heard* the sights (an analogy for physicality). Spirituality was fully revealed (i.e., they *saw*) at the giving of the Torah, while physicality was concealed (i.e., they *heard*). The truth lit up the world.

There was one problem with this experience: the truth lit up the world so powerfully that the people couldn't handle it. With each of G-d's spoken commandments, their souls left their bodies. The intensity of this powerful revelation was beyond the capacity of their physically limited bodies to contain.

The Mission: Redemption

The purpose of the world is to regain that incredible level of revelation, where the truth is visible to our eyes and our physical beings can clearly perceive *kedushah*-where G-d is no longer hidden or concealed. Then we will know and feel our true selves, experiencing our souls rather than our bodies.

In this purified redemptive state, envy, hatred, war, and competition will cease to exist. We will live in unity, completely connected to the Creator and His will.

We were given the holy task of preparing the world for the revelation of *kedushah*. Our fulfillment of the Torah and *mitzvot* helps prepare the world for this incredible level of G-dly revelation, by revealing light *with every mitzvah we do*.

G-d could accomplish all this without us, but He wanted us to be His partners in bringing about the future redemption. In this way, all of our Torah and *mitzvot* are an opportunity to emulate Him by being "cocreators" who truly influecne the world.

This is our task: to prepare world to receive the revelation of the truth. G-d is already here and ready to be revealed to us, as He was when He gave us the Torah. But are we ready? Is the world prepared?

The future revelation depends on what we do here in the present. The "reward" that awaits us in the time of redemption will not be a prize for what we are doing now, but rather a *direct outcome* of our work today.

Wages and Harvests: An Analogy

A teacher working in a school receives a salary at the end of the month. The money is not a direct outcome of his work, but rather the payment owed him for the hours of work he gave. On the other hand, a farmer sows his field and the harvest he reaps is a direct outcome of the sowing. The way he sows and tends his crops determines what he will reap.

The same idea applies to the redemption. At that time, it will be revealed to us how all of the deeds and efforts we made had an impact on the world throughout the long darkness of exile.

In other words, redemption is not a "salary" for all the hours of effort we invested, but rather a direct outcome of the work we do every day. Every *mitzvah* we do today prepares the world for the future revelation of Divine light. And when redemption comes and the light is revealed, we will see with our eyes what we have contributed all our lives!

This is why the Torah teaches us that the reward of a *mitzvah*...is a *mitzvah* ("*mitzvah goreret mitzvah*"). On a simple level, this means that by doing a *mitzvah*, we get rewarded with the privilege of doing more *mitzvot*. But the deeper interpretation is that the reward for the *mitzvah* is the *mitzvah* itself. Because, as we now understand, "*mitzvah*" means preparing the world for the future revelation of light; and its reward is the actual revelation of light. As such, the reward for doing the *mitzvah* (revelation of the light) and the *mitzvah* itself (preparing the world for that revelation) are the same.

Mashiach Times

When we yearn for the *geulah*-the final redemption-we are yearning for the era when we will see G-d everywhere, and there will no longer be any concealment.

Our anticipation and hope for redemption is more than just seeing all the Jewish people return to Israel, and it's more than receiving the abundance of good things promised to us in the Torah. It's even more than experiencing true peace in the world. We are awaiting the great revelation of infinite light that will be revealed here in our world, when the truth of G-d's infinite light will shine forth and the entire world will bask in its brilliance.

Since this revelation will occur specifically in the material world, our physical efforts in this world of physicality are incredibly important. The ultimate revelation of light will come specifically out of the darkness of concealment that exists in our physical world. Each and every one of our physical actions therefore has the greatest significance.

This is why nearly all of our *mitzvot* involve physical objects. *Tefillin* and *mezuzot* are made from cow skin, the four species used on Sukkot are plants, and we celebrate Shabbat and Yom Tov by eating special meals.

For this reason our Sages teach us, "Actions are the most important thing." With our actions, we are preparing a "home" for G-d's presence; each *mitzvah* helps prepare the world for His revelation.

In the next chapter, we'll explain how this works in practical terms.

In Conclusion

G-d created the world because He wanted it to exist-beyond rational explanations or reasons. And it was created in a way that His presence is concealed, in order to fulfill the purpose for which He created it.

G-d made a world of spiritual darkness and concealment, a world that could be harnessed to serve as a vessel for the incredible ultimate revelation of light. It is our deeds that prepare the world for the great revelation of truth that will exist in the time of Mashiach.

Chapter Twenty-Six

Purifying the World

Torah and mitzvot are our list of instructions for purifying the world and preparing it for geulah.

(Tanya, chap. 37)

In the previous chapters, we explained that the purpose for which the world was created is the transformation of darkness (concealment of G-dliness) into light (revelation of G-dliness). We learned that this world represents the lowest of all of G-d's created worlds, and that our task is to specifically be involved in the revelation of the truth in our physical world of concealment.

We also learned that what applies to the spiritual worlds applies to our souls: the purpose is to reveal G-d's light specifically in this lowest, physical world with our deeds, and we work through our Animal Soul, the lower level of soul, to do this.

We also elaborated further on our responsibility to prepare the world for the great revelation of light that will happen at the time of the future redemption. At that time, the entire world will be illuminated with G-d's light, but not as a reward for the work we did throughout our lives, but rather as a *direct outcome* of it.

Every *mitzvah* we do readies another part of the world to receive the Divine light, drawing G-dliness into another part of the globe. And then, when Mashiach arrives, we'll see clearly with our own eyes the results of all our efforts.

In this chapter, we will begin to explain how this actually takes place.

Kedushah and Kelipah

In the first chapters, we explained that *kedushah*, or holiness, refers to G-d being present in a revealed way in a particular thing, while *kelipah* is that which conceals and covers G-dliness (like the peel that covers a fruit).

Kedushah resides only in that which is nullified before G-d-in a person who "makes space" for G-d by removing his own selfish interests. By making G-d's will his will, he desires what G-d wants. On the other hand, arrogance, ego, and "I" repel G-d's presence.

Levels of *Kelipah*

We also said that *kelipah* itself subdivides into two groups. The lower group is referred to as the "three completely impure *kelipot*." They cover G-d's light so powerfully and completely that they effectively "bind" it from shining and render it inaccessible. This is why forbidden things are called *"asur,"* which also means bound. And since it's impossible to free the spark from within the three completely impure *kelipot*, those items are forbidden to us by the Torah.

For example, the G-dly vitality contained in non-kosher food comes through the three completely impure *kelipot*. This is why we're forbidden to eat non-kosher food: their light is bound up and inaccessible, and thus unable to be elevated to *kedushah*. Light is revealed when we *don't* eat these foods, by obeying G-d's Torah commandment to *avoid* these things.

The higher level of *kelipah* is *kelipat nogah*. As a *kelipah*, it also conceals G-dliness, but not absolutely. It can be worked with. If we use something that receives its vitality from *kelipat nogah* in the proper, holy way-i.e., in the service of G-d-then its spark of holiness is separated out, freed, and elevated. This is why permitted things are referred to as *"mutar"* in Hebrew, which also means "freed" and "untied".

Kosher foods receive their vitality from *kelipat nogah*. When we say a blessing before we eat, and have in mind the intention to use the food to have energy to serve G-d (rather than just to fill our stomachs), we infuse the food with a higher purpose, and its sparks rise to *kedushah*.

All of this was already discussed in earlier chapters. Now we'll take a deeper look at the subject.

Elevating the Physical to *Kedushah*

As previously mentioned, *kedushah* is G-d's will-His inner will-in a revealed state that's free from concealment. *Kelipah*, even *kelipat nogah*, hides G-d's will. What is G-d's will? G-d's will is for the Jewish people to observe the Torah and its *mitzvot*. When we do the *mitzvot*, we are fulfilling His will.

The vitality in permitted foods comes from *kelipat nogah*. When we first approach food, the level of *kelipah* covers the food's G-dliness and prevents us from seeing in it G-d's will. But when we recite a blessing beforehand and eat it for a purpose loftier than satisfying bodily cravings, such as to gain strength to serve G-d (or on a higher level, when we think only of the holiness contained in the food and not its fragrance and taste), in that moment we are eating "for the sake of Heaven," and G-d's will is revealed.

And by helping a Jew serve G-d, the food too has fulfilled its purpose and it is elevated to *kedushah*.

This process is even more pronounced when we do a *mitzvah*. By using an *etrog* to fulfill the *mitzvah* of shaking the four species on *Sukkot*, or turning the skin of a cow into a *mezuzah* or *tefillin*, we take a permitted physical object from *kelipat nogah* and use it to fulfill G-d's will. As a result, the item gets elevated to *kedushah*. Our actions revealed the item's purpose-its inherent truth.

This process can happen only with permissible items from *kelipat nogah*. If we tried to do a *mitzvah*, for example, with a forbidden *etrog* (i.e., one from a tree that's less than three years old, which is called "*orlah*," or one that was stolen), the three completely impure *kelipot* that give the forbidden item its vitality bind and shackle the item's *kedushah*, and we can't elevate it.

The same problem exists when we try to do any *mitzvah* or good deed with something forbidden. It won't work. Because the means are forbidden, all the blessings and good intentions in the world won't help-the holiness is bound up and unable to rise to *kedushah*.

Such an act is called a "*mitzvah* performed by way of a sin"-a *mitzvah* that takes place by means of a sin, or at the same time as committing a sin. Examples include feeding poor people non-kosher food or *chametz* on Passover or giving charity from stolen money.

Purifying the World

Thus far we explained that specifically the physical performance of a *mitzvah* reveals the *kedushah* found in the material object that was used for that very *mitzvah*. On a deeper level, we can say that the act of doing a *mitzvah* affects not only the object used, but also ourselves and all the kosher food we ate earlier that gave us the strength to do this *mitzvah*.

Let's look more closely at the *mitzvah* of *tefillin* as an example. First, the skin of the animal used in making the parchments and the boxes rises to *kedushah*, because it was used to make something that was used for a *mitzvah*-which is the will of G-d. In addition, the energy the body expended in donning and praying with the *tefillin* also rises to *kedushah*, since that is its purpose and thus it revealed the will of G-d. Moreover, everything we ate earlier that gave us the strength to perform the *mitzvah* also rises to *kedushah*. This is the whole reason the food exists, and when used this way it reveals G-dly light and energy.

In earlier chapters, we explained what a *mitzvah* is and compared it to the parts of the body-just as they each absorb into themselves a different dimension of the soul, so does each of the *mitzvot* attract and draw down G-dly light. We can now understand this on an even deeper level: the G-dly light is drawn into the physical object used to do the *mitzvah*, the energy used by the body to perform the *mitzvah*, and the food eaten earlier that gave the body this energy.

Purifying Our Part of the World

When we say that a *mitzvah* has an impact on the energy that moves our body and on the food we ate that produced that energy, we are referring to the Animal Soul (the energy that moves our body) and the part of the world (the food we ate that produced that energy) it was created to influence.

Each of us is responsible for a particular part of the world-an area that G-d put us in charge of refining. By successfully performing our life's work, we influence and elevate our section. And once we all finish our work and complete our personal mission, the outcome will be revealed: *geulah* (redemption).

Chassidim call this "slaughtering the world," from the word "*hamshachah*"-to draw or pull something out. The word "*shechitah*"-meaning "slaughter"-is connected to this idea of pulling something up to a higher level, in this case, the level of *kedushah*.

When we perform *shechitah,* that is, kosher slaughter on a cow, and then eat the meat in a holy way that fulfills G-d's will (i.e., by first saying a blessing and having in mind that we are eating "for the sake of Heaven," for a higher purpose than to satisfy our cravings), the meat unites with our bodies and rises out of the animal kingdom. It is absorbed into our human bodies, thus becoming one with the level of mankind (there are four levels of creations-from lowest to highest, inanimate/mineral, vegetation, animal, and human). And from there it gets completely absorbed in *kedushah*. As such, *shechitah* elevates the animal kingdom to a higher level.

Similarly, we "slaughter" -i.e., draw out-the *kedushah* in the world, by using the world for a holy, higher purpose. This is how we elevate the world to a higher level and transform it into a holy place, a place where the *Shechinah* can reside, thus fulfilling the purpose for which the world was created.

The Impure *Kelipot*

The three completely impure *kelipot* receive their vitality through *kelipat nogah*, because they can't receive it directly from *kedushah*. It has to pass through the concealment of *kelipat nogah* first. As such, as soon as the entire *kelipat nogah* is purified we enjoy a twofold profit.

When each of us refines the part of the world that is our responsibility to elevate, we are refining the *kelipat nogah* and elevating it to *kedushah*. At the same time, it can no longer serve as a pipeline to vitality for the three completely impure *kelipot*, rendering them nullified and extinct.

This also happens to us personally in our service of G-d. The three completely impure *kelipot* siphon vitality from us through *kelipat nogah*. When is this possible? When we use something permissible that gets its vitality from *kelipat nogah* only for pleasure, without including G-d in our intentions. Then the three completely impure *kelipot* still have a hold on us.

But if we remain focused on *kedushah*, whenever we use something permissible (i.e., *kelipat nogah*) for a higher, holy purpose rather than mere personal enjoyment, then the three completely impure *kelipot* have no influence on us.

This is why we not only avoid the forbidden (the three completely impure *kelipot*), but we also need to avoid using the permitted for unholy reasons (the three completely impure *kelipot*, through *kelipat nogah*), because this doesn't contribute anything to our service of G-d. As the *Chassidic* saying goes, "Whatever is forbidden...is forbidden, and whatever is permitted...is unnecessary."

We also learn from this why Jews tend to sway and move during Torah study and prayer. It's because we want our learning to also influence our bodies and Animal Souls, and therefore we get them involved in our *mitzvot*. Our learning is not just an intellectual endeavor; we want both our body and soul to be involved.

In line with this, our Sages taught that study done with vitality and enthusiasm-with our entire body and being-will not be forgotten. Forgetfulness is caused by the concealment of *kelipah*. But if the entire body is involved in *kedushah*, in doing *mitzvot*, then the *kelipah* is nullified and we remember what we learn.

Different Ways to Purify the World

According to what we have explained, we can understand why *tzedakah* is considered such a great *mitzvah* and why it specifically has the power to bring the redemption closer.

Tzedakah is different from other *mitzvot*. When a person takes money he earned and donates it to *tzedakah*, he instantly raises to *kedushah* his act of giving as well as all the work and effort he put into earning the money. And even if he won, inherited, or received the money as a present, the fact that he could have used the money for his own enjoyment and instead gave it away to charity raises it to *kedushah*.

And what about Torah? On the one hand, it's written that the *mitzvah* of Torah study is equal to all the *mitzvot*. At the same time, the law is that a person must stop his Torah study and help someone if asked to assist with a *mitzvah* when no one else is available. If Torah study is equivalent to all of the *mitzvot* together, why would it be permissible to stop learning to perform another *mitzvah*?

To answer this, we need to revisit the purpose for which the world was created: to prepare the world for the revelation of G-d's light.

This point actually comprises two main parts. The first is the purification of material things, which is primarily accomplished by doing material acts with material objects. And because these acts are in accordance with G-d's wishes, they transform the material object into a vessel that receives holiness. The second part is drawing G-d's light down into the world.

While every *mitzvah* contains these two elements, physically performed *mitzvot* emphasize the first part (the purification of the world), and Torah study emphasizes the second (drawing down the light).

Consequently, when a person studying Torah is asked to perform another *mitzvah* that no one else can do, he has to stop and go lend his assistance, because purifying the world (and not drawing down the light) is the main purpose. Still, drawing down G-dly light is also part of the purpose for which the world was created, and if there's someone else who can do the *mitzvah*, he should continue his Torah study-for it draws down G-dly light.

Studying Torah draws down a higher and loftier level of G-dly light than the *mitzvot*. As we said, *mitzvot* are like G-d's limbs, while Torah study is His will and wisdom. And just as in a person, the level of vitality found in the mind is loftier than that found in his limbs, so is the light drawn down by Torah study loftier than the light drawn down by performing a *mitzvah*.

Moreover, Torah study enables us to reach a higher level of union with the Creator. Because its wisdom can be grasped in our intellect, it permeates deeper into the soul than *mitzvot*.

In Conclusion

The main purpose of the Creation is found specifically in elevating the material world-when we take material items and perform physical actions that conform to G-d's will. As a result, we transform those items into fit vessels for G-d's light and draw that light down into the world. This is why actions are of primary importance, and most of the *mitzvot* that we do focus on physical items.

Every *mitzvah* refines the object being used, the person performing the task, and his part in the world. When we succeed in purifying all of *kelipat nogah* and elevating it to *kedushah*, the impure *kelipot* will lose their life force and vanish from the world.

Thus far we emphasized the importance of deed. In the coming chapters, we will emphasize the importance of intention.

The Fifth Gate

Intention

Tanya, Chapters 38-50

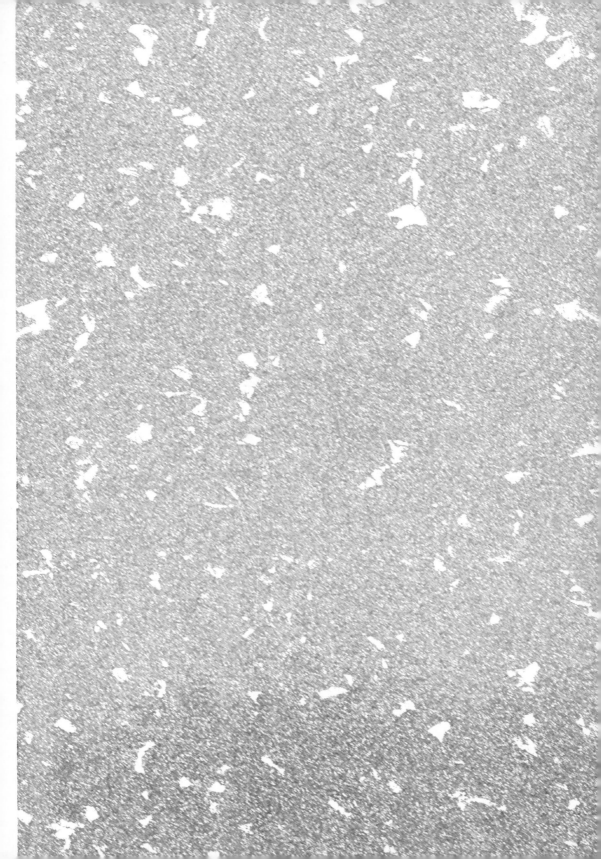

Chapter Twenty-Seven

The Power of Intention

Action is the main thing, but intention
elevates it-like the wings of a bird.

(Tanya, chaps. 38–40)

Now that we have explained the purpose for which the world was created, and how we fulfill that purpose specifically through our physical actions, we will focus on the tremendous importance of the *kavanah* (intention) that accompanies each of our deeds.

We can't emphasize enough the power of intention! First we must internalize the awareness of how each and every action we perform has an incredible impact on the world, creating a home for the Creator. Then we can internalize how our intentions, our *kavanot*, illuminate G-d's home.

What Is *"Kavanah"*?

Every *mitzvah* should be accompanied by a feeling of love or awe for G-d. These feelings are the *kavanah*-the intention.

When we do a *mitzvah* motivated by love for G-d, we feel a strong desire to give G-d pleasure and happiness. We want to rise above the material world and joyously devote ourselves to G-d.

When we do a *mitzvah* motivated by awe of G-d, we fear being separated from the Creator, disappointing Him, or causing Him "distress."

The Body and Soul of a *Mitzvah*

Every *mitzvah* has two components: the action and the *kavanah*, the intention. Although both of them draw G-d's light down into the world, having *kavanah* draws down a loftier light than the physical deed. However, intention can't exist alone. It has to be clothed in a *mitzvah*.

A *mitzvah* done with *kavanah* is like a body with a soul. The act of doing a *mitzvah* influences and refines the world-even if it is done without *kavanah*. What *kavanah* contributes is the ability to draw down a far more brilliant light.

When we do a *mitzvah* without any intention, it's like a body without a soul. It's a lifeless body, but there is a body-i.e., a deed was done that affected the world and moved it closer toward realizing its purpose.

On the other hand, having *kavanah* without performing an action is like a soul without a body-lofty and spiritual, with zero impact on the world. The *kavanah* needs a *mitzvah* in which to dwell.

Therefore, tons of intention and no *mitzvah* = nothing accomplished.

Even the smallest *mitzvah* and no intention = impact on the world.

And a *mitzvah* done with intention = the highest impact on the world with a far greater Divine light revealed.

The Analogy of Numbers

This can be compared to numbers. The *mitzvah* is like the number's first digit, and the intention is the zeroes that follow it. When we do a physical action (number 1), it impacts the world. The more intention (zeroes) we have, the larger the number grows-from 1 to 10, to 100, to 1000, to infinity.

There are two types of *mitzvot* that we perform. There are *mitzvot* performed only in action, such as giving a coin to *tzedakah*, and there are *mitzvot* performed in speech and thought, such as prayer and Torah study.

The differences in G-dly light drawn down by action *mitzvot* versus speech and thought *mitzvot* is like the difference between the vital energy found in inanimate objects such as stones, water, and earth versus plants like trees, flowers, and fruits. Just as plants have a higher level of vitality than inanimate objects since they can grow, so do speech/thought *mitzvot* draw down a higher light than action *mitzvot*, because they are infused with a greater vitality from the impact of our thoughts.

And when the *mitzvot* are performed with intention, the light is even greater.

Inherent vs. Intellectually Aroused Love

We also explained in the earlier chapters that there are two types of emotions. There are emotions that we naturally have within us and we only need to access them. This includes the natural love that every Jew has for G-d as an inheritance from our forefathers, Avraham, Yitzchak, and Yaakov.

This inheritance is called the *"pintele Yid,"* the spark hidden within each and every Jew. As soon as we remember who we are-children of G-d and the descendants of our illustrious spiritual ancestors-we rediscover this love. And even when we don't actually feel this love in our hearts, it's still strong enough to inspire and motivate us to action.

The higher level of emotion is generated by our intellect. By deeply contemplating G-d's greatness and identifying the G-dliness around us, we generate feelings of love for G-d in our hearts. These feelings originate in our minds. In comparison to simply arousing the first, inherent love, this is harder work and is known as the "long, shorter road." Though it's harder to achieve these feelings that arise from the intellect, they are more reliable, "stable," and longer lasting than the naturally based feelings.

The light drawn down by *kavanot* that are generated by intellectual contemplation is far loftier than the light drawn down by the *kavanot* that are rooted in natural feelings. The difference is so vast that it parallels the difference between animals and humans. In the same way that lofty human attributes have energy that exalts us above all of creation, so too the light drawn down by intellectually inspired intention is far superior to that which is drawn down by intentions generated by natural, inherent emotion.

One of the primary differences between humans and animals is in our ability to choose, to make decisions based on rationality and not out of impulse. When a person's performance of a *mitzvah* includes *kavanah* generated by contemplation-and not merely from aroused innate love for G-d-he achieves a far higher impact and level of revelation of light in this world.

Four and Ten

It's not a coincidence that there are four worlds (*Atzilut*, *Beriah*, *Yetzirah*, and *Asiyah*), four categories of creations (inanimate, plant, animal, man), and many other aspects of reality that are divided into four: four elements, four directions, four sons in the Passover *Haggadah*, four cups of wine at the *Seder*, four species waved on Sukkot, etc.). Obviously, this is part of G-d's plan.

Division into four corresponds to the four letters in G-d's Name, spelled *Yud-Hey-Vav-Hey* and pronounced "*Havayah*." From these four letters derive all things that divide into four, including the four primary worlds: *Atzilut* from the *yud*, *Beriah* from the first *hey* in the Name, *Yetzirah* from the *vav*, and *Asiyah* from the second *hey*.

When we previously discussed the ten *sefirot*, we divided them into two main groups: the attributes of the intellect, which include *Chochmah*/wisdom, *Binah*/understanding, and *Da'at*/knowledge; and the emotional attributes: *Chesed*/kindness, *Gevurah*/severity, *Tiferet*/glory, etc. Here we will see that the *sefirot* can also be divided into four groups corresponding to the four worlds and the four letters of G-d's Name.

Chochmah (the source of the intellect) corresponds to the world of *Atzilut* and the letter *yud*. The connection is that both *Chochmah* and *Atzilut* are nullified and self-less before G-d. Similarly, the letter *yud* is a small letter in the simple, humble form of a dot-representing the stage before and above conscious understanding (i.e., a sense of self).

Binah (intellect) corresponds to the world of *Beriah* and the first *hey* in the Name. Going from the first letter of G-d's Name (*yud*) to the second letter (*hey*) requires expansion in length, breadth, and depth.

Similarly, *Beriah* is the beginning of self-awareness and independent existence-an expansion on *Atzilut*'s nullification.

The six emotional faculties, also called **middot**, correspond to the world of *Yetzirah* and the letter *vav*. The numerical value of *vav* is six, a clear hint to the six *middot*. Its shape-a simple vertical line-parallels the work of the *middot*: drawing the intellect down into action.

Malchut (kingship; the garments of thought, speech, and deed) corresponds to the world of *Asiyah* and the second *hey*. Just as the first *hey* indicates expansion, the second *hey* (corresponding to our conscious, action-oriented dimension) develops the six emotional faculties and translates them into deed.

These four worlds are not far away in outer space-they are right here, though in a different dimension. We can't see them because they are spiritual worlds. Our relationship with them consists of affecting them through our spiritual activities in this world and entering these spiritual worlds that we influenced when our soul leaves its body at the end of its time here-enjoying the fruits of its labor on earth.

Heichalot and Sefirot

Every world contains *heichalot*, chambers, as well as the *sefirot*, that give live to that world. Our world has a material component and a spiritual dimension that gives life to the physical. In the spiritual worlds there is no physicality, but their more external dimension contains *heichalot*.

When we perform a *mitzvah* with the lower level of intention (naturally occurring emotion not born of intellectual contemplation), then our soul will rise to the world of *Yetzirah* after leaving the body. This world is also called the "lower *Gan Eden*"-a lower level of spiritual paradise. Because we only activated our emotional faculties, the soul arrives in the "world of emotions"-i.e., the world of *Yetzirah* where the emotional attributes, the *middot* reside.

When we do a *mitzvah* with the higher level of intention (emotion generated by contemplation), by deeply contemplating G-d's greatness to generate strong feelings of love and awe in our hearts, then the soul rises to the world of *Beriah,* also called the "higher *Gan Eden.*" Because we used our intellect for *kavanot,* the soul arrives in the "world of intellect"-i.e., the world of *Beriah* where *Chochmah* resides.

But even when a person served G-d with only innate love and awe (reaching the level of *Yetzirah,* the lower *Gan Eden*), at special times like Shabbat and Rosh Chodesh the soul can rise higher to *Beriah* by way of the pillar connecting the two worlds at these times.

Even though the person's Divine service was based on natural love and awe, he still used the emotions he felt for G-d to help him overcome his *yetzer hara* and its cravings. He behaved as a human being, using his ability to choose and activating his intellect. Therefore at special times he is granted the opportunity to enter the world of *Beriah.*

Reaching *Atzilut*

There is an even loftier *kavanah* that we have yet to discuss. It's a level of intention that's reserved for the great *Tzaddikim.* There is a way in which the fulfillment of a *mitzvah* attains an even higher level than intention born of contemplation. This is when a *Tzaddik* nullifies himself before G-d and devotes himself to Him so completely that he becomes His "chariot."

A chariot is completely subservient to its rider. A *Tzaddik* is completely subservient to G-d. He's so absolutely devoted to Him, far beyond the level of intellectual contemplation, that he enters the world of *Atzilut,* where the *sefirah* of *Chochmah* (the source of intellect that transcends comprehension) resides.

In other words, the *beinoni*'s highest level of intellectual contemplation of G-d's greatness leads to feelings of love and awe for G-d: he understands and therefore he loves G-d. But for the *Tzaddik,* contemplation of G-dliness is unnecessary because he *sees* it. And seeing is higher than intellect, just as *Chochmah* is higher than *Binah* and *Atzilut* is higher than *Beriah*.

A Bird's Wings

Let us further examine what happens to all the Torah we studied and the *mitzvot* we performed in our lifetime when the soul leaves the body and enters the spiritual worlds.

What happens to all the energy we invested in our life's work?

Just as the *mitzvot* and Torah study draw down light into the world, they ascend to the worlds in preparation for when the soul leaves the body after it dies; the higher the level of intention, the higher the *mitzvah* flies.

The *Zohar* compares a *mitzvah* to the body of a bird and the *kavanah* to its wings. The bird has wings, but it can't use them. It can live and be acceptable for kosher slaughter-but it cannot fly.

Mitzvot work the same way: they can exist without intent, without the wings created by love and awe for G-d, but they can't "fly" and reach the higher worlds. They remain stuck down here.

Thus Torah that was studied with feelings born of contemplation rises up to the ten *sefirot* of *Beriah* (i.e., *Beriah's* inner, spiritual core). When the soul itself rises to *Beriah*, it "basks in the radiance of the *Shechinah*," enjoying the light of the *sefirot* that give life to the world of *Beriah*.

Torah that was studied with feelings inspired by our inherent emotions rises to the ten *sefirot* of the world of *Yetzirah*. And when the soul rises to *Yetzirah*, it enjoys the radiance of the light from *Yetzirah's* ten *sefirot*.

Torah and *Mitzvot* without *Kavanah*

Mitzvot without *kavanah* are divided into several types. One is when we do a *mitzvah* without *kavanah* because it's what we were raised to do. It's a familiar habit, a comfortable routine. The prophet Yeshayahu describes this as "going through the motions because we were taught to follow commands."

In such a case, the Torah one studied is unable to rise and connect with the *sefirot* in the higher worlds. The *sefirot* represent the spirituality of each world. For Torah study to reach them, it also has to be spiritual-clothed in the "spiritual garments" created by our *kavanah* and not done from habit.

A *mitzvah* done without *kavanah* lacks its inner dimension; the reward waiting for the soul in *Gan Eden* also lacks its inner dimension because it's disconnected from the *sefirot*. The soul will still rise to that world, but will not enjoy that world's innermost dimension, because its Torah study lacked inner feeling.

A Dream about G-d

A Torah-observant Jew woke up in the middle of the night in a panic. He told his wife he had dreamt about G-d.

"What's the problem?" she asked. "Our dreams are a mixture of everything we thought about during the day."

"That's what scared me," replied the husband. "I haven't thought about G-d in years!"

This isn't really a story-it's a joke. A sad joke. We don't want to live our lives doing *mitzvot* without any connection to G-d, without any feeling of love or awe for our Creator. What a loss!

Even sadder then doing *mitzvot* by rote is doing them for unhealthy, inappropriate reasons, like a desire to be a Torah scholar in order to be honored or to look down on others. These motivations derive from *kelipat nogah*. When we do *mitzvot* for egotistical, self-serving reasons, *kelipah* is injected into those *mitzvot*.

In such a case, not only does the Torah remain below and is unable to rise to the higher world of *sefirot*, but it's even clothed in *kelipat nogah*. It's not *kedushah*.

A Synagogue Full of Prayer

The Baal Shem Tov once entered a synagogue and asked to speak with the rabbi.

"I see that this synagogue is full of Torah and prayer," he said.

The rabbi beamed at the compliment.

But then the Baal Shem Tov added, "The synagogue is full because all the Torah and prayer is lacking kavanah, unconnected to the purpose for which we learn Torah and do mitzvot. So it's all stuck down here and it's filling up the synagogue!"

Mitzvot done without *kavanah* are stuck in this world, unable to fly. But there is hope for these *mitzvot* and the person who performed them.

"Done for the Wrong Purpose" Leads to "Done for the Right Purpose"

When a person contemplates his Torah study and finds it lacking in *kavanah*, or he senses that he learned out of arrogance instead of selfless dedication, he can do *teshuvah* by regretting the past and firmly resolving to do things differently in the future. The pain he feels about the past motivates him to change. Then, when he resumes his Torah study with true concentration and focus-i.e., real *kavanah*-all the Torah that he previously studied "for the wrong purpose" is immediately released from the *kelipat nogah* imprisoning it and it is retroactively able to rise.

For this reason, it's worthwhile to learn Torah and do *mitzvot* even if our intentions aren't completely *"l'shem Shamayim"*-for the sake of Heaven. Our efforts can retroactively be redeemed in the future and still have the potential to make a profound impact.

The Torah perspective is that *all of our actions* have tremendous potential. There is always the gift of *teshuvah* to become more aware and improve in all areas of our service to G-d. The next time we learn Torah or do a *mitzvah,* this time with *kavanah,* they rise to holiness along with the Torah and *mitzvot* that were of lesser quality.

It's better to have done these actions, which fulfill G-d's will and purpose in the world, than to not have done them at all, because there is the significant possibility that we will feel regret and do sincere *teshuvah*. And as we have learned, even if our original actions lacked *kavanah,* our future *teshuvah* will release the concealed light and let it rise to the higher worlds.

In Conclusion

We live in a physical world that is changed by our actions. All of our deeds have a transformative, powerful impact on the world.

We try to have *kavanah* before we learn Torah and do *mitzvot*. When our actions lack the vitality infused by *kavanah,* they have less impact. Torah study, *mitzvot*, and *kavanah* work together to influence reality and fulfill G-d's vision for the universe.

Chapter Twenty-Eight
Two Wings

Love (ahavah) is not enough-you also need awe
(yirah). First comes awe, and then comes love.

(Tanya, chap. 41, part 1)

Now that we've explained the importance of *kavanah*-that without it our actions are like a body without a soul, or a bird without wings-we will examine the different levels of *kavanah* more closely.

Love and Awe

Feelings of awe and love for G-d are like the bird's wings of a *mitzvah*, which enable its body-the physical act of doing the *mitzvah*-to soar and rise up. In the coming chapters, we will discuss these emotions and how to create them in the soul. First we will discuss the unique qualities of each one.

Which one is more important-love or awe? Love inspires us to perform the positive *mitzvot*, while awe motivates us to avoid the negative *mitzvot*, or prohibitions. Both are necessary in our service to G-d. On a deeper level, even our fulfillment of the positive commandments requires awe; and in fact it's the starting point.

When the *Tanya* talks about *yirah*, it's not referring to worries about getting punished, just as *ahavah* doesn't mean expecting to get prizes and rewards. Earlier we defined *yirah* as a fear of separation from G-d and a fear of disappointing Him. But now we'll give it an additional definition.

Yirah means understanding that the world has a Master Who created it, manages it, recreates and renews it every moment, and gives us the strength to live in it. This understanding leads us to the conclusion that we need to accept Him as our King and take upon ourselves the responsibility of serving Him by fulfilling His will.

Today awe and fear have fallen out of style; it's not popular to talk about awe and fear. Love is the hot topic of the day. Some people claim that G-d Himself is love, and serving G-d out of love is all that is required of us. Although this idea isn't completely wrong, it's problematic. In a sense, it limits the depths of our ability to serve G-d with all our inner attributes and emotions, which include fear and awe. It makes G-d "smaller" in our eyes.

At the same time, we don't want fear of punishment in our spiritual future to be the motivation for performing *mitzvot*. Serving G-d from *ahavah* is considered a higher level. But it is *yirah* that usually motivates us to be subservient to G-d. If we do *mitzvot* only out of *ahavah*, without any feeling of *yirah* or understanding that we need to be nullified before G-d and do His will-something significant may be lacking.

Firstborn Daughter: A Sign of Sons to Come

Our intellectual faculties, *Chochmah* and *Binah*, are called "father" and "mother." Proper meditative contemplation with the intellect produces emotions, as parents produce children: *chesed*, love, also called "son," and *yirah*, awe, also called "daughter."

There is an old Talmudic saying: *"Bat rishonah siman lebanim*-A firstborn daughter is a sign of sons [to come]."* On a spiritual level, this saying refers to our service to G-d: feelings of *yirah* (the firstborn daughter) will lead to *ahavah* (sons).

But in the spiritual order of our emotions, *ahavah* does not necessarily lead to *yirah*. If the order is reversed and the first child is a son (love), there is no guarantee that daughters (awe) will follow.

The Feeling of Love

Love feels great. When we love G-d, we feel close to Him. We feel that He is our loving and caring Father, and as His children we love Him back and are willing to do anything for Him. But love that is not preceded by fear is usually incomplete.

The feeling of love derives from our sense of self: *I* love G-d, and the more *I* love Him, the more *I* want to do for Him. And sometimes, when we only have love for G-d, we do *mitzvot* only because we enjoy them. We view it as a game: if it's fun and entertaining, we'll do it.

In addition, because love is a feeling of closeness, we may come to feel so buddy-buddy with G-d that we may think we are on His level. We may become too casual in our *mitzvot* observance and lose our sensitivity to the fact that G-d is infinitely beyond us.

Without *yirah*, our sense of *kabbalat ol Shamayim*-our commitment to doing His will-is absent, and we run the risk of not accepting His authority.

Worker and Volunteer

A factory worker receives a salary from the factory owner and uses it for living expenses. He understands that he must follow the factory manager's instructions. He knows that if he doesn't fulfill his work obligations, he won't get his salary and he won't be able to pay his bills. In contrast, a volunteer doesn't get paid for his efforts, and therefore he feels less of a sense of obligation.

Each of these situations has an advantage and a disadvantage. The worker does everything that's asked of him, but he might constantly look at the clock and look forward to the workday being over. The volunteer isn't obligated to be there since he *chose* to be there. This is a great advantage, because it's likely that the volunteer will give more of himself than the paid worker does. He will truly put himself into the work and look for opportunities to help as much as possible.

But the volunteer's advantage is also a disadvantage. He chose to be there, and he can also choose *not* to be there-he can up and leave at any moment. As long as he has not accepted the authority of the manager like paid workers do, he isn't committed to the company. Practically speaking, such a person is not really working-he's entertaining himself.

These differences also apply to love and fear. So long as there are feelings of love, the person will choose to serve G-d. His service is not built on true commitment; he's involved out of choice, and he will stay as long as it "feels right" to be there. Like the volunteer, he could leave at any moment. It's not the same dedicated service of the paid employee. He could make a different decision and move on, leaving it all behind and ending his volunteer service.

An example of this could be someone who has begun to learn about Judaism, has started studying Torah, and is fulfilling some *mitzvot*. He's involved and interested but has not yet fully committed himself to G-d. He may put on *tefillin* and keep Shabbat, but he has not yet decided to accept upon himself the "yoke of Divine service" (*kabbalat ol Shamayim*).

Each one of the individual *mitzvot* that he does has incredibly potency, influencing and elevating the world, even though he himself is not yet "serving G-d." Even without total commitment and acceptance of G-d's sovereignty, each *mitzvah* has incredible significance.

And yet, this person hasn't begun to truly serve G-d. It's still just an interesting game to him, and it's unclear how far he'll progress (if at all) in his commitment. We see that this is the "fun stage," when things go smoothly because it's still the early initial stage. Once the person decides to jump in and fully assume the yoke of commitment, dedication, and responsibility for serving G-d, he may encounter real challenges and obstacles. Because now the real work has begun! Before that, it wasn't quite real.

Yirah: The True Connection

This is similar to a couple before they decide to get married. They think they get along, that they have a good connection, but they haven't yet encountered the true test of their compatibility. Only after they've made a lifetime commitment to each other, only after the wedding, does the real work begin.

This also applies to our "marriage" with G-d. Until the wedding takes place-when we make a commitment to accept His sovereignty over us-true commitment is lacking, and real Divine service has yet to begin.

When the Alter Rebbe's student Reb Hillel read the *Tanya* for the first time, he said, "Until now I thought I was a *Tzaddik*. Now I'm hoping to be a *beinoni!*"

Before we truly begin serving G-d and completely accept His authority, we think we are *Tzaddikim* and every *mitzvah* we do is a pleasure. The true work begins only after we accept the commitment to truly serve G-d. It is only then that we realize how far we are from the level of *Tzaddik* and begin working toward the level of *beinoni*.

That is why *yirah* is so essential. Awe and fear are the beginning of everything-and love will follow afterward. True, lasting Divine service begins with *yirah*.

Obtaining *Yirah* through Contemplation

Our feelings are born out of the intellect. Contemplation leads to emotions, and the more intensely we contemplate G-d's greatness, before Whom we stand and to Whom we are praying, the more we'll feel awe and fear of G-d.

The most opportune time for such meditative contemplation is before and during prayer. One of the main purposes of prayer is to arouse our emotions toward G-d and spirituality. And once these feelings are ignited, they continue to inspire us throughout the day.

But before we can contemplate, the thoughts racing through our head need to be tamed so that we can fully concentrate on the subject of our meditation: G-d. Once we are ready, we can begin the process of contemplating G-d's greatness.

Start with this meditation: Think about how G-d recreates the world anew at every moment, infusing His life force into all of creation, and life energy into each individual. Think about how G-d is present everywhere. He is simultaneously within the boundaries of time and completely beyond it. He is completely aware of every aspect of everything, thinking about each one constantly, and tending to their particular needs, as it is written, "He counts the number of stars; to all of them He assigns names" (*Tehillim* 147:4). At the same time, He is also "above" all of the creations-and they have no impact on Him.

According to the *Zohar*, two different types of G-dly light and energy are found in the world: *memalei*, filling the worlds, and *sovev*, surrounding the worlds.

Memalei, or inner light, is a reduced level of light and energy, which enables it to be grasped and received in the "vessels" of whoever "receives" it and unites with it. Like water changing to fit the shape of the glass it's poured into, *memalei* light conforms to the needs, limitations, and dimensions of each recipient.

This is similar to the relationship between soul and body. Not only is the soul inside the body, but it also unites with it. The soul completely fills up every bit of the body so that they can't be separated.

How does the soul clothe itself in the body? It infuses itself into every limb according to its needs and ability to receive (i.e., its vessels). For example, the mind possesses more light than the legs, the head more than the hands, etc. The more a limb or organ can handle, the bigger its vessels, the more light it receives.

In a similar way, G-d fills the worlds and all of His creations. Each of them receives G-dly vitality that becomes clothed in them and united with them. But each of them gets a different amount of vitality because it's distributed according to what they can handle-according to their "vessels." Therefore, animals have more vitality than plants, but plants have more vitality than stones.

The other type of light is **sovev,** or external, surrounding light. It is also known as *makif*. This light is beyond the limitations of *memalei* light-it is "unlimited" and equally present everywhere. As a result, *sovev* light doesn't get absorbed into the recipients' vessels, and thus can't be grasped by the worlds or the creations in them. This is why it's called "*sovev*," surrounding light. It doesn't submit to the worlds' boundaries and dimensions; it's beyond their reach.

If *memalei* is like water fitting into the cup, *sovev* is like a wood block resting on top of the cup and refusing to change in order to fit in. It can also be compared to the experience of learning something very deep and esoteric, where we can't seem to wrap our minds around it and understand it. The G-dly light in the concept is too lofty to be held by our intellect-by our mind's vessels.

On a soul level, *sovev* corresponds to the attribute of *ratzon*, will. Unlike intellect (mind) and emotion (heart), will does not have a particular place in the body. Rather, will is equally distributed across the body, surrounding it instead of filling it. In other words, it is such a lofty power in the soul that the body can't receive it and hold on to it in its "vessels." As such, it's called "*sovev*."

It has to be kept in mind that despite G-d's greatness, He "puts it all down," so to speak, in order to tend to the Jews in general and to each individual Jew in particular. He knows us, our names, what we like, and what we need.

On a deeper level, He created everything in the world for us. Not so that we should feel proud and arrogant, but so that we will humbly accept responsibility for our mission. Everything we see when we look around us was created by G-d specifically for us to use in our Divine service. Some things help us directly, while others initially seem to hinder us, yet ultimately also help us-by overcoming them, we grow and progress in our service of G-d.

Kashering Dishes for Pesach in Siberia

Two Chassidim were incarcerated in a Russian prison for the crime of spreading Judaism. As Pesach neared, they lacked matzah, wine, and all the symbolic foods for the Seder.

All they could do was clean and kasher a pot for cooking potatoes. After preparing the pot, one of the Chassidim burst into tears. "We could be at home with our families celebrating the exodus from Egypt. But how are we supposed to celebrate when we are in prison?"

The second Chassid calmly responded, "Think about it. Perhaps the whole purpose of our souls' descent to earth was to prepare a pot of potatoes for Pesach in this Russian prison and thereby reveal its Divine spark."

Each of us needs to feel that the world was created just for me. With this awareness comes the understanding that something is expected of us and we have a responsibility to act accordingly.

Until we grasp and appreciate this point, it's likely that our feelings will remain "stuck" in our mind and fail to reach our heart. For the heart to also feel it, we need to do deeper contemplation.

In Conclusion

Feelings of *yirah*, accepting G-d's dominion over us and thus the need to serve Him, and feelings of *ahavah*, the desire to unite with G-d, are both necessary in our service to G-d. Generating these feelings requires meditative contemplation, but the place to begin is with *yirah*.

Chapter Twenty-Nine

For the Sake
of Unification

Uniting with G-d is a goal in itself
and not just for personal gain.

(Tanya, chap. 41, part 2)

We began discussing the meditative contemplation that leads to awe of G-d. Now we will continue our exploration of this topic.

The Starting Point

After our initial contemplation that G-d created the entire world, is everywhere at all times, and yet is actively involved in caring for us, we will now emphasize that He's not far off in space, but rather right here with us in the room, at this very moment, examining us.

His examination is deeper than that done by people who only see with their eyes. G-d also looks into our hearts. He sees our actions as well as what's going on inside us, what motivates us, what we think and what we feel. There's no hiding from G-d; there are no facades or deceiving Him.

As a result of deeply meditating on this fact of reality, we can conclude that we must serve G-d with a feeling of *yirah*, as if we were standing before a mighty and powerful King, which indeed we are.

It's difficult for us to envision what it means to stand before an earthly king, as there are few monarchies in existence in our day. But if we can imagine the fear and awe we would feel before a judge who has the power to decide our fate, we may be able to sense what it means to stand before the true Judge, in awe of His authority over everything that happens to us.

This is the starting point for serving G-d-the feeling of awe.

Drawing Down Infinite Light

The contemplation doesn't stop there. It needs to be expanded and deepened by each person in proportion to the time he dedicates to this endeavor and his ability to envision the reality of these concepts.

A meditative contemplation can be done before praying, putting on *tallit* and *tefillin*, giving *tzedakah,* lighting Shabbat candles, or doing any other *mitzvot*. This applies equally to men and to women-everyone is obligated to love and fear G-d.

Here is what we can think about before doing a *mitzvah*:

Each *mitzvah* draws an infinite light into the world. The *mitzvot* are G-d's inner will, and He is united with them and revealed through them. When we fulfill a *mitzvah*, we draw His light upon ourselves and get absorbed into it.

It gets more specific when we apply it to an individual *mitzvah*.

The *tefillin* worn by men have four compartments, each of which houses a piece of parchment with a portion of the Torah written on it. The parchments each correspond to one of the *sefirot*.

As we mentioned before, our intellect is divided into three parts: *Chochmah* (wisdom), *Binah* (understanding), and *Da'at* (knowledge). And because the role of *Da'at* is to translate our comprehension into the emotions of love and awe, it contains both of them. Of the four Torah portions contained in the *tefillin*, the one beginning, "Sanctify to me every firstborn," corresponds with *Chochmah*. The portion of "When you will bring" corresponds to *Binah*. The portion of "*Shema Yisrael*" corresponds to love, and "When you will listen," with awe.

As such, by wearing *tefillin*, not only is infinite light drawn down in general, but also light is drawn down directly into the minds and hearts of those who wear it. In this way, we commit, dedicate, and subjugate our minds and hearts to the service of G-d-using them exclusively for G-d. This is what we can contemplate before donning *tefillin*.

The meditative contemplation connected to the *tallit* focuses on G-d being our King. Wrapping ourselves in the *tallit* corresponds with drawing His Kingship down upon us, as we are commanded in the Torah, "Surely you will make a king over yourself." This refers not only to a physical king in this world, but also to G-d, Who is called the "King of kings."

Everyone Can

The story is told of a Chassid who prayed that he would be able to feel the same level of awe of Heaven as the righteous Tzaddikim. When his prayer was answered, he felt such fear and terror that he hid under the table and prayed to have it taken away.

This contemplation of G-d's kingship is possible for everyone, and each of us can achieve the feeling of awe it produces. Just as a soldier can feel fear of the army's commander-in-chief even before entering his room-just by thinking about his lofty position-so we can feel awe of G-d by contemplating Who G-d is, how great He is, how life and death are in His power alone, and how He is nevertheless right here with us.

Even if someone is unable to generate heartfelt feelings of awe, it doesn't detract from the *mitzvah* to be in awe of G-d. Intellectually understanding that the world has a Master and that we need to accept His authority and be nullified before Him is the beginning of learning to fear G-d. With this awareness, we perform the *mitzvah*.

But if even this level of understanding is lacking and awe is missing, then the *mitzvot* we do cannot be called "service of G-d." As we explained previously, Divine service done only out of love, without self-annulment and acceptance of G-d as King, is not yet serious-it's more like a game.

Contemplation Is a Prerequisite

Deep contemplation is not needed to generate a feeling for what our eyes can see. G-d, on the other hand, is completely abstract, without form or image. Thus, arousing feelings for Him takes more than a simple thought. We need to deeply contemplate G-d's greatness, each person according to his ability, in order to generate feelings of awe for Him.

The *Zohar* addresses this by saying that in order for an ox to plow land, he first has to have the yoke of the plow placed upon him. Without it, he will accomplish nothing by walking up and down the fields.

In the metaphor of the bird, it needs both wings to fly-it cannot do so with only one wing. The same applies to doing a *mitzvah* (the body of the bird): with only one wing (love), it cannot soar to the higher worlds of *Beriah* and *Yetzirah* and be included in their ten *sefirot*. But *yirah* alone is also not enough. We also have to arouse feelings of love and a desire to connect to G-d.

Uniting G-d and the Shechinah

This approach is not about our individual feelings toward G-d, but rather the view of each of us as a part of the collective Jewish people who all connect to G-d.

Every Jew contains the entire Jewish people within him, and every Jew contains the *Shechinah*. "Shechinah" is the name given to G-d's light after it descends into our world and gives it life-i.e., *memalei*, the filling light. "*Hakadosh Baruch Hu*" (the Holy One, blessed be He) is the name given to the G-dly light that transcends the world-i.e., *sovev*, the surrounding light.

We primarily encounter the *Shechinah* in our world and *Hakadosh Baruch Hu* in the Torah. When we do a *mitzvah*, we bring *Hakadosh Baruch Hu* and the *Shechinah* together.

This is a different approach to *mitzvot*. Here, the intent is not to connect to G-d or to quench our thirst for *kedushah*. Instead, we are speaking of a higher level where there is no "me." Rather, I seek only to "help" G-d by uniting Him with His *Shechinah*. It's comparable to a child who wants to help his parents because they need help, and not for his own benefit.

This is a very lofty level that is clearly not everyone's position. It's not something that we all truly feel. A sincere person is likely to feel dishonest if he tries to imagine that every *mitzvah* he does is for G-d's benefit alone. But actually, he's not being dishonest. Deep inside, we all possess the desire to do things "for the sake of Heaven."

Sanctifying G-d's Name by Living

In his inner self, every Jew loves G-d and is even willing to die for Him. This is the true essence of a Jew. Our history has demonstrated this many times. Jews were willing to die rather than be separated from G-d by bowing down to idols, converting to other religions, or desecrating His Name. Jews willingly died even when they were "simple" Jews who kept Torah and *mitzvot* and were not considered outstanding righteous *Tzaddikim*.

But we don't need to die to sanctify G-d's Name. We can also sanctify G-d's Name by *living*. This should be our approach to Torah and *mitzvot*-seeing each *mitzvah* as an act of self-sacrificing devotion. Every *mitzvah* we do can be filled with our readiness to give everything we are to G-d, looking only to give and not to receive.

This is how our prayers begin each morning. The first thing we say upon waking is *"Modeh Ani"* (I gratefully acknowledge), the prayer thanking G-d for purifying my soul during sleep and restoring it to me in the morning. We also acknowledge in this prayer that one day G-d will take our soul back. And therefore we resolve that as long as we have our soul within us, we will be completely devoted to G-d and make it our life's work to be connected to Him via prayer, Torah, and *mitzvot*.

The Baal Shem Tov's Prayer

It was said of the Baal Shem Tov that before he would begin praying, he would wonder whether his soul would remain in his body until the end of the prayer. Would he experience such intense kelot hanefesh (expiry of the soul due to its yearning to unite with G-d) and give himself so totally to G-d that his soul would leave his body, or would he "survive" the prayers?

Even after we finish praying, the same idea applies-we want to remind ourselves that throughout the rest of the day, when we study Torah and do *mitzvot*, we are not seeking personal pleasure, but rather devoting ourselves to G-d in our daily life.

And even more than that, our intent is to give pleasure to G-d. Just like the great joy felt by the king when his son is released from imprisonment, so is G-d (the King) very happy when we (His children) rise up out of the confines of the physically restricting world by learning Torah and doing *mitzvot*.

In Conclusion

There is a deeper level of reality beyond our own personal view of the world. Not only do we have our own individual connection to G-d, we also have a connection to the entire Jewish people. As Jews, we are children of G-d, and in our essence we are ready to give our lives to Him as a child who devotes himself wholeheartedly to the care of his parents.

Our devotion to G-d is to please Him and not for personal gain. Though this is a high and lofty level, we each have within us the ability to soar. However, this essential truth is concealed and requires meditative contemplation to be revealed.

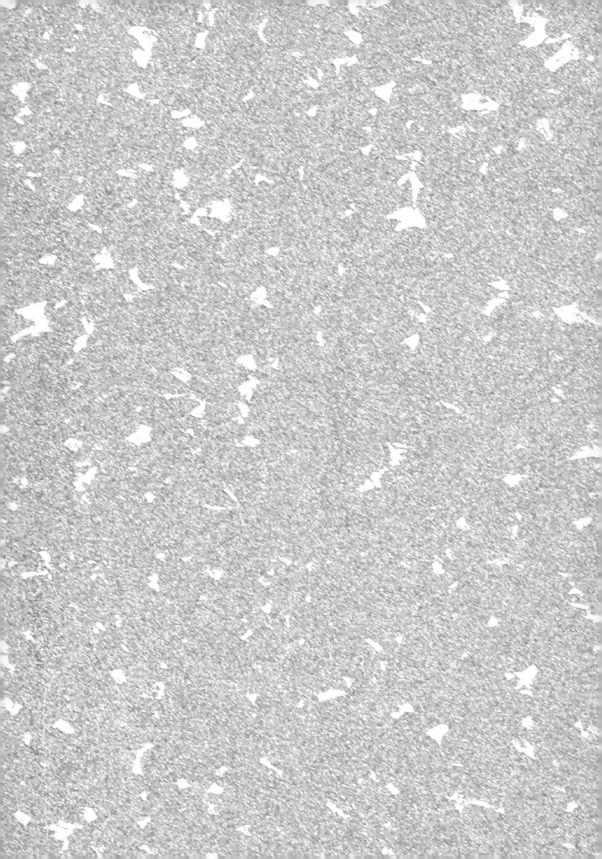

Chapter Thirty

Yirat Shamayim

There are two levels of awe: yirah tata and yirah ilah.

(Tanya, chap. 42)

We briefly examined the need for both love and awe, and explained a level of Divine service that's higher than both of them: pleasing the Creator. Now we will discuss in depth the two levels of *yirah* and the meditative contemplation necessary to achieve them.

Yirat Shamayim and Moshe

As mentioned before, "*yirah*" doesn't mean feeling scared, and it certainly doesn't mean self-centered worries. Rather, it means accepting G-d's authority and committing to serve Him and fulfill His commandments. It's an understanding that the world has a Master Whom we need to listen to.

Contemplating a concept in order to generate feelings about it is a difficult task- especially when it comes to G-d, Who is abstract, without shape and form. We can't imagine what He looks like or what it means to be "standing" before Him.

But G-d didn't leave us on our own. In order to help us accomplish this difficult task, He sent us help in the form of our *Tzaddikim*.

The first *Tzaddik* we learn from is Moshe Rabbeinu (Moses, our teacher), who is often referred to as the "shepherd of the Jewish people." Just as a shepherd feeds his flock and looks after their needs, Moshe was a devoted shepherd of the Jewish people. Not only did he oversee their physical needs, making sure they had food and water, but he also "shepherded" them spiritually.

As mentioned, the soul attribute of *Da'at* takes the comprehension produced by *Chochmah* and *Binah* and becomes united with it by deeply grasping it until it generates heartfelt emotions. Moshe strengthened the Jewish people's *Da'at* so that they could deepen their contemplation and successfully produce emotions that helped them serve G-d. As the verse states, "*Know* the G-d of your fathers and serve Him wholeheartedly." When there is *Da'at*, there is also wholehearted service with all our emotional attributes. This is how Moshe spiritually "shepherded" the Jewish people.

In the generations after Moshe, G-d-sent more *Tzaddikim* whose souls contained a spark from his soul. They also strengthened our *Da'at* and helped us achieve heartfelt emotions for G-d.

Just to make sure we're clear-*Da'at* is not understanding or simply amassing information. It is a deep bond, an intimate awareness of a concept. It's not enough to understand the greatness of the Creator; we must *know* Him by investing time to think about His attributes. We need to free up time in our busy lives by stepping back from all of our engagements, clear out our mind and thoughts, and make an effort to think deeply about G-d's greatness.

Difficult Work

Just understanding His greatness or simply contemplating it is not enough. Rather, each of us must also contemplate our personal connection to G-d's attributes-where we are in the picture. This is what makes it such hard work, and this is why we need a Moshe to help us do it.

There is a dimension of Moshe found in each of our souls, and through its connection to Moshe we get the power to deeply invest our *Da'at* into contemplating G-d's greatness.

Still, even though we have a dimension of Moshe within, it's difficult to just meditate. This is because the part of our soul that is nourished and draws strength from the soul of Moshe Rabbeinu is in our bodies, and the body is material and interferes with our ability to focus on contemplation.

It requires a real effort to counter the distractions of the body, as it uses a wide range of techniques to disturb our contemplation. Our body complains of hunger, thirst, fatigue, headaches, and weakness. It's too hot, it's too cold, it's too sweaty. The body wants us to focus on its physical needs more than the soul's spiritual need to connect to G-d.

This is soul work-not allowing our thoughts to confuse us and distract us from our meditations. In our generation, it's widely known just how difficult it's become to concentrate for even a few moments at a time, and even on material matters. All the more so when contemplating something spiritual. Therefore, successful contemplation requires great exertion of the soul.

The Analogy of the Magician: Everyone Can

When we see a magician pull a rabbit out of a hat, we understand that this is an illusion. We watch carefully, fascinated, in an effort to figure out the tricks he uses. The same approach applies to our contemplation of the world. We know that G-d is everywhere. We just have to observe carefully, fascinated, to figure out how to find Him.

Some souls are so lofty, pure, and refined by nature that they don't need lengthy contemplation to find G-d. As soon as they wake up in the morning, they feel G-d's presence is close. Their feeling of awe is instantly generated, and they begin to serve G-d with joy.

But there are souls on a lower level who don't feel this when they wake up, and they don't instantly spring out of bed ready to begin serving G-d. It takes much more effort for such souls to contemplate G-d's greatness and produce feelings of awe.

King Shlomo said of this, "If you seek it like silver and search for it like hidden treasure, you will understand the awe of G-d and discover the knowledge of G-d" (*Mishlei* 2:4–5). When someone hears that he has a treasure buried in his yard and all he has to do is start digging, he immediately starts shoveling with all his might. He knows it's there. Even if it takes time to find it, it's worth the effort and the energy he invests.

This is what Shlomo is telling us: there is buried treasure in our souls, a wealth of awe and fear of G-d-*yirat Shamayim*-and if we start to "dig," using meditative contemplation, we'll reach it. As the Talmud teaches us, "One who says, 'I labored and succeeded'-believe him" (*Megillah* 6b).

With effort, the treasure within us is reachable.

With the Help of the *Tzaddik*

Tzaddikim help us by guiding our efforts to search for and find G-d. When people look for valuable, precious gems within the earth, they need an expert geologist to guide their efforts in the right direction, or they won't know where to dig. They'll waste time sifting through the sand. A *Tzaddik* is an expert guide in the innermost map of the soul.

There is no doubt that each of us possesses *yirat Shamayim* within us, but a *Tzaddik* helps us find our inner way. Without the help of a *Tzaddik*, we could have "theoretical" awe-we may think and speak of it, but practically speaking it doesn't impact on our conduct.

There are people who make *Kiddush* and have a Shabbat meal on Friday night, but then they turn on the television. They know G-d exists and want to live according to His wisdom and directions, but there is an obstacle between theory and practice. The *Tzaddik* helps us strengthen our *Da'at*, our contemplation of G-d's greatness, which in turn aids our efforts to make awe of G-d part of our daily life.

"Turn from Evil and Do Good"

When we achieve the desired awe, it guides and inspires us to behave properly. We will want to avoid transgression and do good with all three garments of the soul: thought, speech, and action.

A person standing before a king, or someone else he considers important, won't behave like he ordinarily does among friends. He won't allow himself to act however he wants or say whatever he thinks. All the more so when a person deeply contemplates the reality of G-d and *knows* that G-d is right beside him. He is empowered to control his thoughts, speech, and deeds. His *yirat Shamayim* consciously influences his behavior.

Some wonder, How can G-d hear and see everything? Is He really able to supervise everyone at all times? And even if He can, the universe is so vast-why would He be interested in what I do?

The answer is simple. G-d is not *outside* the world looking down at us. He is *here*, one with the world. G-d's presence infuses every corner of creation! Just as a person's body has billions of molecules and cells, and the body is conscious of every single one of them because it is united with them, so is G-d aware of each of His creatures at every moment. That is what it means when it says, "*Ein od milvado*-There is nothing but G-d alone."

In actuality, this is far too lofty a matter for our understanding; we cannot truly understand how G-d is aware of every part of His creation. But just knowing that He does leads us to *yirah*.

Observation in Prayer

The main meditative contemplation each day occurs during morning prayers. If we prepare ourselves for prayer and then pray properly with *kavanah*, succeeding in generating a feeling of awe, that morning contemplation can spiritually sustain us all day. All we need is a brief contemplation to refuel the feeling.

And anytime we feel ourselves slipping-and our thoughts, speech, or deeds are not what we want them to be-we can recall our meditation, "regenerate" our awe, and draw new strength to cope with our challenges.

The simple meaning of "prayer" is to cry out to G-d in times of trouble and ask for what we need. On a deeper level, however, prayer is not (only) about receiving; it's also about giving.

The Hebrew word for prayer, "*tefillah*" is related to the word "*tofel*," which means "attach" or "join," like the pieces of a broken vessel that are pieced together to make it whole again. With this insight, we can add that the deeper meaning of prayer is forming a connection with G-d. And we do this through contemplation that produces heartfelt emotions.

Faith: A Form of Training

To be strong, healthy, and functioning optimally, our muscles need a daily workout. Training-"*imun*" in Hebrew-has the same root as "*emunah*," faith. Meditative contemplation and daily observation of the world also requires practice and training, "*imun*," which leads to faith, "*emunah*."

With daily training in our beliefs, we become more proficient at focusing on the inner core of everything we see and hear. We learn to see the G-dliness everywhere and in everything.

The Inner Vitality

So how do we achieve this deep level of contemplation?

We feel awe in the presence of a great king because of his inner vitality and soul powers, not his body. It's his authority, abilities, and the control he wields that makes an impression-not his muscles. It's not what our eyes see that inspires our awe, but rather what we understand to be behind it. Nobody was ever fearful of a great and powerful person's clothes! Garments only testify to what's inside. Similarly, it's not the body that inspires fear, it's the inner persona and vitality.

Imagine entering the king's castle. The servants in the king's vicinity fulfill his requests with awe and admiration. Before you even see the king, you feel awe and respect for him, just by your observations of his servants' behavior.

A similar phenomenon occurs when we observe all the stars and galaxies in the universe, and the millions of diverse creatures filling the earth. We contemplate the fact that it's all an external expression of the Creator. Looking at the king's servants causes feelings of awe of the king; studying the complexity of the world leads to awe for G-d, Who is the inner vitality of the world.

When we tour a large city and see its tall buildings, the awesome greatness of it all instills us with wonder. We are impressed not only by the outer impressive appearance of the buildings themselves, but by the intricate planning that was needed to create the city.

So too, when we observe the magnificent complexity of the created world, from the tiniest microscopic cell functioning and the harmonious balance of the organs of our body to the vast expanse of the solar system and beyond, we begin to feel a growing sense of awe toward the Creator Who made everything. Meditative contemplation on the works of creation, called "*bechinah*," leads to awe.

Further contemplation of the fact that G-d created all of creation, and continues to sustain and recreate it anew every moment, leads to even deeper awe.

Yirah Tata and *Yirah Ilah*-the Lower and Higher Awe

In *Pirkei Avot*, we are taught, "Without fear there is no wisdom, and without wisdom there is no fear" (*Avot* 3:21).

If we need wisdom to achieve fear and we need fear to achieve wisdom, how do we begin? The answer is that there are two levels of *yirah*.

The lower level of awe is called "*yirah tata.*" This is the *yirah* that is a prerequisite to wisdom, where wisdom results in good deeds, as stated in the verse "The purpose of wisdom is repentance and good deeds."

Then, after achieving this level of wisdom, we can use it to reach the higher level of awe-*yirah ilah*.

The lower level of awe, and the contemplation needed to attain it, involve G-d's external garments (i.e., His creations). Thinking about them gives us clues to the inner vitality of G-d. However, there is a higher level of contemplation, which requires wisdom to attain it.

Another *mishnah* in *Pirkei Avot* teaches, "Who is wise? He who sees what will be." The simple meaning of this statement is that the wise person imagines what will be the future consequences of his actions. The deeper meaning is that the wise man sees the world being born-he contemplates how G-d creates the world anew every moment.

Based on this insight, he concludes that from the Creator's point of view the world is not an independent reality, and the creations within the world do not move independently without G-d sustaining and directing them. G-d "pulls the strings" behind the scenes. Moreover, if He stopped creating it for a second, it would cease to exist.

On an even deeper level, the real existence of the world is through "G-d spoke and it came into being"-the words by which G-d created and sustains the world.

As such, it's obvious that not only is the world subservient and dependent upon G-d, but we too are subservient and dependent upon G-d. We, too are being recreated at every moment.

This contemplation generates the higher level of awe.

Two Levels of Accepting His Authority

These two levels of *yirah* lead to two levels of accepting the yoke of G-d's kingship, two levels of commitment to serving Him.

On the first level, *yirah tata*, we contemplate the fact that the world has a Master Whom we need to listen to and obey. The starting point is that there is a world and I exist, but then I realize that there is Someone above me whose authority I need to accept and before whom I must "annul myself."

This level of self-nullification is called *"bitul hayesh"* (nullification of my sense of self)-meaning, I exist, but *I* understand that *I* need to do what G-d is telling me.

On the second level, *yirah ilah*, we contemplate the fact that from G-d's perspective there is no world! The entire existence of all of creation is of no comparison or value next to G-d-including myself. Therefore, not only do I need to push aside my arrogance and nullify myself before G-d, but in actuality there is no "I" at all.

This level of self-nullification is called *"bitul bimetziut"* (nullification of my sense of separate existence). Unlike the first level, where I have my own will and desire that I forego in order to fulfill what G-d wants, here there is no "me" to have a desire.

This is a very lofty level that not everyone reaches.

In Conclusion

Yirah tata, the lower level of awe, is the understanding that G-d is the Master of the world and we should obey Him. This understanding serves as the basis for serving G-d. Without it, all of our efforts are incomplete. As such, we have to invest time and spiritual labor to acquire this level of *yirah*. Once it is achieved, we have to train ourselves to hold it in our hearts constantly.

Yirah ilah, the higher level of awe, is the understanding that G-d is continually bringing all of creation into existence out of utter nothingness and that we do not exist separately from Him at all.

Chapter Thirty-One
Five Levels of Love

There are five levels of love: *ahavah rabbah, ahavat olam, Nafshi iviticha, Av* and *ben,* and *rachamim*-aroused love.

(Tanya, chaps. 43–44)

The *Tanya* teaches that there are five levels of love. The highest, and hardest to achieve is *"ahavah rabbah."*

Ahavah Rabbah

Ahavah rabbah means "great love" and refers to delighting in love, delighting in the connection. It's an ecstatic feeling of connection with G-d. It's not a love of yearning for something that we don't yet have, the love of longing and thirsting for something we are eagerly expecting. Delighting in love is complete, fulfilled love. We are together, my beloved and I.

A person who has achieved perfection in his *yirah* may receive this level of love as a gift from G-d. This is an extremely high level of connection that few attain.

Ahavat Olam

Ahavat olam, "love that's of the world," results from serving G-d. It's a deep love born by contemplating spiritual truths: that G-d continuously renews the world's existence every moment, that He is found in every aspect of creation, that there is no place without G-d, that He creates the world through Divine speech, and that His G-dliness sustains everything.

It results from the knowledge that the world can't exist without G-d constantly willing it to be. And this awesome G-d personally created the miraculous, intricate complexity of my mind and body and intervenes in my life every second with *hashgachah pratit*. G-d loves and cares about me with an unfathomable love; I am surrounded by His *ahavah rabbah* for me personally.

These meditative contemplations can bring a person to the understanding that we have so much to be grateful for. All physical desires are insignificant in comparison to the "real thing"-the *ahavah rabbah* of G-d and His Divine light.

With this line of thought, a person ultimately discovers that physical desires are insignificant compared to the deep satisfaction one has in an eternal relationship with G-d. These meditations help a person aspire to something greater-G-d, the only truly lasting thing in life. In comparison, bodily pleasures are temporary and don't provide eternal satisfaction.

This understanding helps a person move toward G-d and *kedushah* and wean himself away from the temporary pleasures of this world.

Wanting the Real Thing

A young child longs for toy cars. When he grows up, he longs for a real car. He isn't looking for toy cars anymore, and he'll be upset if you offer him a toy now.

We need to intellectually understand G-d's reality so that our Animal Soul will be subordinate to the knowledge that G-d is the "real thing" and the only worthwhile desire, while the pleasures of the world are like a breakable toy in comparison. Such knowledge will help us to naturally feel love for G-d.

Imagine you are looking at a plate full of delicacies. Your mouth waters as you inhale the enticing fragrances. You experience a strong desire to eat it all.

But what if it were a plate full of plastic food? We wouldn't crave the plastic, because intellectually we know it isn't real, and we have no feelings for something we know isn't the real thing.

As we work on appreciating that the world is "plastic" and G-d is the truth, our physical addictions fade-replaced by a desire for G-d.

We Both Have Desires

A Jew visited a Tzaddik because he was very disturbed by how his desires were distracting him from real service to G-d.

"Rebbe! I crave food, money, honor, pleasure, but the Rebbe craves holiness! We are both full of desires. How can I change mine to be like yours?

The Tzaddik looked at the Jew sympathetically and answered, "For you to begin to desire kedushah, you have to pray to G-d as sincerely for spiritual things as you do for physical things. Then G-d will help you!"

Love of G-d is not compatible with other loves. If we're focused on our love of food, money, and honor, there is no room for love for G-d to coexist.

"For I am G-d, I do not change; and you, the sons of Yaakov, have not been consumed," writes the prophet Malachi (in *Malachi* 3:6). The simple meaning is that G-d tells the Jewish people that they exist in the merit of G-d's unchanging nature: He made a promise to our ancestors, and He will not rescind it.

On a deeper level, G-d is telling the Jewish people, "I have not changed. I am beyond the world, which is infinitely insignificant compared to me, for its creation has not at all impacted on Me." And He thus wonders, "You, the Jewish people, who pray and contemplate this awesome fact, how can it be that such an awareness does not lead your soul to be consumed in its love for Me?"

Avraham and Yitzchak

In *sefer Bereshit* (25:19), the Torah says, "These are the chronicles of Yitzchak, the son of Avraham; Avraham fathered Yitzchak." Yitzchak corresponds to *yirah* (awe and fear) and Avraham to *ahavah* (love). Viewed in this light, the verse is teaching us the typical order of our Divine service: first Yitzchak (*yirah tata*, the lower level of awe), then Avraham (*ahavat olam*, love that's of the world). Next is Avraham again, but at a higher level (*ahavah rabbah*, great love), and then comes a higher level of Yitzchak (*yirah ilah*).

Although this is the usual order, it can be "bypassed." Sometimes (and in our generation, often) the process of returning to G-d, Judaism, and our souls begins with love for G-d. And while an element of awe is surely there, it's concealed and only gets revealed later on as a person grows in his intellectual understanding of who G-d is.

Many Jews return because they "remember" G-d and feel a strong longing for Him. This love motivates them to change even long before they feel awe and understand what it means to accept the "*ol Shamayim*" of G-d's authority. Once a Jew has returned via *ahavah,* his increased understanding will arouse him to serve G-d first with *yirah tata* and then with *ahavah.*

Inherited Love

Beyond the two levels of love-*ahavah rabbah*, which comes to us as a gift from Above, and *ahavat olam*, which is born of meditative contemplation-there are many additional "sublevels" of *ahavah*. These differ from one individual to the next.

One of these is accessible and common to us all. This is the love we all received as a spiritual inheritance from our ancestors, the *Avot* (Avraham, Yitzchak, and Yaakov). It is an inherent, naturally occurring love that is concealed within us. It's up to us to use our intellect to find a way to reveal it.

Everyone wants to live. Everyone goes to sleep at night hoping to wake up in the morning. Every sick person longs to be healthy again. In the same way that we have an inborn desire to physically be alive, so too can we desire G-d. The inner core of our being, our "I" that we naturally desire, is G-d! This love is referred to as "*Nafshi iviticha*-My Soul [i.e., G-d], I desire You" (*Yeshayahu* 26:9).

The contemplation leading to such feelings of love touches on our inner essence, where we ask, Who am I? What is life?

When we realize that the answer is contained within the truth that all of our souls are literally "a part of G-d Above"-that G-d is in us-then this means that the love we have for ourselves is really love for G-d. In this way we "transfer" our self-love and desire for life to love for G-d and a desire for *kedushah*.

In addition, in our inner core we are *bnei Yaakov,* G-d's children. And like a child who loves his parents so much that he will devote himself to them, so too when we are in contact with this inner core of ourselves, we discover how much we love our Father in Heaven and are prepared to do anything for Him. This is the love referred to in the *Tanya* as "*Av* and *ben.*"

Verbalizing Awakens Intent

There is a level of love expressed in connection with Moshe Rabbeinu that would seem to indicate that it's out of reach for most people, because none of us are on his level. But we can achieve higher levels of love in some small measure by accustoming ourselves to verbalize that G-d is indeed our Father and the Source of our lives.

In the beginning, we may not feel we can say this sincerely: "G-d, You are my Father and You love me so much!" We may feel embarrassed or afraid to express something we don't yet connect with, that such a verbalization is only external-it's not real and we're only mouthing the words.

But even if it's not something we really feel yet, verbalizing awakens intent; it can help us get in touch with our inner truth. Thus there is no need to be embarrassed or fear we are bluffing, since deep down inside our souls, it *is* the truth.

Verbalizing brings these different types of love out of concealment to a state of conscious awareness, and enables them to be felt in our hearts and translated into action in the form of Torah study and *mitzvot*. This gives G-d immense pleasure, like the happiness of a father whose imprisoned son has finally been released. As a result, this awakened love serves as wings for our *mitzvot* to fly.

Compassion

It takes concerted, invested effort in deep concentration for us to awaken the emotions of awe (corresponding to Yitzchak) and love (corresponding to Avraham). Besides this awakening, there is another emotion that can inspire us to perform *mitzvot*: the emotional attribute of *rachamim* (compassion), which corresponds to Yaakov.

Compassion has a unique quality. It is easily roused and doesn't require the same deep contemplation as love and awe. We don't need to meditate when we see someone injured; we naturally feel compassion and want to help. If we see someone is suffering in some way, and we have the means to help him emotionally, spiritually, or physically, we naturally feel aroused to do so.

Compassion…for Whom?

The very same approach applies to the soul-we feel compassion for a Jew who appears far from G-d, and we can feel compassion for the G-dly spark in our own souls when we feel estranged from G-d.

If we feel compassion for our souls, we will more selflessly and more easily want to fulfill *mitzvot*.

How do we do this? First we meditate on the fact that we have a G-dly spark within us that is one with G-d Who gives us life. We consider how our soul descended from the *heichal neshamot* (chamber of souls) on High into the world of concealment. Now our soul is clothed in a physical body full of physical desires that conceal that spark. The body causes the spark of *kedushah* to be painfully distant from its Source and holy origins.

Next, we contemplate the sad state that it is not just a *possibility* that the body has distanced the spark from G-d, but in fact it has happened. Our thoughts, words, and actions are not always connected to G-d and have caused us to be estranged from our G-d. We are disconnected from *kedushah*, and we take G-d down with us, so to speak. We have banished the Divine spark into darkness.

The book of *Yeshayahu* (55:7) states, "The wicked will abandon his path...and return to G-d and be merciful." The simple meaning is that when a person returns to G-d in *teshuvah*, G-d has mercy on him. But the deeper meaning is that the person has mercy for G-d-i.e., for the Divine spark in him that is part of G-d and that he is now returning to G-d.

Compassion arouses a person to return to G-d and cling to Him. And since the arousal of compassion doesn't require deep contemplation like love, this path is open and available to all.

In Conclusion

Ahavah rabbah is an experience of love that can come only as a gift from Above. *Ahavat olam* is generated by contemplating just how insignificant the world is in comparison to G-d. "My soul, I desire You" and love for G-d as our Father are types of love that naturally exist within us and need only to be revealed. Compassion arouses love more easily than contemplation.

We can strive to achieve all these levels of *ahavah*.

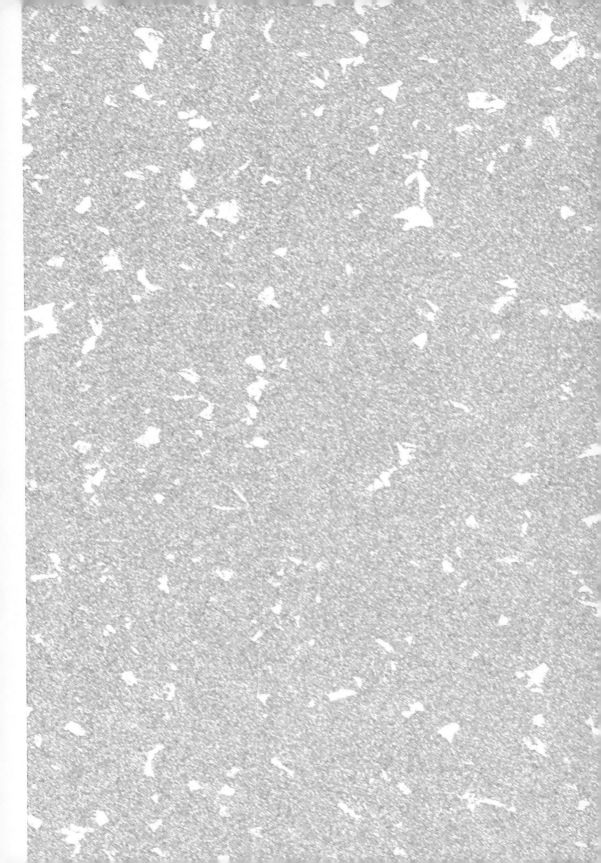

Chapter Thirty-Two

Like a Face Reflected in Water

An additional level of love: "Like a face reflected in water, so is a person's heart reflected in another heart."

(Tanya, chaps. 46–49)

There is yet another way to achieve love of G-d, which is available to everyone. King Shlomo wrote, "Like a face reflected in water, so is a person's heart reflected in another heart" (*Mishlei* 27:19).

The simple meaning is that when a person looks into the water, he sees his reflection. If he smiles, he sees the image in the water smiling, and if he's angry, he sees an angry image in the water. The same phenomenon occurs between people. When a person looks lovingly at others, they sense his love and respond lovingly toward him. And if he looks at them with hate or jealousy, they feel the same way toward him.

The deeper meaning is that this applies to our relationship with G-d. The way we behave toward Him is how He responds to us; and the way He behaves toward us is how we will behave toward Him.

A similar reciprocal effect is seen between couples in a marriage relationship. When the husband shows his wife love and affection, almost automatically she feels a need to respond with love and affection toward him.

We find this in a relationship between two people, but it's even more pronounced when one person has higher rank. If, for example, the principal of a school praises a student in front of her classmates, the student feels a strong sense of affection for the principal. The head of a corporation who notices an employee's perseverance and praises him in front of his colleagues, has also acquired the employee's loyalty.

And if the employer also gives a "small token of appreciation"- such as a raise or an invitation to a special event-then he will have literally "acquired" the employee's affection and loyalty. The worker will automatically respond with admiration and respect for his boss.

A teenager enamored with a particular athlete would be overwhelmed with joy if that sports star met him, expressed an interest in his life, and invited him to sit with the team during the game. Even a stoic youth would feel inspired to increase his admiration.

Us and G-d

If we contemplate how much G-d loves us, how much He is interested in our lives, and the depth of His personal involvement in supervising us every second, we would feel an overwhelming joy. We would want to respond with a heightened reciprocal love.

The mere contemplation that G-d is infinite and beyond measure, and presides over every aspect of the physical world and the spiritual worlds of countless angels, *sefirot*, and emanations of holiness, and yet He choose *us* as His beloved children, can arouse greater and greater love.

From G-d's perspective, the universe is not as vast at it appears to us. And in the midst of all of creation, the higher and lower worlds, G-d chose us. When we were enslaved in Egypt, He himself-not an angel, seraph, emissary, or anyone else-came down to the physical world, to the lowest of places called Egypt, a place of impurity and idol worship, and personally liberated us to be His people and bring us closer to Him.

Forty-nine days after leaving Egypt, G-d gave us a very special gift: the Torah. The Torah gives us 613 *mitzvot*. By learning Torah, we discover His will and wisdom, and each *mitzvah* is an opportunity to be intimately bonded with Him. We are given 613 opportunities to express the special closeness we have with G-d.

For this reason, we recite a *brachah* before performing *mitzvot*: "*Asher kideshanu bemitzvotav*-Who sanctified us through His *mitzvot*." In Hebrew, the word "*kideshanu*," sanctified, is the same word used for the marriage ceremony, which is called "*kiddushin*"-sanctification. A man sanctifies a woman and thereby makes her his wife. Similarly, G-d sanctifies us through His *mitzvot*, and we become His beloved ones.

This also explains why our Sages instituted that we stand in respect for someone engaged in Torah study. We are standing in honor of the *Shechinah* that is with him at the time that he is united with G-d through his Torah study.

Even though we have explained the ideas that a person can contemplate in order to feel love for G-d, it doesn't mean we will always feel it. Our physical body interferes, acting as a wall that blocks spirituality and *kedushah*. But even though we don't always feel this love, we can know and keep in mind that the reality is that the *mitzvot* we do unite us with G-d. A lack of feeling doesn't change this truth.

Exodus from Egypt Every Day

We've been discussing the meditative contemplation that G-d "stopped everything" He was doing in order to take us out of Egypt, and that when we realize how much He loves us we will be inspired to love Him in return.

But we could ask, If I wasn't personally in Egypt, and I didn't personally witness this redemption, how can this meditation help me?

The answer involves understanding that the exodus from Egypt is much more than just a historic event that occurred thousands of years ago. It's a current event that happens in our soul every day, for "every day a person must see himself as if he had left Egypt" (teaching from the *Haggadah*).

The soul within the body corresponds to the Jewish people enslaved in Egypt. The soul is like a captive prisoner-it's limited by the body, which suppresses the soul's attempts at self-expression. The body opposes the soul's efforts to go free and connect itself to G-d through Torah and *mitzvot*. When a person overcomes his *yetzer hara* (i.e., his negative urges) and succeeds in getting his body to do *mitzvot*-especially reciting the *Shema* prayer-then, at that moment, he comes out of Egypt.

In Egypt, we served the Egyptians and not G-d. Today, too, most of us are servants of our bodies and not G-d. But when we do a *mitzvah*, we are accepting upon ourselves the yoke of G-d's kingship, dedicating ourselves to be His servants. So every time we do a *mitzvah*, our soul is freed from its servitude to the body.

There are no obstacles to this exodus from Egypt, and everyone can experience it at any time. That's why the *Shema* prayer, which symbolizes acceptance of G-d's authority, contains a passage about the exodus: they are the same concept. Each and every one of us leaves Egypt every day, or, more correctly, G-d takes us out of Egypt every day. Contemplation of all the ways G-d frees us leads us to feel tremendous love and gratitude toward G-d.

Our Relationship with G-d

Let's talk more about our relationship with G-d in order to appreciate just how much He "descends" and compresses Himself for us.

G-d is greater than us, the greatest Being there is, and the pinnacle of spirituality. And even more than that, He's beyond great and spiritual; He is the infinite *Ein Sof*. When we describe G-d as being the greatest or the most spiritual, in effect we're saying that He may be greater, but we are still "on the same scale" or "in the same ballpark"-we are the lowest and He is the highest. In other words, despite how lofty He is, we still have some comparison with Him, something in common.

In mathematical terms, a small number such as five and an enormous number like a million have a connection, despite the fact that the million is much greater. Just keep adding five and five and another five...until eventually you get to a million. No matter how great the higher number, it is made up of many times the smaller number.

But G-d is infinite and not just the greatest. That changes everything, because the ratio of infinity to a great number or a small number is exactly the same. Five, a million, and even a billion are all equally insignificant in comparison to infinity. When the Infinite "views" them, He sees them all exactly the same. From His point of view, they are equal-just as from the viewpoint of infinity, a billion is not that different from a million or five.

In other words, from G-d's infinite viewpoint, the earth and all the galaxies look the same, a grain of sand and an entire mountain look the same, a grain of sand and *a million galaxies* are the same. They are all limited, and He is limitless.

This applies to more than just G-d's relationship with the creation. It also applies to the relationship between *sovev*, His infinite light that does not permeate the world-for which there are no vessels capable of receiving, no faculties able to grasp it, since it transcends the world's limitations-and *memalei*, His finite Divine light, which fills and permeates the world. The two have the same infinite relationship.

Tzimtzum

Before the creation of the world, there was "G-d and His Name alone." There was no world and no separate existence, only the Creator. In order to create a world-a world that hides G-d, conceals *kedushah*, enables the creations to feel separate from G-d, and is material and physical-G-d compressed, contracted, and reduced Himself.

If His infinite light continued to be everywhere as it was, there would have been no "room" for the material world. G-d's great light needed to be compressed in order to enable creation.

As we mentioned earlier, when G-d shows us love, it inspires us to love Him back. Two things come out of our understanding that G-d contracted and compressed Himself for our sake:

1. He did it out of love for us, and this appreciation motivates us to love Him.

2. Just as He compressed and contracted Himself for us, so must we compress and contract ourselves for Him.

Making Room in the Heart

There was a school-bus driver whose passenger list kept growing, while his vehicle remained the same size. Within a short period of time, he found that his van, which could hold only ten children, was packed with thirty-two every morning. One day a policeman stopped the driver and began counting the children.

When he reached thirty-two, he arrested the driver.

Later, in court, the driver defended himself by saying, "Your Honor, there could not possibly have been thirty-two children in such a small van. Let's go together and count the places and see if it's possible for so many to fit in."

They went outside, and the judge watched as fifteen children entered the van. It was completely full. Some more children pushed and pushed, but no more than twenty could fit inside.

The judge dismissed the case.

After the trial, the policeman approached the driver and said, "Between the two of us, you know you didn't tell the truth. I counted thirty-two children in your van. I won't tell anyone, but please explain to me how there could have been so many kids inside such a small vehicle?"

The driver answered, "The difference between the children in the morning and the children at the trial is that the morning children want to get in the van together. Because they care for each other, they are willing to be crowded."

Though this is a fable, it illustrates the understanding that when we love someone, we are more willing to "make room" for him. This is understood in marriage, and it applies to our relationship with G-d.

When we understand how much He has compressed and contracted Himself for us-we are ready to do the same for Him.

This contemplation will help us keep our spiritual priorities in focus. When we have a choice between something that seems more important than our connection with G-d, and even if we feel that there are things we can't overcome, this contemplative meditation will help us to overcome our physical desires to choose the higher path.

The Blessings before *Shema*

The main time for contemplation is during *tefillah*-during the time we take beforehand in preparation for praying and in the prayer itself. This is why our *tefillot* contain *tehillim* written by King David, the *Pesukei Dezimrah* that elaborate on the greatness of G-d, His kingdom, and His infinite being.

In general, the *brachah* that precedes a *mitzvah* begins, "Blessed are You, G-d, the King of the universe, Who has sanctified us with His commandments and commanded us to..." The two *brachot* recited prior to saying the *Shema* prayer are not worded this way. They are a different kind of *brachah*. Their purpose is to guide our thoughts during the recitation of the *Shema* by providing us with an amazing meditation to contemplate.

When reciting the *Shema*, we declare the oneness of G-d: "The L-rd, our G-d, the L-rd is one." We say this in order to generate feelings: "And you shall love the L-rd, your G-d, with all your heart, with all your soul, and with all your might." But it takes concerted effort to achieve this level of love. When a person deeply understands that the Creator is with him at all times, everywhere, loving him and caring for him, then a reciprocal love for G-d is awakened in our hearts.

The first *brachah*, "Yotzer Ohr" (Creator of light), is a meditation on how the angels in the spiritual worlds praise G-d continuously, proclaiming His greatness and goodness and giving thanks to "He Who makes the great luminaries, for His kindness endures forever." Inspired by the heightened awareness of the angels, we too will certainly be able to praise our Creator.

The visitor who enters the king's palace, and sees all the servants in their devoted service, is inspired to serve the king. Similarly, we are inspired to serve G-d wholeheartedly when we study the meaning of this *brachah,* where all these entities are serving G-d out of total self-nullification.

"Yotzer Ohr" mentions that the angels say, "Holy, holy, holy-the earth is filled with His glory." "Holy" means separate and removed. In other words, G-d does not dwell with them. So where is He? "The earth is filled with His glory"-all of creation contains Him, and He is with the Jewish people.

Next, we recite the second blessing, *"Ahavat Olam"* (eternal love). It describes G-d's great love and compassion toward us. It declares that He chose us out of all the nations and brought us close to Him and loves us with "an abundant love."

When we read, "You have brought us close to Your great Name forever in truth, so that we can offer praiseful thanks to You and proclaim Your oneness with love," we can deeply internalize the message contained in these blessings. Then, we naturally feel a reciprocal love for our Creator Who loves us so much, like "the image reflecting back in the water."

Drawing Down Infinite Light

But our work doesn't end once we feel this level of love. It's meant to be expressed in our garments (thought, speech, and action). Once we are aroused to respond to G-d's love for us by loving G-d in return, we need to invest it in our garments-by studying Torah and by doing *mitzvot* with our thoughts, speech, and actions.

This is our personal mission: drawing infinite light down into the world through our deeds. But in order to do this we first have to elevate ourselves-through prayer.

The King's Son: An Analogy

A great king, who ruled over a vast empire, sent his son to a distant corner of his kingdom where they had not heard of the king and his laws. His son's mission was to "educate" the locals and teach them the ways of the king.

When he arrived, the king's son found that the people lived as if they were in the jungle. They laughed at his great cape and strange crown. He tried to speak with them and teach them, but they would not listen. As time went by, he tried less and less to influence them, and the less he tried to influence them, the more they began to affect him. Eventually, the king's son became just like them.

One day a letter arrived from the king. The son opened it and read his father's inquiry about the progress he was making. Instantly he remembered who he was and why he was there. He pulled himself together, shed all the new habits he had learned, and put on his old clothes.

He was about to resume his efforts to influence the natives when he stopped and asked himself, "What will be different this time? How will I remember my father and not forget my mission?"

He decided that every morning he would lock himself in his room for an hour and think about the king. This would make him yearn for his father and thereby find the strength to get through the day successfully.

The analogy is clear. The king is G-d, the son is the soul, and the jungle is the body and the physical world. The soul descends in order to impact the body and the world, not the opposite. But as time goes by, the soul may forget its task, and instead of influencing the body, the soul succumbs to the body's influence.

The solution is prayer. If every morning we separate from the world for an hour, and remember who we are and what our duty is-Who our Father in Heaven is, how much we love Him and are ready to do everything for Him, and even to contract and compress ourselves (i.e., resist and relinquish our desires) for Him-this will give us the strength to elevate our body and influence the world.

In Conclusion

An effective technique that reveals our love for G-d is contemplating how much G-d loves us. Then, like an image reflected back in water, this observation will arouse our love for Him. Furthermore, just as He has compressed Himself for us, so should we be inspired to do the same for Him.

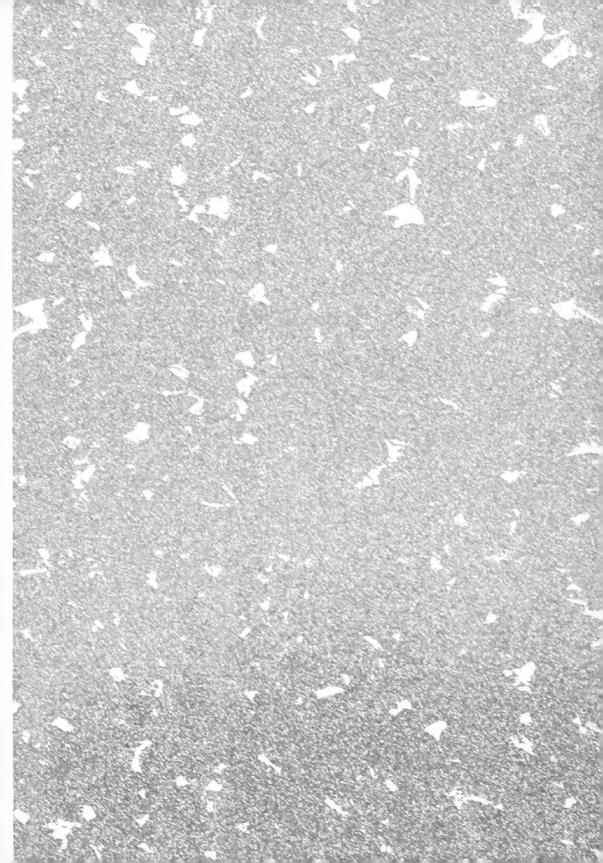

Chapter Thirty-Three

Love That Outdoes Them All

Silver and gold in our service of G-d...

(Tanya, chap. 50)

"And You Shall Love"

Every day we read in the *Shema*, "And you shall love the L-rd, your G-d, with all your heart, with all your soul, and with all your might" (*Devarim* 6:5). The obvious question is, how can we be commanded to love? Love is a feeling and you can't force someone to *feel* something. Either you feel it or you don't!

The answer is, as we've explained previously, that the mind rules over the heart. We develop feelings in accordance with what we think about.

Every *mitzvah* in the Torah (Written Law) has an explanation in the *Talmud* (Oral Law) of how to perform it. For example, the Torah says, "You shall bind them as a sign upon your hand and as frontlets between your eyes." The Oral Law (most of which was given to Moshe on Mount Sinai) teaches us that this refers to *tefillin*, and then explains in precise detail their size and shape and how to make them.

Another example is when the Torah says, "You shall slaughter the animal as I have commanded you." Nowhere else is it written in the Torah how to *kasher* an animal. All the details about *shechitah* are found in the Talmud.

So where does the Oral Law explain how to perform the *mitzvah* of "loving G-d"?

Though the *Talmud*'s discussion of the *mitzvah* to love G-d is not extensive, in the *Sefer Ha'arachim*, the classic work of *Chassidic* teachings, there are over 400 pages discussing this *mitzvah*.

The job of the Torah's inner dimension-the *penimiyut haTorah*-is to guidance on how we can achieve heartfelt love for G-d. The basis for this appears in the Jewish legal work of the famed Rambam (Maimonides), *Mishneh Torah*, in which he explains that the primary way to attain love of G-d is through knowing G-d. The greater the knowledge, the greater the love. However, *actual instruction* and the text to study to obtain this knowledge are found mainly in the teachings of *Chassidut*.

We have so far described six types of meditative contemplation that lead to six different types of love. We will now move on to a seventh type of meditation: contemplating G-d Himself-His essence-which produces a love like fiery flames.

Limited, Unlimited

In the previous chapter, we discussed G-d's great love for us, and that by contemplating this fact we will want to love G-d back.

When we explained how much G-d loves us, we pointed out that He is infinite. We discussed the relationship between that which is limited and that which is unlimited. We offered an analogy of the relationship between small and large numbers-that despite the great difference between them, they are essentially the same. A number in the billions is just a continuum of a small number. No matter how big the larger number is, it can be reached by putting together all the smaller numbers. But an infinite number is unreachable. Tons of limited numbers will never equal a limitless one.

We will now touch on an even loftier level.

Zero and One

Even calling G-d "unlimited" is a form of limit. To say that G-d is specifically unlimited is in effect limiting Him by inferring that He is incomplete-i.e., that He can only be unlimited and can't take on a limited form.

But G-d is the ultimate of completeness and lacks nothing; therefore, we can't define Him as "limited" or "limitless"-He's above them both. This level is called "atzmuto u'mahuto," His essence and being, and it transcends any definition. He's not limited, He's not unlimited, He's not both-He's beyond them all.

This level is difficult to discuss because we lack the capacity to understand it. Even the idea of being "unlimited" is beyond our intellect's grasp, yet at least we understand that we don't understand it. However, regarding G-d's essence, we can't even say that we don't understand it.

Let's go back to the analogy of numbers. Despite the difference between a finite number and an infinite one, and the fact that they have no connection since the infinite number can never be formed by adding together the finite number a great many times-still, *both are numbers*. True incomparability corresponds to the difference between zero and one. Zero is not a number and not in any way part of the one; i.e., no amounts of zero will ever add up to one.

We are accustomed to saying that the world was created *"yesh me'ayin,"* something out of nothingness, where we are the something and G-d is the nothingness. But this is only from our point of view. From the Creator's point of view, it is the opposite — He is the true *"yesh"* (something, existence-the One) and we are in fact the *"ayin"* (non-true existence-the zeroes).

Love Like Fiery Flames

All of the types of love discussed thus far are comparable to silver, *"kesef,"* related to the word *"kisufim,"* longing. We feel a desire to be connected to G-d and clothe our desire in deeds that help forge the bond. These loves are also compared to calmly flowing water, because the person who loves G-d and finds satiation in his Torah study and performance of *mitzvot* attains incredible serenity.

However, this serenity can also be a disadvantage if it lulls us to sleep and ends our efforts of striving to grow even closer to G-d.

There is an additional level of love that is not calm, which makes it loftier than any of the other loves discussed until now. It is a love like fiery flames, and it corresponds to gold-as in the fiery luster that gold possesses.

Its superiority derives from the fact that it employs contemplation of G-d's essence: He is one, the world lacks true independent existence, and creation is nothing in His eyes. Such thoughts can so intensely ignite the soul that it seeks to soar away from the body in ecstatic expiration.

A flame looks like this as it incessantly licks at the sky, attempting to jump off the wick. Love like fire is the same. It contains immense enthusiasm and passion, tremendous thirsting and yearning to near expiration. It is a craving to leave the world and physicality and return to its source.

This was what Nadav and Avihu, the sons of Aharon the *Kohen Gadol* (High Priest), experienced. They so yearned to transcend the limitations of physicality for the freedom of pure spirituality that it actually happened. When they entered the holiest part of the Tabernacle, their souls left their bodies.

Lovesick

The Baal Shem Tov once met a doctor and asked him to diagnose his illness. The doctor examined him and agreed that the Baal Shem Tov was sick, but he didn't know what it was.

"I love G-d so much," the Baal Shem Tov told the doctor, "I have an illness that's not discussed in medical books. It's the lovesickness described in Shir HaShirim."

The Baal Shem Tov didn't need the doctor to examine him and tell him what was wrong. He wanted the doctor to understand this kind of Jewish "illness." When a man so greatly loves a woman, he thinks about her all the time, and yearns to be with her so much that if the yearning is not fulfilled he feels terrible, not only in his spirit but in his body. So too a Jew can arrive at this level of yearning for his

Creator. If the love is not fulfilled, it will bother him so much that he will feel "sick" enough to seek help.

We too can love G-d so much that it will affect us physically until we remedy the "illness" by doing *mitzvot* and achieving a very close relationship with our Loved One. The only way to be "healed" is by attaining a very high level of connection with G-d.

Against Your Will Do You Live

As we said, love like water (the six kinds of love discussed in previous chapters) leads to closeness and connection to G-d via Torah and *mitzvot*. Love like fire works differently.

Love like fiery flames comes from the soul's desire to expire into G-dliness. The person isn't satisfied with the connection He has formed through Torah and *mitzvot*. He wants even more.

But the stage of thirsting (called *"ratzoh"*) is followed by return (*"shuv"*)-i.e., coming back down to earth. The person recalls that ultimately the purpose is down here in the physical world, drawing down G-dly light, and not in escaping from it. In this way, the intense energy and craving of *ratzoh* is harnessed by his daily performance of Torah and *mitzvot*.

In Conclusion

Contemplating G-d's essence, which is higher than even His infinite light, leads us to feel a love for G-d like fiery flames. It features immense enthusiasm expressed in the form of the soul's desire to be consumed in G-d, and it is loftier than the other loves.

We have thus far discussed several types of contemplation that inspire our learning of Torah and performance of *mitzvot* for higher, selfless purposes:

Meditative Contemplation	Intent
"G-d is everywhere in the world, and His light fills it (memalei)."	Yirah tata (lower awe) and bitul hayesh (nullification of our sense of self).
"We are part of the entire Jewish people, and together we unite G-d with His Shechinah via mitzvot."	Self-sacrifice and dedication to Torah and mitzvot.
"The world is nullified before G-d and realizes that it is dependent on the G-dly life force it receives from sovev, the light that envelops the world."	Yirah Ilah (higher awe) and bitul bimetziut (nullification of our existence as independent entities).
Not a contemplation, but rather, when a person achieves perfection in yirah, this level is granted as a gift.	Ahavah rabbah (great love).
"G-d is the One and only true good."	Ahavat olam (love that's of the world).
"G-d is our life."	"Nafshi iviticha-My Soul, I thirst for You"; a desire for G-d, as we have an inborn desire to live.
"G-d is our Father."	The love of a child for his parent.
"I should have compassion for my soul, which is entrapped in the body."	Love born of compassion.
"G-d shows us His love with all the things He does for us, such as taking us out of Egypt and giving us the Torah."	Love compared to an image reflected in water.
"Everything is insignificant and nothing exists before Him; the world doesn't exist compared to His essence and existence, which transcend even the light of sovev and can't be grasped. In that case, I wish to transcend physicality and join with my source."	Love as fiery flames.

The Sixth Gate

"Make for Me a Sanctuary"

Tanya, Chapters 51-53

Chapter Thirty-Four

A Sanctuary in This World

Building a spiritual temple in one's own heart…

(Tanya, chaps. 51–52)

We established that action is the main thing that transforms the world into a dwelling place for G-d and draws *kedushah* down into it. We also explained the various levels of intent (love and awe). We learned that when our actions are accompanied by the appropriate intention, or *kavanah*, this draws down G-dly light into the dwelling place we are creating for G-d by our actions.

In the final chapters of the *Tanya*, which act like a summary of the book, the Alter Rebbe returns to emphasizing the value of deed.

Man's Soul Is a Candle of G-d

In chapter 23, we explained that a person can be compared to a candle. Just as a candle requires a wick and wax, so does the soul require a wick (the body and the Animal Soul) and wax (*mitzvot* and good deeds). We emphasized the fact that the wax is not just feelings and emotions-love and awe for G-d-but also, and mainly, *mitzvot*.

The essential point discussed was that emotions, including love for G-d, come from the person ("I" love G-d, "I" fear G-d), and this self-awareness opposes the fact that there is nothing else in the world but G-d. The *mitzvot*, on the other hand, are commandments from G-d, Who is unlimited, and therefore they can connect us to Him in an unlimited way.

Now we need to answer an often asked fundamental question: how can we say that G-d is everywhere and at the same time say that He is found in a particular place, like the *Beit Hamikdash* in Jerusalem, or in physical objects used for *mitzvot*? If He's everywhere, why do we keep emphasizing the need to do *mitzvot* in order to be connected to Him?

When we talk about G-d's existence, then we say that He is concealed in all of creation-that He is everywhere at all times, equally. But when we speak about *revealing* His presence, there are differences. There are times and places where G-d is more revealed.

"From My Flesh I Perceive G-dliness"

The *Shechinah* is the Divine revelation of G-d's presence in the world, and in each place and time it is revealed differently.

To better understand this, let's contemplate the human soul. Because G-d made us in His image, we can examine the soul and gain some insight into what's happening in the higher worlds.

Our infinite soul is spread equally throughout the body, yet it's also revealed uniquely in each of the different organs of the body. The soul's power of vision is in the eyes, the power of hearing is in the ear, the power of the intellect is in the mind, and so forth. But can we say that part of the soul is in the eye and not in the ear?

Here, too, the answer depends on whether we are discussing the essence of the soul. If so, the answer is definitely that it is everywhere equally. But if we're discussing the *illumination* of the soul-how its powers and attributes are manifest in the body-then the answer is different. The various dimensions of the soul are revealed differently in different areas of the body.

Based on this explanation, it's understandable why we view the mind as the sanctuary of the soul. We aren't talking about the essence of the soul, since it's equally in all parts of the body. Rather, the mind is a sanctuary for the soul's initial revelation, and from there it spreads to the entire body.

The Beginning of Revelation

There are also two main levels to the soul's revelation.

Before the soul's unique investment in each of the body's limbs and organs, its various attributes are revealed in the mind. We're not talking about how the soul sustains the entire body; from that aspect, it's found everywhere in the body equally. However, the soul's *powers* are first revealed specifically in the mind.

In the mind, they have begun to be revealed and differentiated, but remain a part of the mind. This is why the mind can feel and move every organ.

In other words, the soul's power of vision that is revealed in the eyes is already in the mind, but its presence there doesn't enable the mind to see. This is because the mind is not the proper "vessel" to contain the power of sight.

In addition, the way the soul's attribute of sight is present in the mind is different from the way it's found in the eyes. In the mind, the attributes are still in their potential form. In that state, they are too spiritual and abstract to be revealed in the physical world. But once they separate and spread to their specific organ, they "descend in level" and can be revealed.

Thus the revelation of the soul in the body begins in the mind. It's the body's main organ and the soul's starting point, from which it then spreads to the rest of the body. It is the mind that sends vitality to every organ in accordance with its needs, since it feels each organ and knows its state.

Like the mind, the heart is also a central organ in the body, and through it the mind sends vitality to every limb and organ. It is the heart that actually distributes the soul's powers throughout the body. In the mind, the powers exist in a general, all-inclusive state, but are not yet revealed. By passing through the heart, and from there to the other organs, each of the powers is revealed.

In summary, there are three levels:

1. The *essence* of the soul, which is equally distributed throughout the body.

2. The *attributes* of the soul, as they are found and unified with the mind.

3. The *attributes* of the soul as they are revealed in the organs of the body after passing through the heart.

G-d's "Mind"

We can use this analysis of our own souls to gain insight into the way G-d works.

The Creator's existence is everlasting and everywhere at all times, but it is concealed and undetected by us. Nonetheless, G-d is present in our world exactly as He is in the higher realms-because *He's concealed in both*.

The various worlds don't differ in whether or not G-d is present, or to what extent He is present. He is present everywhere. The only difference is how revealed He is. The more He is revealed, the more spiritual that world is; and the more He's concealed, the more material the world is.

In the soul, the mind serves as the bridge between the soul's concealed essence and its revelation. There, the soul's attributes become noticeable but in a general, undifferentiated manner. From there, they individualize and spread to each part of the body. Similarly, the Creator has a "mind" where revelation begins and from which it spreads to the entire world: the *sefirah* of *Chochmah* (wisdom) in the World of *Atzilut*.

Chochmah of *Atzilut*

Earlier we explained that there are four general worlds that subdivide into myriads of worlds. The highest world is *Atzilut*. It is entirely good, saturated with G-dliness, and fully united with G-d. In this world, G-d reveals His ten *sefirot*, through which He created and recreates the world.

As the first *sefirah*, *Chochmah* serves as an intermediary that connects the higher infinite realms with the world of *Atzilut* and those that follow it-*Beriah*, *Yetzirah*, and *Asiyah*. And at the very bottom of *Asiyah* is our physical world.

Chochmah of *Atzilut* is about annulment before the Creator, because the only way to receive the Infinite is through total nullification and absence of any sense of self. Since this is the personality of *Chochmah*, it can serve as the intermediary, bridging the gap between the worlds and our infinite G-d.

More specifically, the revelation of the infinite realms into *Atzilut* begins in the attribute called *Keter* (will, desire; literally, "crown"), which transcends the intellectual faculties, and *ChaBaD*-the intellectual faculties of *Chochmah*, **Binah**, and **Da'at**-which play the role of the "mind" for G-d in general, and for each world in particular.

This revelation then descends and becomes differentiated into the other *sefirot-Chesed*, *Gevurah*, *Tiferet*, *Netzach*, *Hod*, *Yesod*. Then, through the final *sefirah* of *Malchut*, the revelation passes on to the next world and the process repeats. Essentially, the world after *Atzilut-Beriah*-is brought into existence via *Malchut*.

Your *Malchut* Is *Malchut* for All the Worlds

Another name for *Malchut* of *Atzilut* is *Shechinah*, and it is the initial revelation of G-d liness in the lower worlds.

The first thing it makes is intellect-*Chochmah*, *Binah*, and *Da'at*-in the world of *Beriah*. Then, the rest of the *sefirot* are fashioned, ending with *Malchut*, which helps create all of *Beriah*'s inhabiting creations. *Malchut* of *Beriah* is also used to create the next spiritual world, *Yetzirah*, using a similar process to that in *Beriah*. First the intellect is created (*Chochmah*, *Binah*, and *Da'at*), and then the rest of the *sefirot* until *Malchut*. And on and on.

Based on this, we understand that *Malchut* of *Atzilut*, which comes from the intellectual attributes of *Atzilut*, and is connected to G-d's infinite light through *Chochmah*, illuminates each world through various garments: *Malchut* of *Beriah* in the world of *Beriah*, *Malchut* of *Yetzirah* in the world of *Yetzirah*, and *Malchut* of *Asiyah* in the world of *Asiyah*.

And though this fact is not felt or detected, it's not because the

Shechinah is not present here, but rather because it's clothed (i.e., concealed) in the *sefirah* of *Malchut* in each world.

The Holy of Holies

The intellect of each world-*Chochmah*, *Binah*, and *Da'at*-is also called the "Holy of Holies." This is the same name as the most sanctified part of the Holy Temple in Jerusalem, which contained the Ark of the Covenant, which contained the original tablets that Moshe received from G-d. This chamber was off limits to everyone except the *Kohen Gadol*, the High Priest, who entered only on Yom Kippur.

Israel is the Holy Land, where the revelation of G-dliness is loftier than anywhere else in the world. And Jerusalem is the Holy City, where the loftiest revelation in Israel is found. The greatest revelation in Jerusalem is in the *Beit Hamikdash*, and within the *Beit Hamikdash*, the part with the greatest revelation is the Holy of Holies. The Holy of Holies of our world, the most sanctified part of the Holy Temple where the *Shechinah* dwelled, was the place from which *kedushah* spread to the entire world.

In the time of the first Temple, the *Shechinah* (*Malchut* of *Atzilut*) illuminated the Holy of Holies in our physical world in the same measure as it did in *Atzilut*-without the garments of *Malchut* of *Beriah*, *Malchut* of *Yetzirah*, or *Malchut* of *Asiyah*. This is why constant miracles occurred in the Holy of Holies during the times of the first Temple.

For example, the tablets of the Ten Commandments that were in the Ark of the Covenant contained a constant miracle. Its letters were carved in stone all the way through from one side to the other. This enabled them to be read from either side. Logic would dictate that the writing on the back of the Tablets should have been backwards, but in fact they read the same way from both sides. This phenomenon, in which nature and logic were ignored, was a result of the revelation of the *Shechinah*, the highest of powers, down here in our world.

The second Temple, however, was on a lower level, and the *Shechinah* that was revealed in its Holy of Holies was also lower. Instead of a direct revelation, *Malchut* of *Atzilut* first clothed itself in *Malchut* of *Beriah* and *Malchut* of *Yetzirah* (but not *Malchut* of *Asiyah*). As a result, there were fewer miracles during the second Temple period. Nevertheless, there was still a revelation of the *Shechinah* in the Holy of Holies, and it was still off limits to everyone except the *Kohen Gadol* on Yom Kippur.

In Conclusion

The dimension of the soul that sustains the body is found equally throughout the body. However, the revelation of the soul's individual powers, which are invested in each organ and limb of the body, begins in a general way in the mind. The mind serves as an intermediary between the soul's essence and its revelation into each part of the body.

Similarly, G-d's essence is found everywhere equally; G-d's is present in every world and creation. However, His presence is revealed via the intermediary of the *sefirah* of *Chochmah* in the world of *Atzilut*. The *Shechinah*-i.e., *Malchut* of *Atzilut*-is where Divine revelation into the world begins.

Chapter Thirty-Five

"And I Will Dwell in Them"

The Shechinah is specifically found in our actions.

(Tanya, chap. 53)

When we say, "G-d is everywhere," we mean His essence. But "Shechinah" is the term for His revelation in the world, and that differs among the various worlds and creations. In the more spiritual worlds, G-d is more revealed. The more physical the world, the less revealed He is.

In the times of the *Beit Hamikdash*, the Holy Temple in Jerusalem, the *Shechinah* was revealed in the inner sanctum of the *Beit Hamikdash*- the Holy of Holies. What happened to the *Shechinah* after the *Beit Hamikdash* was destroyed? Where is it now? Where is the *Shechinah* found today, during our exile? Where does G-d reveal Himself to us without the *Beit Hamikdash*?

The Paradox of Revelation

When we watch a video on the computer, it shows us a moving picture, even though there aren't any pictures on the computer. Rather, there is an application on the computer that translates the data in the file into visual imagery.

If we saw the programming language being used by the application, we wouldn't see any actual pictures. The visual imagery can only be seen when their "source"-the coding language in the file-is hidden.

Our world works like these videos. Just as the images we see on the screen are a result of computer language, so the world we see is a result of the Divine word with which G-d creates it. Where the computer works on computer language, the world works on the letters of the Hebrew alphabet through which the world was created.

If we could see the "code" behind the world, in that very moment we would stop seeing a world. This is exactly what happened in the Holy of Holies when the *Shechinah* was revealed. Everyone saw miracles, while nature and the world disappeared from view.

In other words, if every creation in the world could feel its source- the *Shechinah* that gives it life-the world would no longer conceal G-d.

Everything would look completely different. The world wouldn't exist in the way we currently experience it.

Mount Chorev

One of the reasons Mount Sinai, where we received the Torah, is also called Mount Chorev is because the root of the word *"chorev"* is related to the word *"lehachriv"*-to destroy. The Torah gives us the power to destroy the world. Not literally to destroy the world (*olam*), but rather to destroy the *"halam"*-the way the world conceals G-dliness.

The future redemption will be marked by the destruction of the "world"-i.e., the concealment will be nullified. Until we reach that future time, the Creator of the world *wants* the world to conceal His G-dliness, so that we have free choice. This is part of the necessary process that enables us to be copartners with G-d in bringing the redemption.

If we could already see the *Shechinah* everywhere, it would (to a certain extent) remove our ability to choose evil-the opposite of G-dliness. If G-d was obvious, then how could anyone choose to go against G-d?

Therefore, the concealment of G-dliness in the world is necessary. It's specifically a result of the concealment in the world that we have two options from which to choose: the truth that we know and believe in, or the concealment that we see and feel, that appears real.

The Solution to the "Problem"

We understand that the *Shechinah*'s revealed presence in our world would nullify the concealment, and along with it all the pleasure G-d receives from our efforts to choose the good and right path. On the other hand, without any revelation of the *Shechinah* at all, the world is too dark. What is the solution?

G-d needed a way to conceal the *Shechinah*, but nothing in the world is capable of hiding it. The *Shechinah* is the source of everything, and therefore everything is nullified to it. Therefore, G-d used something higher than the *Shechinah* to conceal it-the Torah.

Because the Torah preceded the world and the *Shechinah* is not its source, it can serve as a place to reveal the *Shechinah* in a concealed way.

Now it is true that the Torah contains very lofty light, rooted in *Chochmah* of the world of *Atzilut*, and thus the world is nullified before it. Nevertheless, the Torah descended through the steps and stages of the various levels of worlds, in which it became clothed in many different garments-in stories and laws that deal primarily with very material matters-until it reached our physical world.

The Torah: G-d's Will and Wisdom

In essence, G-d wanted to throw us a lifeline through which we could rise above the material, limited world and connect with the unlimited infinite. If He had sent us limited wisdom, we would understand it but not be able to use it to connect with the infinite. On the other hand, if He had sent us infinite wisdom in the same revealed state as it is on High, we wouldn't understand anything.

So G-d compressed and contracted Himself in a way that His entire infinity was infused into wisdom that's on a level we can grasp. This is the Torah that we have: on the one hand, it deals with worldly matters that our minds can relate to, while on the other hand, it's saturated with the infinite.

Can't Free Yourself from Prison

A prisoner can't free himself from prison. He needs someone from the outside to redeem him. Similarly, someone who is drowning in the ocean can't grab on to his own clothes to save himself. He needs someone who's not drowning to rescue him.

The same idea applies to our situation here in the physical world. We can't break free of its limits and boundaries on our own, and neither can we do so through any power that comes from the world. Only a Higher Power can elevate us beyond the physical.

The Torah is the lifeline that G-d sent us to release us from captivity and extricate us from the sea.

The Torah is rooted in G-d's will; it is the *Keter* (crown) of the world of *Atzilut* and wisdom, of the *Chochmah* of *Atzilut*. If we want to know how G-d can help liberate us from the captivity of the physical world, we study and understand the Torah, where His wisdom is accessible. And we learn how to do His will, which is the *mitzvot*.

Two Torahs

Torah study involves both the Written and the Oral Law.

When Moshe Rabbeinu went up to Mount Sinai, G-d gave him two Torahs: the Written Law and the Oral Law. The Written Law is passed down from generation to generation in its written form, while the Oral Law was originally passed down verbally from teacher to student. It was only after the *Beit Hamikdash* was destroyed, nearly two thousand years ago, and the Jews went into exile, that Rabbi Yehudah HaNasi decided that the Oral Law needed to be written down. This was called the *Mishnah*.

During the next several hundred years of learning and discussing the *Mishnah* in the study halls of Babylon, two Sages, Ravina and Rav Ashi, recorded the discussions in a work known as the "Babylonian Talmud." Later generations continued the discussion, and the recording of them. These records include works of legal rulings such as the *Shulchan Aruch*. All of the records of the Oral Law became known as the *Talmud* that we have today.

Although the Written Law is short and concise, it contains every potential detail that might be mentioned and discussed in the Oral Law.

The Written Law and the Oral Law can be compared to a father and mother. In the creation of a child, the father contributes a tiny drop, but it contains the entire blueprint for all the organs, limbs, and traits of the child. The mother carries the embryo and all this hidden potential develops until it is completely expressed in a fully physically formed child. So too the Written Law has the entire blueprint of creation contained within it, which is revealed in the details of the Oral Law.

Direct and Indirect Light

While Moshe received the Written and Oral Law on Mount Sinai, part of the Oral Law was give only in a general manner: Moshe received the rules that explain how to study the Torah and extrapolate the laws and the various details needed to fulfill the *mitzvot*. Sages in subsequent generations used these rules to discover and reveal many layers of depth in the Torah, which became documented in the Oral Law.

Our Sages were taught the method of how this type of revelation occurs from the guidelines of derivation that G-d established when He taught Moshe Rabbeinu. Thus the Oral Law has a unique, precious quality: it demonstrates the power G-d gave to our Sages to be innovative and reveal His Torah in the world.

The Written Torah and the part of the Oral Law given to Moshe in a general manner are called *"ohr yashar,"* direct light. Using this and the rules of derivation that G-d gave us, the Sages and the *Tzaddikim* make new discoveries and determinations of *halachah* as needed in each generation. This is called *"ohr chozer,"* returned or indirect light. It is G-d's will that our Sages are able to determine and establish the laws-meaning that what our Sages decide is in fact G-d's will.

There are people who accept the Written Law as G-d-given, yet reject the Oral Law. However, connecting to G-d and His will, as well as drawing down His *Shechinah* into the details of the world, occurs primarily via the Oral Law, where everything is learned, discussed, and revealed in great detail.

Drawing Down and Revealing the *Shechinah* during the Exile

Now we can answer the question that we started this chapter with. Since the destruction of the second *Beit Hamikdash*, the *Shechinah* lacks a physical place in which to be revealed. Where is the *Shechinah* now?

It is revealed in the Torah-particularly the part of Jewish law that explains what we need to do and how to do it. In other words, the *Shechinah*, which is the Divine revelation that begins to radiate in the *Malchut* of *Atzilut*, is clothed in the Torah, whose source is *Chochmah* of *Atzilut* and even higher, the *Keter* (will) of *Atzilut*.

For these reasons, drawing the *Shechinah* down into our world is specifically done via fulfilling G-d's will: by Torah study and, even more, in performing *mitzvot*. Just as a person's will and wisdom are revealed in their deeds, so is the *Shechinah* revealed when we express the Divine will in action by doing *mitzvot*.

Man's Soul Is a Candle of G-d

We can now better understand something explained in the previous chapter.

The Animal Soul was compared to the wick of a candle, the *Shechinah* to the flame, and G-d's wisdom (Torah and *mitzvot*) to the wax. If the wick was lit without wax, it would quickly burn out. We're not interested in burning out the Animal Soul, since it sustains our body. We want it to continually burn, drawing and maintaining the *Shechinah* (flame) in the world.

Just as it is due to the wax that the wick is not consumed, so the Torah-G-d's wisdom and will in the form of the *mitzvot*-and especially fulfilling it in action, prevents the consumption of the Animal Soul.

Doing the *mitzvot* purifies the Animal Soul and enables it to stay lit and draw down the light of the *Shechinah*.

And as mentioned above, when we talk about the performance of *mitzvot*, we mean doing the *mitzvot* commanded in the Written Torah according to all the details found in the Oral Torah.

Beinoni and *Tzaddik*

We began the book with a discussion of the levels of *Tzaddik* and *beinoni*, and so will we conclude.

As mentioned, the *Tzaddik* succeeded in transforming his being, both the external (thought, speech, and deed) and the internal (intellect and emotion). The *beinoni* succeeded in controlling his external dimension at all times, but because he has not transformed his internal dimension, he still possesses an evil inclination and must continually struggle to control his thoughts, speech, and deeds.

As such, the *Tzaddik* has achieved such an incredible level of purity that he is entirely *kedushah*, and he draws down the *Shechinah* in his external and internal self. The *beinoni*, however, has overcome his externality (thought, speech, and deed), but not his internal self (intellect and feeling). Therefore, only his garments "burn" in the flame-but they still serve as fuel for drawing down the *Shechinah* into the world.

Despite the fact that the *beinoni* has not changed his entire essence like the *Tzaddik*, he still draws down the *Shechinah* into the world through his performance of *mitzvot*.

Thus, in the analogy of the candle, the wax symbolizes not only wisdom but also deeds (which are an expression of the wisdom). And based on this, we conclude that the primary way in which the *Shechinah* is drawn down into our world is not via emotions or intellect, but rather actions. Otherwise the *beinoni* would not be able to draw down the *Shechinah*, since he still has not perfected his emotions and intellect.

In other words, if we only "felt" or "studied," we might encounter the *Shechinah*, but we would not draw it into the world. That is specifically the job of our deeds.

In Conclusion

G-d's will is revealed in the two Torahs, both the Written Law and in the Oral Law, which provides far greater detail of the Written Torah.

Drawing the *Shechinah* into the world is accomplished by doing G-d's will in action, even if the essence of a person has not been transformed. As such, deed is the main thing-even loftier than the emotions and intellect.

The Seventh Gate

The Gate of Unity and Faith

Sha'ar Hayichud Veha'emunah,
Chapters 1-12

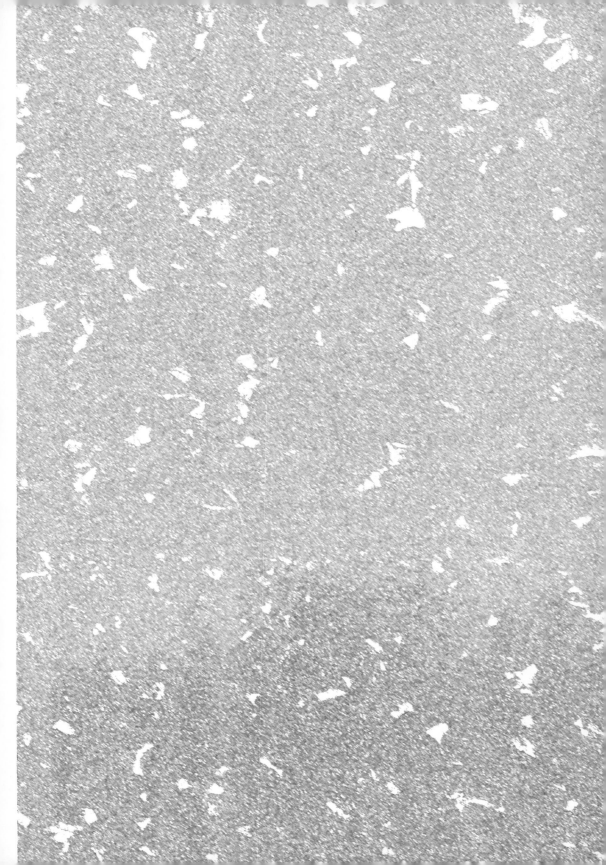

Chapter Thirty-Six

Internalizing Faith

Faith alone is not enough. It has to be brought into the world of comprehension and understanding in order to be internalized.

(Tanya, Sha'ar Hayichud Veha'emunah, Introduction and chap. 1)

Our emotions are a product of knowledge. When we know that something is good for us, we are drawn to it and it generates a feeling of *love* within us. And when we know that something is not good for us, we are repelled by it. It generates *awe and fear*.

At the wedding of a close friend we celebrate his joy, and the closer we are to this friend, the greater our joy. Ordinarily we might not feel this heightened joy when we pass by the wedding of a stranger, but if we think, *These aren't strangers, these are members of the Jewish people-they are our extended family*, we'll feel joy for them as well.

It's the *knowledge* that the groom is a good friend that *creates* the feeling of joy. And it's the *knowledge* that all Jews are one family that creates the feeling of joy even for "relatives" we haven't met yet.

"Know the G-d of Your Father"

The Torah tells us that Adam was intimate with his wife Chavah by saying that he "knew" her; that is, he related and connected to her. The same can be said for the soul. Knowing something means you connect to it and feel that it is a part of you and belongs to you.

The expression that encapsulates this general principle in our service of G-d is that knowledge of G-d "gives birth" to feelings toward Him. The closer we feel to Him, the more we feel that G-d is good for us and we feel more love for G-d. The more attracted we feel, the more we are drawn to Him. And as our feelings of closeness to G-d grow stronger, we feel more and more repelled by anything that obscures and conceals Him.

Therefore faith alone is not enough to serve G-d. Faith without any knowledge or understanding is incapable of generating emotion. It takes intellectual understanding to develop deeper feelings.

This explains why the famed thief of the Talmud could pray to G-d for success before going to steal. Does he truly have faith in G-d? And if he does, why does he steal when the Torah commands us not to steal? And if he doesn't, why does he bother to pray?

The answer is that he does have faith, but it's not an internalized part of his conscious thoughts-it has not really entered his mind. He believes in G-d, but he doesn't understand and know Who G-d is and what He expects of him. As a result, his "faith" has no impact on his emotions, and it is certainly not enough to influence his behavior. He's not repelled by the idea of violating G-d's commandments.

Faith and Knowledge

Faith is abstract and beyond intellect-it can't be grasped in the mind. We have faith in G-d even though we can't see Him. We can use our brains logically to deduce that just like a painting can't appear without a painter, so the world can't exist without a Creator. Yet logic and reasoning isn't enough when dealing with an infinite Creator of the world Who is far above our understanding. We have to activate our internal faith system.

Faith starts in the very place where *the intellect ends*. But in order for it to have an impact on our daily life and every aspect of our behavior, we have to draw it closer to our intellect.

The more we understand and "know" about G-d, the stronger our faith will be and the stronger our emotions, our love and awe for G-d, will be. And as our love and awe for G-d are generated and increase, this will lead us to want to fulfill G-d's will by doing *mitzvot* and good deeds.

Knowledge of G-d Leads to Love and Awe

In his famous work of Jewish law called the *Mishneh Torah*, Rambam explains how to perform *mitzvot* with love and awe for G-d. Contemplating G-d's greatness generates feelings of love and awe for G-d in us; the stronger and more vivid the meditation, the stronger the feelings produced.

In other words, when the Torah commands us to *feel* love and awe for G-d, it's actually commanding us to *contemplate* the greatness of G-d.

Thinking about His infinite greatness and the fact that He nonetheless personally looks out for us generates *love* for Him. Contemplating the fact that He brings us into existence and sustains us arouses feelings of *awe* for Him.

Feeling love and a desire to connect with the Creator motivates us to perform the positive commandments-*mitzvot* that connect us to Him. Feeling awe stimulates a repulsion toward anything that threatens to disconnect us from G-d, and fear of "disappointing" Him prevents us from doing actions that He has forbidden us to do-the negative commandments, or prohibitions.

Emotion breathes life and vitality into our actions. A *mitzvah* performed without emotion is mechanical and devoid of enthusiasm. Although the actions were done, "we" weren't there. To truly perform a *mitzvah* means that all our attributes are involved-faith, will, knowledge, emotion, and deed.

The Foundation of Faith: "There Is None But Him"

If it's true that general, abstract faith in G-d is not enough, and we need to understand what exactly it is we are having faith in-what then do we mean when we say there is only one G-d? What does *"Ein od milvado*-There is nothing but Him" mean?

As we'll see, by properly understanding and internalizing the answers to these questions, we can generate in ourselves the desired emotions.

The *Midrash* teaches us how our ancestor Avraham realized at a young age that there was a Creator of the universe. He realized that the idols being worshipped by his family and the entire world were false gods that had no real powers. He studied the complexity of the natural phenomena around him and deducted logically that there had to be one Creator of everything and not many gods.

After he reached this conclusion, Avraham smashed all the stone idols in his father's idol store. He then began teaching everyone he met that the world had one Creator and He alone should be worshipped. Worshipping idols was pointless-they had no power of their own.

This is the meaning of "*Ein od milvado*": there is no other source of power in the world besides G-d. No person or being has any power that does not stem from G-d. G-d is the source of *everything*.

There is also a deeper meaning: not only is there no other force in the universe other than G-d, but G-d is the only reality in existence. In other words, the entire world we see around us *is* the Creator; there is nothing separate and independent of Him. Not just that everything is subservient to Him, but rather in comparison to Him *they do not exist at all*.

This is why we say that "G-dliness is everything" and "everything is G-dliness." There is nowhere in the universe where He is not found.

When G-d created the entire universe, this had absolutely no effect on Him. It did not impact or change Him in any way. "He was, He is, He will be"-G-d before and after Creation is exactly the same.

Creating the World...with the Word of G-d

How is it possible to be completely unaffected? When we make something, whether we build a table or a stone wall, the act has an impact-we are tired, we have used up resources, our hands are dirty. We are not the same as before we began. And there's another before-and-after difference: we now have a table. How then is it possible to say that G-d is not changed or affected by the act of creation?

In chapter 13, we pointed out that G-d is infinite and unlimited, while the world is finite and limited, both in terms of time (the world was created at a particular time) and in terms of place (the world has physical boundaries). Even the entire expanse of solar systems and galaxies, though exceedingly vast, is still finite and limited.

When we look at the relationship between the infinite and the finite, we discover that *it itself* is also infinite. In other words, the relationship between infinity and any finite number is an infinite one-they are infinitely incomparable regardless of how big the finite number is. No matter how big or small the finite number is, the distance between it and infinity is always the same-infinite.

To say it another way, every finite number is completely incomparable and totally insignificant in comparison to infinity. They have no connection, no relationship.

This also applies to the relationship between the infinite Creator and His limited creation. The world is completely insignificant and incomparable. And given this fact, it's easier for us to appreciate that G-d can create the entire universe and no matter how vast it may be, the process of creating does not "fatigue" or change Him. Since the world is limited, it's exactly the same for G-d to create a grain of sand or an entire galaxy. In comparison to infinity, they are the same-equally nothing.

This is the idea that's conveyed when the Torah teaches us that G-d created the world via speech. "Speech" in this context is an analogy for the relationship between Creator and creation. When a person speaks one word, it's completely insignificant in comparison to his vast ability to speak and certainly doesn't take anything away from his capacity for speech.

In Conclusion

The creation of the world had no impact on Him, He's not missing anything, and the process didn't make Him "tired." G-d is infinite and unlimited way beyond our finite and limited ability to comprehend Him. This knowledge leads us to love and fear Him, which leads to wholehearted *mitzvah* observance.

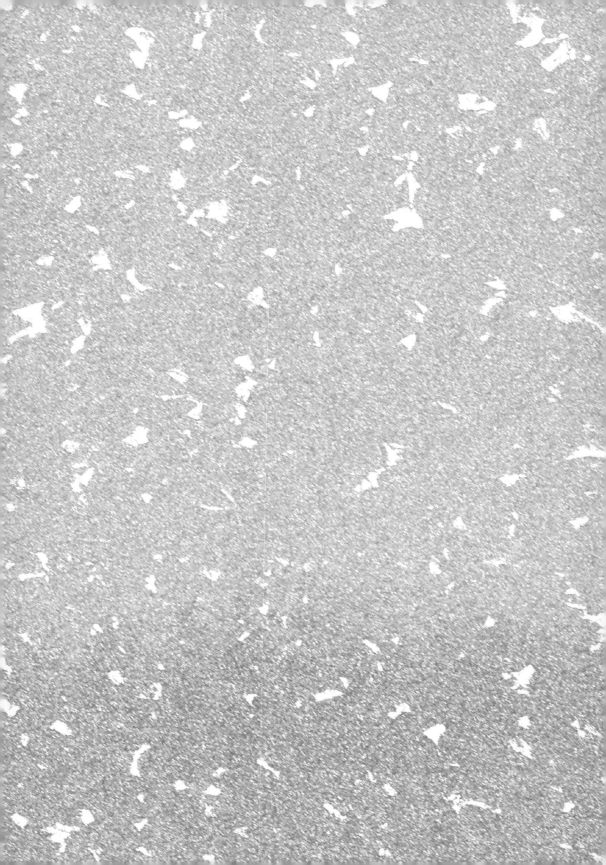

Chapter Thirty-Seven

Something Out of Nothingness

The world is created anew every moment.
If not, it would cease to exist.

(Tanya, Sha'ar Hayichud Veha'emunah, chaps. 2–4)

"Forever, G-d, Your word stands in the heavens" (*Tehillim* 119:89). The simple meaning of this verse is that what G-d said stands. G-d doesn't regret or retract anything He created.

The Baal Shem Tov gives this verse a deeper explanation. As we've discussed, G-d created the world using Divine speech. We read in the first chapter of *sefer Bereshit* that G-d used ten sayings in creating the world: "G-d said, 'Let there be light'"; "G-d said, 'Let there be a firmament in the midst of the water'"; and so forth.

These Divine statements, explains the Baal Shem Tov, continue to be uttered by G-d every moment. Thus, "Your word *stands forever* in the heavens." As we speak, G-d is repeatedly uttering His creative statements. He's saying, "Let there be light" and creating light anew. "Let there be a firmament," and creating it it anew, and so on.

Moreover, if these sayings weren't continually uttered, the entire creation would cease to exist. The universe is completely dependent on G-d's speaking it into existence at every moment. Take away those words, and it all disappears as if it never existed.

A Lightbulb

In the physical world, an electric light bulb stays lit only as long as there is a flow of electricity into it. Turn off the current and the bulb goes dark. The spiritual realms work similarly, though with some differences.

What's similar is that the world continues to exist as long as the ten creative utterances are being said. When they stop, the world stops, like turning off a lightbulb.

Where they differ is that even after turning off the electric current, the bulb is there. It's turned off and it's dark, but it still exists. Creation works differently. Not only do the creative statements give vitality and "energy" to the world, they actually constitute its very existence. The world doesn't just "turn off" or stop developing. It disappears completely and returns to its original state of nonexistence before it was created.

The natural inclination of everything in creation is to return to its original state. Since the entire world was created out of a state of nothingness and nonexistence, it all, by nature, constantly longs to return to that state of nothingness and nonexistence. The only thing preventing that from happening is G-d's continual reinvestment of the creative power initially used to create the world.

G-d Brings Creation into Existence

In the relationship between the body and the soul, the body is subservient to the soul. After the soul leaves, the body disintegrates. However, the soul does not *bring the body into existence*. It merely *sustains* it. In other words, the body needs the soul in order to be alive. Without the soul it still exists, but in a form that will now begin to disintegrate and return to the elements of the earth from which it was formed.

The relationship between the Creator and creation is different. It is not the case that the world exists and G-d only sustains it. Rather, G-d also *brings it into existence anew* at every moment, as a Jew says every morning in the blessings of the *Shema*, "He who continually renews in His goodness every day the acts of creation."

This is the meaning of the Sages' commentary on the verse "And You give life [*mechayeh*] to everything" (*Nechemiah* 9:6). They teach, "Read it not as '*mechayeh*,' gives life, but as '*mehaveh*,' brings into existence."

And the Hebrew word "*ve'atah*," and you," in the verse is comprised of the letters *vav, alef, tav*, and *hey*. These letters hint at the way Creation occurred. The straight line of the letter *vav* indicates the Divine light drawn down into the world during Creation. The letters *alef* and *tav*-the first and last letters of the Hebrew alphabet-stand for all twenty-two Hebrew letters, which were used to create the world. And the letter *hey*, whose numerical value is five, corresponds to the five levels of *Gevurah*, the attribute that represents contraction and compression, which G-d employed in the creation of the world.

What are those five levels? People form spoken words by exhaling breath through the throat, where it is restrained by one of the organs of speech: the palate, lips, tongue, throat, and teeth. Just as these five organs of speech block the breath in various ways and compress it into various letter forms, so are the Divine letters of speech altered and impacted by the five levels of *Gevurah*.

Something Out of Nothingness

Why does the world have to be created anew every moment? Why wasn't the first creation enough? To understand this, we have to clarify what it means to create something out of utter nothingness.

Some people claim that the creation of the world occurred in the same way as man-made creations. In the same way that a craftsman takes natural resources and builds furniture, G-d took natural elements and created the world. In other words, creation was *yesh meyesh*, "something out of something"-there was some kind of physical something in existence and G-d turned it into the physical world.

Naturally, according to this comparison, just as the furniture has no need for its craftsman that created it since it exists on its own, so does the world have no further need for G-d once it was created-it exists on its own.

But we have another approach: before the creation of the world there was no physical matter with which to work-no "something," only nothing. Not only was there no matter to use, there simply was *nothingness*. There was no time, no place, no rules of nature or even of logic. All of these had to be created by the Creator out of "absolute nothing," from total nonexistence.

According to this approach, we understand that the world does not and cannot exist independently. From this perspective, it's clear that creation needs G-d to recreate anew every moment. Otherwise it won't exist.

The World's Existence—Like Pictures on the Web

Let's compare this explanation to the Internet.

How many pictures are on Facebook? Countless. And are those pictures real? When we see a picture on the screen, is the actual image truly there? Of course not. Is there any reality to that picture? Could it exist without the computer like a physical printed picture? Again, no. The picture on the screen has no reality, no independent existence.

In essence, the online pictures don't truly exist. They are files made up of letters and numbers, which are decoded by a program on the computer. The letters and numbers get translated into the images we see. But there's no actual picture there, only data.

Can any of the billions of images found online exist without the letters and numbers behind them? Certainly not. Not one tiny part of it or even one single pixel can exist without the series of characters in the file. It's the data with its letters and numbers that generate the images that we see. Erase that code and the picture disappears.

The Torah explains that the creation of the world occurred in a similar way. The truth of the world around us is not the images our eyes see or the physical world we experience daily. The truth of the world is everything behind the scenes, the Divine code that creates the pictures we see. This code is called the word of G-d, and it is made up of the letters of the holy Hebrew language.

A particular Tzaddik was known for his ability to see the Divine code that created the world. It was not concealed from him. He could see the code clearly at all times. He actually said of himself that if not for the fact that the Torah stated, "In the beginning G-d created," he would not have believed that the world existed.

He Even Brings Inanimate Matter into Existence

This explanation of creation includes every aspect of the world around us. The Divine code of G-d's word is embedded in absolutely everything, from the smallest inanimate object to a fiery planet orbiting the sun; otherwise it doesn't exist.

If the unique series of numbers and letters in a picture's file would be erased, the picture would disappear. Similarly, if G-d would stop saying one of the creative statements with which He created the world, that part of the creation would cease to exist.

The Name Is the Essence

Hebrew is unlike other languages. Every other language in the world is a collection of man-made words agreed upon to be the verbal and written symbols that represent the language. However, Hebrew-*lashon hakodesh*-is the language that preexisted creation; it was not made up by people. Instead, each object received its name from the letters G-d assigned to create and sustain it every moment, and each name describes its essence.

In Hebrew, the word for chair is *"kisei"* (*chaf-samech-alef*) because those are the letters G-d used to create the existence of chairs. A *kelev*, a dog, is *"ke-lev,"* like the heart of its master-by nature a devoted creature.

The *Midrash* explains that Adam Harishon, the first person, was on such a lofty spiritual level that he could see the inner essence of everything that G-d created. Based on his ability to see this spiritual root, he named everything in the world.

Gematria and Letter Exchanges

The ten creative utterances mention general categories of creation: the heavens and the earth, light and darkness, evening and morning, the firmament in the midst of the waters, vegetation, the great luminaries, every type of animal, and then the human being. The ten Divine statements were then later utilized to create all the details.

The finer points and details of every aspect of creation were contained within these primal ten statements, from which the "voltage was lowered" from high-powered intensity to lower dosages.

No one plugs a small lamp directly into a power station. The voltage is way too high and would cause the lamp to explode. Instead, the electricity from the power station has to pass through transformers, which reduce the voltage.

In a similar way, the details and particulars of the world's creation stemmed from a "lower dosage" of the ten Divine statements. The details couldn't be created directly from the ten creative statements; they were way too powerful and intense. First, the voltage needed to be lowered.

The Hebrew language's equivalent of "transformers" is *gematria* (numerology) and letter exchanges. Based on different Torah systems of calculation, certain letters in a word can be switched with other letters. One example is the *at-bash* system (*at = alef-tav*, *bash = bet-shin*) where we can switch the first (*alef*) and last (*tav*) letters of the alphabet, the second (*bet*) and second to last (*shin*), etc. And using these rules, the more exchanges that are made, the lower the "voltage" becomes. In this way, even the lowest of elements in the world can be created.

The Torah and G-d

The ten Divine creative statements that G-d used to create the entire universe were invested with high-voltage intensity power. These ten utterances are found in the Torah, comprised of letters in the Torah. The *Zohar* teaches, "The Torah and G-d are one." As such, the Torah clearly has the power to create.

In Conclusion

G-d created the world with ten utterances and is constantly saying them to recreate them anew. If G-d would not continue saying them, creation would cease to exist and return to its original state of nothingness.

Chapter Thirty-Eight

Built with Kindness

The concealment in the world is also part of the Divine plan. In fact, the concealment itself comes from Him.

(Tanya, Sha'ar Hayichud Veha'emunah, chaps. 5–6)

Let's clarify a bit further our explanation of creation out of nothingness.

A stone resting on the ground is in its natural state. No repeated effort or action is necessary to ensure that the stone remains on the ground. On the other hand, when a stone is thrown and flies through the air, it is "something new"-i.e., its nature is to sit on the ground, and now it's going against that nature by flying in the air.

Since this is new and not part of the stone's nature, it can't last. As long as the power of the throw propels the stone through the air, it will stay aloft. As soon as the energy diminishes, the stone returns to its natural resting state on the ground.

But while it was flying, did the stone's nature change? Did it switch to a flying nature and lose its resting-on-the-ground nature? Of course not. Its nature remained the same throughout. How then could it fly? Not because its nature changed, but rather because the thrower infused his energy into it, which enabled it to fly. So why did it then fall? It fell because the invested power ran out, and once it did, the stone reverted to its own nature.

Creating the World, Changing Nature

This provides us with an insight into the explanation of the "something created out of nothingness" concept by which the world was created.

The world's nature is not to exist (i.e., nothingness)-to "be" nonexistent. The fact that we see it existing runs contrary to its nature, like a stone flying through the air goes against its nature. Just as the stone will fly only as long as the power of the throw is in it, so does the world exist only as long as the power of creation is in it.

The world does not exist independently-it exists because G-d created it. Therefore, if He would stop creating the world, it would simply disappear, returning to its natural state of nothingness and nonexistence as it was before Creation occurred.

If we accepted the approach that creation existed in some primeval form, and that G-d merely changed existing material into a different state, creating *yesh meyesh*-something out of something-then we would assume that the world doesn't need His ongoing intervention to continue to exist.

But the correct approach is, as we said, that the world was created out of nothingness and constantly depends on G-d to sustain it. Otherwise it would return to nothingness.

This explanation helps us more easily understand how G-d creates wonders and miracles in the world. If G-d were far away and uninvolved in the daily renewal of creation, how could He affect a particular situation here? How could He influence our own individual lives with *hashgachah pratit*, where we experience illnesses that "mysteriously" disappear, or where couples who are told they can't have children actually do, and countless other examples.

But since, in fact, His presence fills every corner of the universe, and it is only by His constant will that creation continues to exist, we can understand that it's no problem for G-d to intervene and change nature when needed. This is why we see wonders and miracles occurring, like the ten plagues in Egypt and the parting of the Red Sea to let the Jewish people escape unharmed.

Life and Death by the Power of the Tongue

This also gives us insight into the power of the letters we say in prayer, Torah study, and everyday speech. Creation occurred through the letters of the Hebrew alphabet-the same letters we use when we speak. For this reason, every letter we utter can affect the world in a positive or negative way.

The master kabbalists, who knew the secrets of the letters and of creation, knew which letters to say and when in order to influence reality. But we don't have to be kabbalists to appreciate the power in our words. When each of us prays, we can use the carefully crafted wording of the prayers in our *siddur* that were written by the *Anshei Knesset Hagedolah*-the *Sanhedrin*-and have been passed down from generation to generation. The precise words and letters of our daily prayers can effect a positive change in the world.

And by learning and adhering to the prohibitions against *lashon hara*-slander, gossip, and the like-we can avoid having a negative impact on the world.

Creation: Like Sunlight

In the previous chapters, we learned that the world we see is a nullified nonexistence before the Creator. G-d is everywhere and found in everything. At this point, however, a simple question arises: If He fills everything-where are we?

We can compare this to the relationship between sunlight and the sun. The sunlight that hits the earth's surface doesn't exist independently-it comes directly from the sun. Sunlight reaches our world, which is so distant from the sun, and sunlight also surrounds the sun itself.

The light close to the sun is nullified, insignificant because of its proximity to the sun. To an observer close to the sun, individual rays of sunlight would be unnoticeable. We wouldn't be able to differentiate between the separate rays of light and the sun itself.

G-d and His creation are similar. Creation corresponds to the rays of sunlight, and the Creator corresponds to the sun. Just as the sunlight is nullified before the sun and undetectable when in close proximity, so the world is nullified before G-d and undetectable in His presence. But from our perspective, things seem different. The rays of sunlight appear to be separate and distinguishable from the sun. In fact, we don't even notice that a connection between them is essential. To us, everything appears to exist independently from G-d.

However, the G-d-sun parallel is not precise. The ball of the sun is very far from Earth, and only its rays reach us. These rays *are actually far from and outside the sun* by the time they reach Earth, and this makes them seem to exist separately and independently. But the world is not outside the Creator, because the Creator is not far from us-rather, He's here at all times. That means that the world is actually *always inside its source*, and thus always nullified before the Creator.

If this is the case, the question stands: If the world is indeed nullified before its source (the Creator) and inside its source at all times, how is it that we see a world that seems separate from G-d?

The Lower World: Feeling Independent

Before we give the technical explanation of how G-d created such an illogical reality in which He is our source and we are always inside Him yet we don't feel it, let's first explain the rationale underlying this.

A world that can feel its source is incapable of existing as ours does. If the world were aware of the fact that it is a nullified nonexistence before the Creator, it would surrender its existence. But G-d wanted a dwelling place in the lower world (see *Tanya*, "The Fourth Gate"). Therefore He created a world that is lower, material, physical, and coarse-one that sees itself as independent from the Creator.

Chesed and *Gevurah*

Chesed is the power to reach out and give. *Chesed* is the attribute, the power, that G-d uses to bring things into existence. For this reason, *Chesed* is connected to the Divine Name *Havayah* (spelled *yud-hey-vav-hey*). The last three letters of this Name (*hey-vav-hey*) spell the word "*hoveh*," which refers to the present, and the *yud* in the beginning of the Name indicates continual, ongoing performance (in Hebrew, the letter *yud* before a verb turns it into a constant action).

Essentially, this Name relates to G-d's constantly creating the world anew, as explained in the previous chapter.

On the other hand, *Gevurah* is the power to compress, compact, hide, and conceal. For this reason, *Gevurah* is connected to the Name *Elokim*-spelled *alef-lamed-hey-yud-mem*, with the same *gematria* as the word "*hateva*" (literally, "the nature"), because it is precisely within nature and the natural order of things that G-d hides His presence in the world.

Both *Chesed* (the power to bring into existence) and *Gevurah* (the power to contract and compress) are G-d's powers, and therefore they are both equally infinite-neither is "stronger" than the other. This means that G-d has an infinite ability to create the world out of nothingness, as well as an infinite ability to hide and conceal it all. He can hide His creative power from us.

It also means that we are completely nullified and nonexistent (like rays of sunlight while they are still in the sun), and the world is dependent on and nullified before G-d's infinite creative power of *Chesed*, which brings it into existence anew every moment. At the same time, G-d uses His infinite power of *Gevurah* to contract and compact Himself and His infinite creative power of *Chesed*.

The World Is Built with *Chesed*

According to the *Midrash*, G-d wanted to create the world with judgment (i.e., *Gevurah*), but saw that the world wouldn't be able to exist, so He added the attribute of love (*Chesed*). If *Gevurah* had been the dominant attribute in the creation of the world, G-d's creative power would have been completely concealed and we would be left thinking that there was no Creator. Therefore, G-d partially revealed Himself in the world through the *Tzaddikim* and the wonders and miracles documented in the Torah.

G-d first uses *Gevurah* to conceal the attribute of *Chesed*, and then He reveals *Chesed* in the world, piercing through the concealment. In kabbalistic terms, G-d first hides His great light (referred to as "*tzimtzum harishon*," the first compression), and then He draws down His attribute of *Chesed* in a way that it is obscured by *Gevurah* (referred to as "*ohr hakav*," the ray of measured light).Only then does He reveal some of the light by way of the *kav*.

Based on this, we see that the *Chesed* (kindness) with which the world was created is actually the attribute of *Gevurah*. Meaning, the world couldn't exist without the concealment-for, as we explained, without concealment the world would cast off its sense of self and existence and vanish into G-d's existence. This means that the attribute of *Gevurah* is really kindness, because it is responsible for enabling the world to exist.

This is also why *Gevurah* is connected to the Divine name *Elokim* (numerically equivalent to "*hateva*"): nature and the natural order are what hides the Creator.

In our world, *Chesed* and *Gevurah* oppose each other, like fire and water. But just as G-d can bring fire and water together, so can He unite *Chesed* and *Gevurah*. Because He is more exalted than them-they both nullify themselves before G-d and are merged by Him.

In Conclusion

We know that G-d is everywhere and fills the entire world. In that case, where are we? In truth, all of creation is inside its source, but this fact is concealed because otherwise the world would cast off its existence.

Chapter Thirty-Nine

Celestial Unifications

How the world looks from our point of view and from G-d's point of view…

(Tanya, Sha'ar Hayichud Veha'emunah, chap. 6)

Though the attribute of *Gevurah* compresses and hides G-d's light, it is still just as Divine an attribute as *Chesed*. G-d is everywhere yet undetected by the creations. However, this is only from their perspective. There is no concealment from G-d's vantage point.

The World's Essence: Limitation

What do all creations in our world have in common? Which part of existence is so essential that the world can't live without it? If we removed the color blue from the world, what would happen? What is the one thing that the world has to have in order to exist?

The one thing that all of creation has in common is limitation. Every creation has its own personal limitation and boundaries-beginning somewhere and ending somewhere else, starting at one time and ending at another.

These are the two primary ingredients in the element of limitation in our world: time and place. There is nothing in our world that can say it experiences yesterday and tomorrow as exactly the same, or that north and south are equivalent.

This is because limitation is part of the definition and makeup of both the world and its creations. And without limitation, without time and place, the world would cease to exist. Limitation and existence are interdependent.

Malchut: The Existence of the World and Its Union with G-d

Malchut is the lowest *sefirah* in the world of *Atzilut*, and only it can serve as the starting point for creating the world (see chapter 34). This is because the concept of limitation and the existence of time and space start with *Malchut*. But in the *sefirot* above *Malchut*, from *Chochmah* down to *Yesod*, time and space don't exist.

Thus, there would be no world without *Malchut*. As we explained, time and space didn't always exist-G-d created their existence starting in the *sefirah* of *Malchut*. Thanks to *Malchut*, G-d's infinite light can even be revealed within limited things, in time and in place. And this is exactly how G-d wanted it: a world that feels separate from Him.

Despite the fact that *Malchut* is where limitation beings, it's still part of the ten *sefirot*, which means it's united with G-d's infinite light (the *Ohr Ein Sof*). It simultaneously has a relationship with the realm of limitation and is itself nullified before the higher *sefirot*.

From here we conclude that if the world is nullified and dependent on *Malchut*, and *Malchut* is nullified and dependent on G-d, then the world is actually nullified and dependent on G-d. This is how it all looks to G-d.

The Higher Level of Unity: *Shema Yisrael*...G-d Is One

The meditative contemplation of "*Shema Yisrael*" is that G-d is one. Meaning that there is no other god and no other power besides the Creator. But on a deeper level, the meaning of "one" is a bit different.

The word "*echad*," one, made up of the letters *alef-chet-dalet*, teaches us about the process of creation. *Alef* corresponds to the "*Alufo shel olam*" (the Champion of the world)-i.e., the Creator. The *gematria* of the letter *chet* is eight, corresponding to seven levels of Heaven (as discussed in the *Talmud*, Heaven has seven levels) plus one earth (7 + 1 = 8). The letter *dalet*, whose numerical value is four, corresponds to the four corners of the earth.

Thus, saying the word "*echad*" inspires us to think about the fact that the seven heavens, the earth, and its four corners are all nullified before the *alef*-the Champion of the world.

In other words, meditating on "*Shema Yisrael*" is the highest level of unity. It's how G-d sees the world-that everything is nonexistent before Him; everything is nullified.

The Lower Level of Unity:
"Baruch Shem Kevod Malchuto Le'olam Va'ed"

Immediately after reciting *"Shema Yisrael..."* we say, *"Baruch shem kevod malchuto le'olam va'ed*-Blessed is the Name of His holy kingdom forever." In other words, although there is no world from G-d's viewpoint, from our perspective there is a world, but its entire reality is G-dliness-everything is G-dliness.

In other words, G-d doesn't "see" a world. The boundaries of place and time are subservient to *Malchut*, which itself is annulled before the higher *sefirot*. But on this level, *we* see the world and the limitations of time and place. However, we are aware that time and place don't have an independent existence-they are created by G-d and He is found within them. Therefore, we relinquish our personal desires before Him.

Bitul Hayesh and *Bitul Bimetziut*

Bitul hayesh and *bitul bimetziut* are two forms of contemplation that bring a person to two different levels of self-nullification before the Creator.

When we meditate on the lower level of unity (*yichuda tata*) and internalize the fact that everything is G-dliness, we are still very much aware of our own existence, but we nullify it before the Creator. In other words, we feel our desires, yet we relinquish them because we understand that everything is G-dliness.

However, when we meditate on the higher level of unity (*yichuda ilah*) and understand that nothing *exists* outside of G-d, we are able to distance ourselves from our own existence. We don't feel our personal desires so much; we have no desires or "self" to nullify since we are aware that they don't really exist outside of the Creator.

"I, G-d, Have Not Changed"

The simple meaning of the statement that "I, G-d, have not changed" is that G-d doesn't go back on His word or back out of His obligations to us. The deeper meaning is that creating the world made no change in G-d; He is exactly the same as before Creation.

This is because the contraction and compression employed to create the world's many creations is not separate from Him and is not a true concealment of Him. Even the contraction itself is part of the Creator. As such, the vast amounts of creations He made are unable to hide and conceal Him. In fact, they do the opposite-they reveal Him.

Let's look at a snail that's hiding in its shell. Is the shell concealing the snail? No, the shell itself is a part of the snail. Seeing the shell is seeing the snail. In the same way, a person can't conceal himself. As discussed in Jewish law, a person is not allowed to put his hand on his head instead of a yarmulke. His hand and his head are both him; he can't cover himself with himself!

This also applies to G-d. Everything is Him, including the concealment. How then could He conceal Himself?

Uniting the Names *Havayah* and *Ad-nai*

In many *siddurim*, G-d's Names *Havayah (yud-hey-vav-hey)* and *Ad-nai (alef-dalet-nun-yud)* are written with one inside the other with alternating letters-sometimes it starts with the first letter of *Havayah* (*yud*) and sometimes the first letter of *Ad-nai* (*alef*).

The Divine Name *Havayah* corresponds to the higher *sefirot*, and *Ad-nai* corresponds to *Malchut*. The two methods of combining these names are the two aforementioned approaches to unity. *Ad-nai* within *Havayah* is the higher unity-*Malchut* unites with the higher *sefirot* and the world is nullified. *Havayah* within *Ad-nai* is the lower unity-G-dliness (within the higher *sefirot*) is revealed within *Malchut* and the world; everything is G-dliness.

This brings us back the poignant question: Is there a world or not? The answer is that it depends on the perspective. From the higher view, there's no world. But even from the lower perspective in which the world exists-it isn't meant literally.

Existence, Lack of Existence, and False Existence

Between existence and no existence there is an additional level: false existence. In other words, the world exists but it is not a true existence.

When we speak about creation, we generally employ the concept of *"yesh me'ayin"* (something out of nothingness). Meaning G-d, Who is "nothingness," creates us, the "existence" (limited, finite creations). But from G-d's perspective it's the opposite: He is the real "existence," and we are "nothingness" in relationship to Him.

Since our existence is not a true state of existence like G-d's, it's impossible to say that the world is a true existence. On the other hand, we can't say that the world has no reality, because G-d created it.

The compromise is somewhere in the middle-the world has existence but not true existence. And it's not independent existence, since its existence comes from G-d, as Rambam said, "The existence of creation derives from G-d's existence-the true existence." The world's existence stems from the fact that G-d creates it every moment anew-it is entirely dependent on Him.

He Is the Knower, the Knowledge, and the Known

So far, we're clear that G-d was not changed at all by creating the world, and it didn't detract from His powers or alter His abilities. However, one could still mistakenly think that G-d's *knowledge* changed. In other words, before Creation there was no world that He needed to get to know and learn about, to check up on and see how it's doing-but now there is a world. One could conclude that at the very least, creating the world made a change in G-d's knowledge. But it's not true.

In a human being, we can distinguish between the person (the knower), his intellect (knowledge), and the subject matter (known) because they are all separate. For G-d, however, they are all one completely unified whole. This is called "simple unity." Instead of three things merged together, it's one unit right from the start.

When a person is deep in contemplation, imagining something in his mind, we can say that there is a person who is imagining, there is his mind that he uses to imagine, and there are the images he is thinking of in his mind-three different and separate aspects. These are a united whole in G-d. When G-d "imagines" the world (us), He, His "imagination" and we are all one. Thus, creating the world doesn't add to, take away from, or change G-d's mind in any way.

This is because the world doesn't exist outside of G-d. He's not on the outside looking in. It would make sense to think that the world could change His mind if it was. However, He and the world are one-it can't change Him.

Unity That Is Beyond Comprehension

The fact that in G-d-unlike in a person-the knower, the knowledge, and the known are all one is not something that can be grasped by human intellect. It can't be discussed and verbalized, the ear can't hear it, and the heart can't recognize it.

This is because we generally try to understand things that exist outside of ourselves by thinking about how it is in us, or in relationship to us, and then projecting outward. In this case, however, it's so completely foreign to our comprehension that we can't grasp it.

We can grasp that G-d exists, but we can't grasp His essence.

Imagine two drops of water sliding down a windowpane. The drops can "meet," merge together, and form one drop. In the new drop that's formed, we can't tell that it is two separate drops that merged-it appears to us as one simple drop.

This is a good example for demonstrating unity. The new drop is formed by merging two drops together; it's larger than it was before. But as we said before regarding G-d, adding knowledge doesn't add anything to Him. For Him, "knowing" the world is not learning about something outside of Him. Rather, all He has to do is know Himself.

Divine Providence…Even for an Ant

This discussion also gives us insight into the concept of *hashgachah pratit*, Divine providence, according to the teachings of *Chassidut*.

The Chassidic approach is that G-d can be found everywhere, since He Himself is physical place and location. He doesn't have to watch over us since He is us and we are Him; G-dliness is everything and everything is G-dliness. There can't possibly be a crack or corner in which He is not present, and there can't be a creation that G-d didn't create.

Some may ask, how can G-d keep tabs on every single thing in creation? How can He know that an ant in the Amazon jungle is hungry? How can He see such a small creature? But based on what we have explained, the answer is simple: G-d doesn't have to look down at the ant from outer space. He is also in the Amazon jungle and the ant itself is also a part of G-d. By knowing Himself, He also knows all there is to know about the ant.

To make this more understandable, we can compare G-d's ability to oversee everything to the way a human brain "knows" and feels every cell in the body. It doesn't have to "observe it from above."

But because this level of understanding is beyond our intellect and comprehension, we sometimes forget to see it this way. We mistakenly imagine that G-d is not everywhere and that there are things that happen without His supervision (G-d forbid). And not only simple, unlearned, regular people make this mistake; even Torah Sages could err on this point.

This is why it's so important to study *Chassidut*-to take this awareness that's beyond comprehension and internalize it as much as possible, and at the very least to repeatedly review it.

Sovev and *Memalei*

G-d's existence in the world is described in the works of *Kabbalah* in two ways: He surrounds the worlds (*sovev kol almin*), and He fills the world (*memalei kol almin*).

By surrounding, we don't mean going around the outside. The light of *sovev* is very much found in the world. The difference between them is the way in which they exist in the world. The light of *sovev* is the *sefirah* above *Malchut*. Because it is such a lofty light, the world can't absorb it. Therefore, it brings the world into existence but doesn't get involved in its details-to *sovev*, they all seem the same.

On the other hand, the light of *memalei* is the *sefirah* of *Malchut*, and it's on the same level as the worlds. It "clothes" itself in each and every bit of the world and in each creation according to its level.

Nevertheless, the light of *memalei* is not grasped by the world-it is the place of the world (G-d is the location in which the world is found), but the world is not its place. The fact that it is present in the world and all its details doesn't affect it.

In Conclusion

On one hand, there is a world. On the other, there isn't a world. And on the third hand, both are true...

Chapter Forty

Simple Unity

The Creator is beyond all intellectual
comprehension-direct and indirect.

(Tanya, Sha'ar Hayichud Veha'emunah, chaps. 8–12)

Thus far we have explained that G-d's unity and His knowledge are simple-i.e., not a unity of parts but a solid, seamless whole. In this chapter, we'll show how this same type of unity also exists among the higher *sefirot*.

An example is when the Torah describes G-d as being wise (*sefirah* of *Chochmah*) or kind (*sefirah* of *Chesed*) or powerful (*sefirah* of *Gevurah*). These attributes-like knowledge-don't add or take away anything from Him.

Codes That Help Us Understand

The higher *sefirot*, in the world of *Atzilut*, are also united with Him in simple unity. We can't grasp this unity either. We use analogies and codes in an attempt to analyze the Creator, yet we understand that they are only for us. G-d's actual reality and existence are not the same as in our description.

Take a topographical map, for example. Higher areas are usually colored brown, and areas with plant life are green. Does this color code show what the areas actually look like? No. The color code is only for us, a universally agreed upon map code, so that we know that green represents plant life. We attempt to do the same thing when we discuss the *sefirot*.

Names and analogies are used in order to help us understand, but we have to always remember that talking about G-d does not equal grasping His essence. Even when we praise and exalt G-d, we must remember that He is holy and infinitely exalted over us, completely beyond all our praises. It's impossible for us to grasp His true greatness.

The Chasm between *Chochmah* and *Asiyah*

For us, *Chochmah* (wisdom) is the attribute from which everything begins. It is the first spiritual attribute, and our initial spark of awareness. Next come *Binah* (understanding) and *Da'at* (knowledge), which complete our trio of intellectual attributes. The intellect's conclusions are passed on to the heart and transformed into emotions, which are then invested into the garments of thought, speech, and action, through which the emotions are expressed.

There is a huge difference between the power of the soul found in our actions and the power of the soul found in our speech. The one in speech is clearly more powerful. A similar difference exists between speech and thought, thought and emotions, and emotions and intellect-each of these levels indicate an ever higher power of the soul. As such, it's clear that *Chochmah* is incomparably loftier than the garment of action.

From G-d's perspective, however, there is no difference between *Chochmah* in the world of *Atzilut* (the highest level in the highest world) and the world of *Asiyah* (the lowest level). They are the same to Him.

This is the meaning of the verse "You made [*asita*, related to *Asiyah*] everything with wisdom [*Chochmah*]." That is, the highest and the lowest, *Chochmah* (in the world of *Atzilut*) and *Asiyah*, are equal from His viewpoint.

Nullification of the *Sefirot*

To summarize, we explained that the world is nullified before the higher *sefirot*, and that a person could mistakenly believe that the *sefirot* are the Creator. In actuality, the higher *sefirot* are merely a ray of creative light from G-d and therefore also totally nullified before Him.

G-d Himself is exalted and beyond the world. *Everything* in the world, including the *sefirot*, are nullified before Him. In other words, from G-d's viewpoint spirituality *is no more exalted* than physicality. He so completely transcends them both that when He "looks down from above," spirituality seems just as low as physicality.

In fact, we can't even say that *Chochmah* and *Asiyah* are the same from His perspective. We use it to help us understand, since we perceive the greatest separation to be between *Chochmah* and *Asiyah*. But it doesn't accurately portray the reality-we just don't know any other concepts to use.

Therefore, when our Sages use various terms to describe G-d, such as "wise," "merciful," or "kind," they're not attempting to describe His essence, because it can't be grasped. Rather, the description only refers to a particular way that G-d acts in the world, which *we* perceive as "wise," "merciful," or "kind."

The Secret of Faith

Concealed, unknowable matters are not in our domain. G-d's essence is not knowable and graspable. As such, all we can do is believe with pure and simple faith (which is beyond intellect) that He is united in simple unity with the *sefirot*.

In other words, common sense and logic are enough to understand that there is a Creator and that He sustains the world with a light that fills the world-*ohr memalei*. Yet we can't grasp how the world is nullified to the *sefirot*-i.e., the *ohr sovev*, the light that surrounds the world-or how G-d transcends place and time. All we can do with these concepts is try to understand that we do *not* understand.

In fact, even that which we just explained about us being unable to grasp G-d's *essence* also can't be understood; it has to be taken on faith.

Just as it would be ridiculous to say that we can't touch and hold *Chochmah*, since it's not physical and can't be held like an object, so it would be ridiculous to say that we don't understand G-d. He is simply not found within the realm of comprehension that is completely understandable to finite, limited beings.

Nevertheless, the Sages used the term "lights" to refer to the higher *sefirot* in order to bring the concept of G-d's unity with them just a tiny bit closer to our understanding.

Sunlight in the Sun

The analogy for this is rays of sunlight while they are still in the sun. We used this analogy earlier to understand the relationship between the world and the word of G-d. Now we'll use it to understand the relationship of the word of G-d (i.e., the *sefirot*) and the Creator.

Even in the ball of the sun there is sunlight. However, in the sun the rays are seen as a part of the sun and not something separate. In fact, the rays of sunlight are so intensely "nullified" to the sun that even as they start to leave the sun, they lack a perceptible sense of independent existence. We can't even call them "rays" yet.

The "word of G-d" (i.e., the lofty *sefirot* of *Atzilut*) is completely nullified and absorbed within G-d Himself. And not only as the *sefirot* exist on High, but everywhere. Unlike the sun, which is in a certain point in space and only the rays are nullified, G-d's essence and being is absolutely everywhere, all the time.

The Programmer's Unity with His Program

Let's use the world of computers again to help us understand.

Earlier we explained that an image that we see on the computer screen doesn't really exist, and if we looked at its source file we would see only a series of characters and digits-the source of the image on the screen. Similarly, the world (the image) is nullified to and dependent on its source: the word of G-d (the source file and the program that reads it).

On a deeper level, the program translating the file into an image is itself nullified and dependent on the computer, and even more so on the programmer, who is superior to the computer, since he is the one who gives the computer its instructions. (This analogy has a limitation: although the programmer is above the computer, he's not united with the program, as G-d is united with the *sefirot*. This analogy is meant only to emphasize the great difference between the program and the programmer, between the *sefirot* and the Creator.)

Of course, if the two-dimensional characters in a computer game tried to praise the game's programmer, who comes from a three-dimensional world, they would never be able to find words to truly praise him because their vocabulary only includes words and concepts from their two-dimensional world.

As mentioned, the purpose of this analogy is only to help clarify the concept in a small way. The reality is not like this-it is far beyond our grasp and ability to understand, "for His ways are exalted beyond ours." Only from our perspective is it possible to discuss each of the individual *sefirot* as separate attributes that we can relate to.

The *Sefirot* Conceal and Reveal

This is the same approach we use when we explain the words of Eliyahu the prophet that are quoted in the introduction to *Tikkunei Zohar*. This passage is read before the Friday afternoon prayers: "You are He who brought forth ten *tikkunin*. We call them the ten *sefirot* [meaning, only we call them by this name] with which to regulate hidden worlds that are not revealed, as well as worlds that are revealed. Indeed, it is through these that You are hidden from mankind."

This passage from the *Zohar* means that G-d both hides in the *sefirot* and is revealed through the *sefirot*. We come to know G-d through His acts of *Chesed* (kindness, giving) and *Gevurah* (severity, restraint). However, these acts are not Him. They conceal Him in order to reveal a small fraction of His essence.

Even our description of the world being created through speech is only an analogy to give us a small glimpse to help us understand G-d. A person's emotional attributes are revealed first in his thoughts, then his speech, and finally in his actions. The same process occurs with G-d. In order for His lofty *sefirot* from the world of *Atzilut* to be revealed in the worlds, they first descend to "speech"-letters and utterances.

To express our feelings, we have to clothe them in letters and words, give them some form, and then we can speak and express ourselves. Similarly, G-d's attributes, the *sefirot*, can't be revealed in the world unless they are attired in statements. For example, in order for *Chesed* to create light, it has to be "dressed up" in the words of the statement "Let there be light."

Using Letters to Draw Down G-dliness

For the aforementioned reason, all of the G-dly energy that descends into the world is called "letters," and the letters draw down His will to sustain the worlds. In essence, the twenty-two letters of the Hebrew alphabet represent twenty-two different kinds of drawn-down light. And it is specifically the number 22 because that's exactly what G-d wanted.

The way we write each of the letters indicates to us the particular form of the light each letter draws down. This is the reason each letter has its own unique shape-they represent twenty-two different forms of drawn-down light. Great importance is attached to the precise shape of the letters, and much is inferred about lofty spiritual concepts based on those shapes.

For example, the letters in the words "*Yehi rakia*-Let there be a firmament in the heavens" (*yehi: yud-hey-yud*; *rakia: resh-kuf-yud-ayin*) are the ones through which Heaven was created. Any change in the letters-such as numerical *gematria* adjustments-creates other, different creations. Such changes create new levels of contraction and compression that reduces the amount of revealed light, similar to how the light of the sun that reaches us when it is reflected off the moon is weaker than the light that comes directly from the sun.

As mentioned, creating the world through letters is a creation that is *yesh me'ayin*-"something out of nothingness." The G-dly light and vitality that then descends into the world is dimmed considerably in order to bring inanimate objects, such as stones and dirt whose vitality is totally hidden, into existence.

In Conclusion

The basic fundamental principles of faith have to be intellectually learned and understood as much as possible. This is more than just believing that G-d exists or that He alone is Sovereign over the world. It means understanding that He brings the world into existence and renews the world's vitality at every moment, He is everywhere at all times, and He watches over every creature and every item down to the tiniest, microscopic particle.

When we internalize and live with these principles of faith, we will naturally feel love and awe for Him. It is this knowledge that is the basis of our understanding of how much G-d cares for us, how His *hashgachah pratit* supervises every detail of our lives, how He is close to us, watching over us all the time without cease. With this knowledge, we build a trusting, joyous relationship with Him.

Therefore, it's important to learn as much as possible about our faith, to understand and internalize the strong relationship that exists between our Creator and ourselves, so that we can perform *mitzvot* with the enthusiasm and vitality created by these profound feelings of love and awe.

The Eighth Gate

The Gate of Repentance

Iggeret Hateshuvah, Chapters 1-12

Chapter Forty-One

The Process
of Teshuvah

Changing directions...

(Tanya, Iggeret Hateshuvah, chaps. 1–3)

The first book of the *Tanya* taught us about serving G-d-what this means and how we can do it. The second book, *Sha'ar Hayichud Veha'emunah*, taught us about the Creator-how He creates the world and the fundamentals of faith. Now, in the third book, *Iggeret Hateshuvah*, the Alter Rebbe discusses *teshuvah* (repentance)-what it is and how it's done.

Changing Direction and Returning to G-d

Some people think that *teshuvah* is about weeping, fasting, and asceticism; others believe it's about guilt, sadness, and self-flagellation. While these feelings might accompany the process of *teshuvah*-and we'll learn later which of them are appropriate and which are unnecessary-they don't constitute the essence of *teshuvah*.

Teshuvah means "returning to G-d," from the root of the word "*shuv*," return. A transgression, in essence, causes us to travel *away* from G-d, moving us in the wrong direction and putting distance between us. With *teshuvah,* we are firmly resolving to make a U-turn, to change course and go in the right direction, returning to the path of serving and reconnecting to G-d.

In essence, *teshuvah* is closing the gap created by the sin and replacing it with acceptance of G-d's authority and commandments.

Remembering Who You Are

A couple may be sitting next to each other in the same room, but if they are staring sullenly in opposite directions, they feel a wide distance separating them. Yet all it takes is a small turn of the head and a smile to bridge that gap.

If we, so to speak, turn our head away from G-d, it takes only one small turn, one small decision, to change direction, and in one moment we can return to being one with Him. That "moment" is the decision to not transgress and return to doing G-d's will. This is called *teshuvah*.

On a deeper level, *teshuvah* is returning to ourselves, to who we truly are. Sin can only occur when we momentarily forget who we are and what our purpose is in the world. When we do *teshuvah*, we are returning to ourselves, to our essence, rediscovering our true inner being-the part of us that deeply desires to do the will of G-d.

Fasting

People associate fasting with *teshuvah* because this is what we do on Yom Kippur.

What does fasting accomplish?

Imagine a son didn't listen to his father and acted against his wishes, doing the opposite of his father's request. Even after the son apologizes and promises never to do it again, a blemish in their relationship remains, created by his insolence. There may be some lingering bad feelings and a sense of awkwardness or estrangement. Their bond of trust has been weakened.

If the relationship is important to him, the son will want to appeal to his father to try and smooth things over, repair the breach, and restore the trust-perhaps with a gift.

When the *Beit Hamikdash* (Holy Temple) stood in Jerusalem, a Jew who transgressed was obligated to bring an animal sacrifice to the Temple as an offering after he did *teshuvah*. This offering was in addition to his verbal declaration of *teshuvah*-of saying that he regretted what he did. The offering served as his gift to G-d to help restore the relationship and make amends.

During the long exile, after the *Beit Hamikdash* was destroyed and the ability to bring an offering was no longer an option, the custom of fasting was instituted. For every sin, there were an appropriate number of fasts, and every person knew how many times he needed to fast in order to wipe the slate clean.

Fasting was a substitute for bringing an animal sacrifice. In other words, instead of offering up an animal, we would offer up something of our Animal Soul by fasting and actually losing some of our own body mass during the fast.

However, the situation is sometimes such that not only does the fast fail to give part of the Animal Soul and "reduce" (i.e., humble) it, it does the opposite. Fasting could make a person feel arrogant and full of pride at his accomplishment and level of holiness. "I'm such a *Tzaddik*-look how I fast to repent of my sins!" In that case, the fast actually achieves the opposite of what it's meant to achieve.

Also, with the passage of generations, we are weaker than our predecessors were. They could fast a few times a week without adverse effects, and it didn't disturb their daily routine, work, or Torah study. For them, fasting was indeed a sacrifice to reconcile with G-d.

Since our bodies are not as strong as in previous generations, fasting weakens our ability to work and study, so the original intent in fasting is lost. In order to give something of our Animal Soul in this generation, we give *tzedakah*. This is also a sacrifice-as it involves giving up something of our material possessions. It's our way of giving something of ourselves to G-d.

Special Capabilities to Do *Teshuvah*

The fact that our bodies are weaker and we are unable to fast as Jews did in previous generations is not a disadvantage. One could have thought that because we are on a lower level than those who lived in previous generations, we can "only" give *tzedakah* instead of fasting. That our work of giving *tzedakah* is less valuable than the work of fasting.

But this is not true. Everything that happens in the world is by Divine providence-under G-d's watchful eye and due to His orchestration-and if it happens that we have less strength for fasting, then it has to mean that our generation received special alternative options from G-d. We have different strengths and abilities, and a seemingly lesser act today can have as great an impact, accomplishing the same results that once required whole days of fasting.

The same idea applies to *tzedakah*. A person who has less money to give is not at a disadvantage. If it was determined by Divine providence that he should have less money for *tzedakah*, he gives with more self-sacrifice. He can accomplish with a small sum what others-who have more to give-can accomplish only with a larger amounts.

"Little by Little, I Will Banish It from You"

It only takes a moment to start the *teshuvah* process, from the instant we decide to stop transgressing and start going in the right direction. However, from the point when we make the decision to return, until we are actually fulfilling all of the Torah's commandments, it could take time.

Why? Changing a whole lifestyle is not easy. One should first make a deep, inner decision to change and then start the process in stages, little by little, at a pace that's tailor-made for each individual, with proper guidance along the way.

In Conclusion

Teshuvah means leaving the path of transgression and deciding to change direction. It means regretting what we did in the past and resolving to learn, grow, and begin the process of observing all of G-d's *mitzvot*.

Chapter Forty-Two

Returning the Hey

The incredible, unique quality of the Jewish soul,
and the deeper meaning of *mitzvah* and *aveirah*...

(Tanya, Iggeret Hateshuvah, chaps. 4–6)

We explained that *teshuvah* is the firm resolution that our soul makes to change and return to G-d, forsaking the path that causes separation from G-d. *Teshuvah* can happen in one moment of inspiration, as soon as we make a firm resolution to change. But a resolution can also be dropped in a moment, if the person returns to his habitual, familiar patterns.

In order for *teshuvah* to be strong and lasting, it needs to be preceded by an inner, soulful process of introspection. We need to deeply understand the negative impact of an *aveirah* (sin) and the positive power of a *mitzvah*. This intellectual comprehension can then lead to developing a true, heartfelt desire to leave the path of transgression and follow the path of life-the path of doing *mitzvot*. Without this inner work, any firm decision we make to change remains external, what we call "lip service," without the heart's true resolve.

To better understand the meaning of *aveirah* and *mitzvah*, we need a fuller appreciation of the Jewish soul.

The Source of the Jewish Soul: G-d's Inner Dimension

When the Torah describes the creation of the world, it uses personification. It describes G-d in human terms that serve as analogies to help us understand the essence of creation. But it's absolutely clear that G-d has no physical form or image, and He can't actually be described in human terms. The Torah speaks in human terms only in order to aid our understanding.

As was explained in the first chapters, the Torah writes that G-d created the world with G-dly speech. He spoke and creation came into being: "G-d said, 'Let there be light,' and there was light" (*Bereshit* 1:3). This applied to everything in creation, with the exception of one thing: the G-dly Soul, which is literally "a part of G-d above."

When describing the soul, the Torah uses the word "*vayipach*," exhaled, instead of "spoke": "He *breathed* a soul of life into [Adam's] nostrils." Since G-d doesn't actually "breathe" or "speak," these verses need to be understood as analogies that help us better grasp the concept involved in creating Adam and the rest of creation.

The relationship between G-d and the world is like the relationship between a person and his *spoken word*. The relationship between G-d and the Jewish soul is like the relationship between a person and his *breath*. The difference between them is that speech comes from a more external dimension of the person, while breath derives from a more inner part.

This is also the difference between creation as a whole and the Jewish soul. All of creation derives from G-d's more external dimension, while the G-dly Soul comes from G-d's internal dimension.

The Structure of the Soul

As we explained in *Sha'ar Hayichud Veha'emunah*, the Divine Name *Havayah* refers to G-d's inner dimension, while the Divine Name *Elokim* refers to His external dimension. This means that the world, which derives from the external dimension, was created using the Name *Elokim*, while the G-dly Soul is connected to *Havayah*.

The soul, however, is not considered a creation-it wasn't brought into existence by G-d. It *is* G-d, but in a form that descended into the physical world, into the bodies of the Jewish people.

And since the soul derives from *Havayah* (also connected to the ten *sefirot* of *Atzilut*), it resembles *Havayah*. The soul's different levels correspond to the letters that form this Name of G-d: *yud-hey-vav-hey*.

Chochmah and *Binah*

The letters *yud* and *hey* correspond to *Chochmah* (wisdom) and *Binah* (understanding). *Chochmah* is the starting point of the intellectual process, the initial spark of insight, the abstract idea that emerges in the mind before it gets developed and built up. It's a kind of intuitive, inexplicable understanding. *Binah* is the next stage, where the intellect grasps the abstract idea and develops it.

The letter *yud* is an abstract letter without form and dimension. Therefore, it corresponds to *Chochmah*. The letter *hey* is more developed than the *yud*, as if the *yud* was stretched in all three dimensions of length, width, and depth. This corresponds to *Binah*, which takes *Chochmah*'s abstract ideas and brings them down into examples and analogies so that the intellect can grasp it.

The letter *yud* also features a small crown above it that stretches upward. It's even more abstract than *Chochmah* and corresponds to *ratzon* (will, desire) in the soul-just as our attribute of will transcends our intellect.

Emotional Attributes and *Malchut* (Feelings and Garments)

After *Chochmah* and *Binah* come the emotional faculties (*Chesed, Gevurah, Tiferet, Netzach, Hod,* and *Yesod*), which are generated by the intellect. Our intellectual perspective of each aspect of the world we live in influences our feelings for the world around us.

When we contemplate something in depth and come to understand that it's good for us, we will be drawn to it, or, if it's a person, we'll feel love for him. If we understand that something is not good for us, we'll try to avoid it.

The letter *vav*, the third letter in the Name *Havayah*, has the numerical value of six. It therefore corresponds to the six *middot*, the six emotional attributes.

The form of the *vav* is a straight line that goes from the top to the bottom. This represents how our emotions bring our intellectual understanding down into the world of action.

Emotions are the foundation of how we begin to relate to other people. Comprehension doesn't require another person; we can reason and understand in our own mind. Feelings are an expression of movement toward someone outside of us.

Our emotions are drawn down into our thoughts, speech, and actions, which are the soul's "garments" and modes of expression-not the soul itself. Just as we use clothes to present ourselves to our friends and society, using the appropriate garments for each occasion, so does the soul find expression in the world via its garments of thought, speech, and action.

The second letter *hey* in the Divine Name *Havayah* symbolizes the three garments, because the letter *hey* is made of three lines.

A Constant Connection with G-d's Inner Dimension

In addition to the fact that the soul is derived from the Name *Havayah* and shares the same structure of the ten *sefirot*, even after the soul descends into this world into a body, it continues to receive its vitality via the Divine Name *Havayah*!

This is significant because we might think that the soul's active connection to the ten *sefirot* is only while it is in the higher worlds, and not after it descends into a body. That's incorrect. The truth is that the G-dly Soul, even after entering the body, continues to be directly connected with its source in G-d's inner dimension. It is a piece of infinity-of G-dliness-that has descended into our lowly, physical world. The soul is inseparable from G-d.

To be more precise, almost nothing can separate it. There is one thing in the world that can separate the soul from its source and root, and that is transgression. Although G-d is found everywhere, He decided that His presence would only dwell and be revealed where His will is being done. He will "remove" that revelation from places that don't follow His will or violate it. By doing *mitzvot*, we fulfill His will and get to literally be with Him. But our sins separate us.

613 Threads in the Rope of Connection

There are different levels of *aveirot* based upon their severity. What's common to them all is the basic fact that a sin is a violation of G-d's will. From this viewpoint, there is no difference between greater and lesser sins. However, regarding the intensity of the blemish and the amount of separation from G-d caused to the soul, there are differences between sins.

The soul's connection with G-d is compared to an invisible rope stretching between them. The rope is woven together from 613 threads to create a thick, strong rope. The 613 *mitzvot* are the threads. Whenever a person commits a small *aveirah*, a thread is broken, but overall the rope remains connected. But a severe *aveirah*-like those that the Torah says are punished by *karet*, where "the soul will be cut off"-can sever the entire cord and the soul's connection with the Creator.

A Missed Positive Commandment = Missing Light

The 613 *mitzvot* are divided into 248 positive commandments and 365 negative commandments (prohibitions). They correspond to the body's 248 limbs and 365 sinews.

There's a fundamental difference between positive and negative *mitzvot*. Positive *mitzvot* involve doing an action, and that action has an impact on the world. They are more than a mere "test of obedience" to see if we are following G-d's orders. The positive *mitzvot* change the world because their performance draws G-dly light into the world.

Naturally, if we missed an opportunity to fulfill a positive commandment, then the light it could have drawn down into the world remains absent. This is a missed chance. For this reason, we are taught that a person who failed to perform a positive *mitzvah* should do *teshuvah*, and he will be immediately forgiven. Forgiveness comes quickly in this case because the light is missing, the opportunity passed, and there's no way to fix it.

But, in fact, that's not completely true. In the normal, natural way of things, the opportunity to draw down the light was missed and there's no going back in time. However, there is a way to overcome this. If a person truly regrets his mistake from the core depths of his heart, it's possible to tap into an inexhaustible source of infinite light. And by reaching that point in the soul, he can reveal and draw down a level of light that transcends the light that would have been drawn down by doing the *mitzvah*.

This works because the higher light "fills in the gap." It's like a dried-up river: dig deeper into its source, and eventually a depth is reached where there is abundant water-enough to replenish the river.

This place is found very deep in the soul. It's a place where the most important thing is our connection to the Creator, our essence and mission-something we can't live without. And reaching that point puts us face-to-face with the essence of our soul. In this place, we can't speak, because words only dull the true, pure emotion; they are too "small" to hold our feelings in their entirety. We can't even cry, because tears at that moment would only obscure the inner truth. All we can do is release a still, small wail that emanates from our innermost heart.

It's like a blast from the *shofar*: simple, without words or notes-an expression from the core of the soul declaring remorse for its deeds and longing to return to its Father's embrace.

Repairing the Damage of Violating a Prohibition

The negative commandments, however, are a different story. Violating a prohibition means committing a forbidden act, and that damages the soul by creating separation from the Creator. Such a situation also requires *teshuvah*, and here, too, G-d grants forgiveness and pardon-but we have to wait for Yom Kippur to have our souls cleansed.

On Yom Kippur, the pinnacle of holiness, G-d grants atonement for all of our transgressions throughout the year. On that day we prayerfully ask G-d to "forgive us, pardon us, and grant us atonement."

The Bar Mitzvah Suit: An Analogy

A boy received a new suit for his bar mitzvah, and his father asked him not to wear it until the celebration. But the boy couldn't wait. He put on the suit and snuck out of the house to show it to his friends. He was so excited that he ran, slipped, muddied, and ripped the suit. The suit was ruined!

Embarrassed, the boy humbly approached his father and asked him not to be angry with him, despite having disobeyed his father's request. He pleaded not to be punished and for "the debt to be erased." In addition, the boy even asked his father to fix and clean the suit so it could be worn for his bar mitzvah.

Naturally, the father was willing to forgive his son and overlook his disobedience. This was, after all, his son. Even if he misbehaved, they were still father and son; their deep, essence-level connection remained.

Yes, the father forgave his son, but when it came to fixing and cleaning the suit, he explained that this was a major job that required being repaired by professionals with special machines. It would not possibly be ready until after his bar mitzvah.

This is what happens when we violate the negative commandments. G-d "forgives us"-He's no longer angry. And He "pardons us" by "erasing the debt." But the cleansing takes place only once a year-on Yom Kippur.

That's the reason that we mention "forgive us" and "pardon us" in our prayers throughout the year, but on Yom Kippur we add "grant us atonement."

The Soul's Vitality in the Times of the Temple and Nowadays

When the *Beit Hamikdash* stood in Jerusalem, the Jewish people were on a very high level and received spiritual sustenance directly from the G-dly Soul. No intermediary was necessary. However, it also meant that the life of a Jew who committed a sin punishable by *karet* (soul excision) would end earlier-by the age of fifty or sixty.

During our exile, however, things are different. The soul is still derived from the Divine Name *Havayah*, but the vitality of the soul first passes through the garment of *kelipat nogah* (see chapter 6). It no longer comes directly from G-d as in the times of the Temple, and thus a Jew can sin and still live.

In fact, during our exile, the opposite can happen: a Jew can transgress and apparently live a good, prosperous life, as the verse states, "The way of the wicked is successful." It's possible to see people who transgress and yet succeed and enjoy plenty.

Why is this? Because a Jew is connected to the Creator and *kedushah*, and the *kelipot* (impure, concealing forces) want to siphon off vitality from *kedushah*. As such, they try to "help" a Jew reach the highest levels of *kelipah* in order to take from his *kedushah*. But this is only a temporary condition. A Jew has to be connected to *kedushah* for his vitality. If he continues trying to draw vitality from *kelipah*, he eventually loses the abundance he received for being connected to it.

The Mystical Principle of the *Shechinah's* exile

As mentioned, a Jew's soul comes from G-d's innermost dimension. For that reason, violating G-d's will not only separates us from G-d, but even "drags" G-d down along with us into *kelipah*. *Kedushah* is pulled into impurity. This is why the Hebrew word for a sin is "*aveirah*"- literally, "transfer." Because the act transfers powers of *kedushah* into *kelipah*.

This "pulling down" is called the "exile of the *Shechinah*." When a Jew commits a sin, he takes G-d with him and brings Him into a state of exile in the *kelipah*. In other words, not only is the Jew in exile and his soul concealed, but in that moment, he also increases the concealment of G-dliness.

This is why the verse says, "And G-d will return with you" (instead of "G-d will bring you back"). G-d Himself will also return together with the Jew from exile to redemption, since He was also in exile.

Returning the *Hey* of *Yud-Hey-Vav-Hey* (*Havayah*)

Doing *teshuvah* returns and restores the second letter "*hey*" in the Divine Name *Havayah*. Through *teshuvah*, we change our thoughts, words, and deeds, the garments of the soul, which are hinted at by the three lines comprising the letter *hey*.

In this way, we restore the *Shechinah* from the *kelipah* to *kedushah*. We take G-d out of exile-removing the *sefirah* of *Malchut* (also connected to the same letter *hey*) from the *kelipah* and bringing it back to *kedushah*.

In Conclusion

The soul is a part of the Creator. Doing *mitzvot* connects the soul to G-d and draws light down into the world, while committing *aveirot* disconnects the soul and blemishes it. The lower level of *teshuvah* is when we fix our actions by restoring the lower letter *hey*-the second *hey* in G-d's Name-to its source and root.

Chapter Forty-Three

Simple Teshuvah

True remorse, teshuvah from the depths
of the heart, repairs all blemishes.

(Tanya, Iggeret Hateshuvah, chaps. 7–8)

In the previous chapter, we discussed the uniqueness of the Jewish soul and as a result came to appreciate the severity of sinning. (Kabbalistically speaking, sinning means drawing the second letter *hey* from the Divine Name *Havayah-yud-hey-vav-hey*-which corresponds to the *sefirah* of *Malchut*, down into the *kelipot*).

Now we will explain the soulful process that leads to the two levels of *teshuvah*: *teshuvah tata* (the lower level of repentance) and *teshuvah ilah* (the higher level).

As mentioned, the mystical meaning of *teshuvah* means "restoring the *hey* to the Divine Name *Havayah*." We see this in the word "*teshuvah*" itself, which can be broken into two words: "*tashuv hey*," which means "returning the '*hey*.'" That is, reattaching it to the level it represents in the Name *Havayah* (*yud-hey-vav-hey*), as it was before the person sinned.

This can be understood in two ways: returning the first *hey*, which corresponds to the level of *Binah*, or returning the second *hey*, which corresponds to *Malchut*.

This reveals the difference between the two levels of *teshuvah*. The lower level of *teshuvah* restores the lower *hey* (*Malchut*), and the higher level of *teshuvah* restores the higher *hey* (*Binah*).

Teshuvah Tata

Ultimately, the goal of *teshuvah* is to reach the firm decision to turn away from the path of transgression, which separates us from G-d, and return to the Divine path of accepting G-d's authority and doing *mitzvot*. But the first step begins with an inner, spiritual process.

Personal interests should not be the main motivating factor in feeling regret over the past and making a firm commitment to change. Even though most people are generally interested in enjoying the soul's spiritual paradise in Heaven (*Gan Eden*) and avoiding the cleansing punishment of purgatory (*Gehinnom*), and therefore fear sinning and seek to do *mitzvot*, this is not *teshuvah*.

Instead, part of properly and truly changing ourselves via *teshuvah* is understanding that "it's not all about me." Sinning is not just a personal problem concerning our own individual situation in our relationship with G-d. It's much deeper than that.

Teshuvah is about fixing the higher worlds that have been blemished because of our behavior, *as well* as restoring our connection to the Creator. *Teshuvah* is expressing regret over the "larger" damage we have caused and seeking to rectify it.

When a person is truly remorseful about the transgressions he has committed in the past, the subsequent desire to do *teshuvah* can be immense. The further one is from the proper path, the more intense may be the thirst to return. This gives us an insight into the incredible level of *baalei teshuvah*-returnees who are highly motivated by a strong desire to make amends for the past and restore their damaged connection with G-d.

Teshuvah Requires Deep Contemplation

Reaching a place of truth in our soul, a place where we truly understand what we did wrong and feel the gravity of our deeds, requires deep, self-reflective thinking. We have to continually contemplate what our soul is, where it came from (attached to G-d above, literally a "piece of G-d"), and realize how low we have sunk with our misdeeds: from the highest of heights and a place of purity to the deepest pit.

Following this meditation (regarding where our soul comes from), it's necessary to arouse feelings of mercy and compassion for the soul that is distant from its source and for G-d Who was "forced" to descend into the lowest places because of our *aveirot*.

This compassion stimulates a feeling of *merirut* (bitterness)-i.e., deep pain and remorse over our past. To clarify, this is not a sadness that leads to depression and self-defeating self-castigation. Rather, it's the remorseful bitterness that inspires a tremendous, strong desire to change.

But if our motivation for *teshuvah* is solely a selfish concern for ourselves, then this meditation may lead us to an undesirable, unproductive state of depression and emotional paralysis. Instead, it's more effective if our approach begins with thoughts and concerns for G-d and the damage to the soul (which is part of Him). Then the emphasis is automatically not "Look how bad my personal situation is," but rather, "I need to wake up, get moving, and begin to repair."

True Regret

A father of three drove his two boys to school every morning. His infant always came along, buckled into a baby seat. One hot spring day, on his way home from dropping off his boys, the father stopped to run into a store and pick up a few items. He saw that the baby had fallen asleep, and he thought it was a shame to wake her up since he was only "dashing in and out" of the store.

Once he started shopping, though, he got distracted thinking about other things they probably needed. The line at the checkout counter was quite long, and it was over half an hour before he emerged from the store and returned to his car.

He had forgotten all about his baby! When he reached his automobile, he saw with relief that the baby seemed to be quietly sleeping.

But she wasn't. She had suffocated in the hot car.

One can't possibly imagine the unfathomable depth of the father's regret. Nor can we imagine the intense pain of a mother who leaves her toddler in the bathtub for "just a second" while she runs to answer the door or phone, and her child drowns in that instant!

This is true, heartbreaking remorse that stimulates an intense emotional and intellectual personal accounting of the impact of one's deeds.

A Broken Heart Defeats *Kelipah*

The second part of this inner soul process of *teshuvah* is defeating *kelipah*.

The main cause of our sins is arrogance-the belief that we are the center of the world, that everything is about us and we deserve it all. Such a belief is based on an overexaggerated sense of self–importance, called *yeshut* in Hebrew, or "ego" in modern terminology. In order to overcome *kelipah*, we have to overpower it by nullifying our ego-our *yeshut*-and any unhealthy self-obsession.

What often prevents us from doing *teshuvah* is our ego's arrogance. It is mistaken to think, "Oh, I'm fine, I have nothing to fix." Such thinking prevents growth and spiritual progress. We can't strive for higher levels when we think, "Hey, everything's fine, I'm on the right path, and there's nothing that needs to change." This is our ego speaking and keeping our souls sealed off. If we believe ourselves to be above everyone else, then there is no need to listen to others, and there's no willingness to change the lifestyle to which we are accustomed.

We need to break the ego by laboring to overcome the false sense that we are the center of the universe, that *"magia li"*-I deserve everything. A broken, contrite heart is the pathway to this level of self-nullification.

How can we "break" the ego? One way is to try to assess our state honestly, by trying to view ourselves objectively, as though from an outsider's perspective. Can we step back and see in what ways we are too self-absorbed and self-serving and in what ways we are too self-inflated?

This meditation can help us to break, humble, and subdue our ego. Remorse that leads to self-disgust and bitterness (not depression) helps break the heart. A broken heart becomes humble and helps us to weaken the power of a self-serving, arrogant ego.

A Personal Accounting

In the past, this work of breaking and humbling was done via fasting and self-affliction. In our generation, however, when it's difficult for us to handle fasting (as explained in the first chapter of this section), the main tool for "breaking" is deep, inner self-examination.

It takes unceasingly honest self-assessment, contemplation of our actions, and serious thought about the damage we have caused to our souls and G-d by our sins to awaken the remorse needed to change.

As mentioned, even a sin whose punishment isn't *karet* and therefore doesn't cut the invisible connecting cord between the soul and G-d still weakens our connection. It still "cuts" one of the threads comprising the cord. Our prophets compare the way sin conceals Divine light to the way clouds hide the sun. Many small clouds (i.e., small sins) can obscure the sun (G-d's light) just as much as one large cloud.

There are three daily prayers-*Shacharit*, *Minchah*, and *Ma'ariv*-that are said with a *minyan*. And then there is a private prayer: the bedtime *Shema* that we say at the end of the day, in the privacy of our home, when we have the opportunity for self-examination.

This is a quiet time to review what transpired that day and do a personal accounting of all of our thoughts, words, and deeds. This is when we can contemplate the gravity of our sins and resolve how to make tomorrow different.

Revealing the Source, Awakening Celestial Compassion

Contemplation and personal accounting are the spiritual processes that precede our resolution to change. They also prepare the heart to make a true and sincere appeal to G-d to grant us forgiveness, pardon, and atonement.

This heartfelt, genuine appeal draws down lofty light from the Divine Name *Havayah*, and brings us to a new level of G-dliness that is beyond logic.

This level is called the "Thirteen Attributes of Mercy." From this level, G-d freely grants forgiveness regardless of our worthiness. This level is so lofty that it can erase all of the soul's blemishes, and bypass a slower, "step-by-step" process of *teshuvah*.

According to normal logic, a person shouldn't be forgiven for his *aveirot*, but with deeply felt *teshuvah*, coming from a very deep place, G-d mercifully forgives even a person who doesn't deserve it.

There are rivers that dry up every few years. If we wanted to restore their waters, we would have to dig deeply into the riverbed to rediscover the source of the underground spring. Once we reach it, the river will fill up again.

The same process applies to the soul, as it says, "From the depths I have called You, G-d" (*Tehillim* 130:1). We may have missed many opportunities to draw down G-dly light into the world because of our *aveirot*, and we may think that there is no way to rectify this situation.

But the process of *teshuvah* involves digging deep into the depth of the soul where we discover our inner point of G-dliness. When we reach the source of the light itself, we can (retroactively) draw down the light and fill in all of the gaps that were created by our transgressions and missed opportunities.

Avinu Malkeinu-Our Father, Our King

We call G-d both "our Father" and "our King," because both levels exist in our relationship. He is the King and we are His subjects; He commands and we obey. Someone who doesn't follow the king's orders is considered rebellious, and an estrangement is created that's difficult to repair.

But there is another level in our relationship with G-d-that He is our Father. A father always loves his child and is always close to him. Even if the child rebels against the father's will, he remains his son and the father will find room in his heart for forgiveness.

Throughout the year and on regular days, G-d is primarily "our King," but to be forgiven, we want to awaken the connection we have with our Father, Who is always ready to forgive us. Through *teshuvah*, we awaken the part of G-d that is "our Father." Then He naturally forgives us and helps us repair our blemishes.

In Conclusion

A deep understanding of the essence of *mitzvot* and *aveirot* leads to meditative contemplation that awakens the deepest levels of our soul. This enables us to change direction, reaccept His authority as our King, repair damages, and return to the loving embrace of our Father.

All this comprises the level of *teshuvah* called "*teshuvah tata*." There is an even higher level, *teshuvah ilah*, which will be discussed in the next chapter.

Chapter Forty-Four
Higher Teshuvah

*Teshuvah-return-but not [only] from transgression;
rather [return] to your true self.*

(Tanya, Iggeret Hateshuvah, chaps. 9–10)

The previous chapter described the lower level of *teshuvah* called "*teshuvah tata*," which involves cultivating a deep understanding of the gravity of transgression, true remorse from the heart, a sincere and firm decision not to repeat the sin, and full acceptance of G-d's authority as our King.

This *teshuvah* restores the lower *hey*, the second *hey* in the Divine Name of *Havayah*. This *hey* represents *Malchut* and the soul's garments (thought, speech, and action) that were blemished by the sin and severed from the connective cord between the soul and G-d. Now, thanks to *teshuvah*, the connection has been restored. But this is still only the lower level of *teshuvah-teshuvah tata*.

It's hard to imagine what could be higher than this. We have experienced true remorse that led to the purification of the soul and rectification of the situation. Why do we need another level of *teshuvah* if all has already been forgiven and our sins pardoned?

Teshuvah, but Not from Sins

This concept is part of the *Tanya*'s unique perspective on the *mitzvah* of *teshuvah*.

The main application of *teshuvah* is not for sins, and therefore the *mitzvah* of *teshuvah* doesn't apply only to sinners-it's for everyone. This doesn't mean that a Jew who carefully observes the entire Torah and its *mitzvot* has to dig deep into himself to find things that were done a bit "carelessly." Such a search only leads to the discovery of marginal, trivial things, and such nitpicking *teshuvah* will fail to awaken a desire to return to G-d. Only contemplating how one's sins have pushed one far away from G-d can generate such thirst.

But what is *teshuvah* that's not about sin?

The answer is that sins were never the real problem-only a symptom. While the sins surely have to be addressed via the lower level of *teshuvah*, it still isn't the core issue. For that, *teshuvah tata* is insufficient.

The Root of the Problem: Ego

The real problem here is ego, arrogance, an overexaggerated sense of self, *yeshut*, and feeling as though we are independent of the Creator.

But how can it be otherwise? G-d Himself created the world with concealment, with the appearance of being separate from Him. Even the soul itself, after G-d "exhaled" it into existence, senses itself to be an independent entity, drawn from the Creator yet separate. This sense of independent existence and self-importance is the root of the problem.

In other words, sin is more than just rebelling against G-d's authority and refusing to fulfill His commands. At its core, sinning demonstrates that we have lost touch with our essence. The fact that the sinner doesn't feel his inner essence and doesn't recognize that at the core level he is one with G-d is what enables him to sin.

We regain that awareness and reignite our yearning to unite with G-d through *teshuvah ilah*.

Teshuvah Ilah

With *teshuvah ilah*, we want to rise above our self-absorption and realize that we have a "piece of G-d" within us that thirsts to "return" to G-d. When we long to be connected to G-d, to nullify ourselves before Him, then, as a matter of course, we will not even want to sin.

There are people who grew up secular and then became Torah observant later in life-*baalei teshuvah*. They may talk proudly about their past, boasting about how much they sacrificed to become religious. They left a career and a high-paying job, etc., and now they're "doing G-d a favor" by becoming observant.

There are other *baalei teshuvah* who gave up no less of a career, yet they are ashamed of their past, of having been so far from G-d, and they wouldn't dream of receiving honor because they did *teshuvah*. On the contrary, they feel they have hardly even begun their *teshuvah* process. They have so much to learn, understand, and do; they are just starting to grow closer to G-d.

The Higher Letter *Hey*

As mentioned, the first *hey* in the Name of G-d (*yud-**hey**-vav-hey*) represents the attribute of *Binah*. The soul's attributes can be divided into two main groups: the intellectual powers of *Chochmah* and *Binah*, and the six emotional attributes and *Malchut*.

The primary difference between intellect and emotion is that feelings are outward-toward others. In order to love, there needs to be someone to love. Intellect, on the other hand, exists even without another person-it's entirely possible to learn something on your own.

In general, our ego, self-awareness, and arrogance are mostly found in the heart and emotions, and far less in the intellect. The intellect is more objective and tends to be further removed from self-interest (relatively speaking).

Therefore we need *Binah* to reach a level where we aren't aware of our own existence, the point where the soul truly returns to its roots. So it's not enough in that case to restore the second letter *hey*, the *sefirah* of *Malchut* that corresponds to action. The soul itself longs to be close to G-d, as it was before Creation. This is the level of *Binah*, the level of thoughts, before there is any action.

Binah: The Gateway to *Teshuvah Ilah*

In the first section of *Tanya,* we discussed at length the various levels of love. The most exalted is when intellectual observation produces feelings of love for the Creator. By using our power of *Binah* for holy activities such as Torah study and intellectually generating a love of G-d, we return the higher *hey* to the Divine Name and achieve the level of *teshuvah ilah-teshuvah* at its highest level.

Achieving this level involves returning to G-d and uniting with

Him in an incredible union, just as when the soul was united with the Creator before He breathed it into existence and clothed it in a physical body. That's true nullification to G-d and not merely a feeling that "there is a Creator above me and therefore *I* must serve Him," or "the Creator has commanded me to do something and *I* regret not having done it."

Rather, it is nullification of the sense of existence-*bitul bimetziut*. This is the *teshuvah* we do when we feel separated from G-d and long to return. It's more than fixing deeds and misdeeds; it's a thirst to unite with G-d.

"I Hereby Pardon..."

A young yeshivah student wanted to learn how to properly do cheshbon hanefesh (spiritual accounting) at the end of the day. He arranged an unobtrusive way to observe his rabbi at the time of the bedtime Shema by standing quietly next to the rabbi's door.

He heard his rabbi begin the prayer "I hereby pardon anyone..." that is part of the bedtime Shema, but before he continued with the words "who made me angry or who sinned against me," the rabbi suddenly stopped and began to weep.

"'I hereby pardon'? Me? Who am I to pardon? How could there be someone who angered me that I have to forgive now? This means that I consider myself separate from G-d and from other Jews! For this I must repent and do teshuvah!"

The Way to Return with "All Your Soul"

The higher *teshuvah* is expressed when we study Torah with love and awe. Then we use *Binah* to generate these feelings by contemplating the greatness of G-d. When we do that, the letter *hey* that represents understanding to its source. Then the feelings of love and awe that was generated by this intellectual contemplation become clothed (i.e., are expressed) in our thoughts, words, and deeds-the garments of the soul.

The different dimensions of the soul each connect to the Creator in various ways: in action, by giving *tzedakah* and doing *mitzvot*; in speech, by learning Torah; in thought, by reflecting on the Torah we learn and thinking about G-d and His holiness; in feelings, by working on having good *middot* (character traits) and trying to emulate G-d's attributes of compassion and mercy, etc.; and with the intellect, by studying Torah with *Chochmah* and *Binah*.

The loftiest connection with G-d is created through Torah study. Our involvement in Torah study repairs all of the blemishes, flaws, and damage in the soul. Therefore a person looking to fix his soul will study Torah inspired by intellectually generated awe and love. And if he was already putting aside time to study for one hour, he will try to increase his efforts to study for two. Just as we repair a severed rope with a double knot, we try to double our efforts in order to repair what was broken and regain a strong connection.

Teshuvah Ilah through Torah Study

Studying Torah out of intellectually inspired love and awe is a form of higher *teshuvah*. The Torah is said to have "preceded the world," meaning that it comes before the world in both time and importance. The Torah transcends the world, and by studying it we connect with a reality above nature.

How does that happen?

When we study Torah with humility before G-d, it is as though we open up a channel for G-d to speak through us, because our personal existence is set aside. This is nullification of our sense of existence (*bitul bimetziut*) and thus is a higher level of *teshuvah*.

The key, however, is that the learning is done with the intent to inspire the love and the awe. Someone who has learned the entire *Talmud* has made an impressive achievement. But what's considered truly important is not just what he knows-but what he has internalized. How has the entire *Talmud* made an impact on the person? How has he changed? How has he grown? How much has he internalized his studies and become a different, more elevated person?

When we study with the intention to connect with G-d, and become one with Him, we have more of a chance of experiencing *bitul bimetziut*.

Torah Study versus Prayer

It is, however, possible that this level is unattainable for most of us; it's too lofty for the world and for us. Perhaps our Torah study will not enter and transform our innermost selves. This is because, as we said, Torah is lofty and originates from *above*.

Prayer, on the other hand, originates from *below*, from us. Prayer is the structured order that we traverse by way of various thoughts and intentions (like rungs in a ladder, by which we bridge this world with the higher worlds). Meditating on the verses in prayer leads a person to an awareness of the Creator's greatness and infinite goodness.

Like Torah study, this also generates feelings of love for the Creator in the soul. These feelings are primarily expressed in the *Shema*, where it says, "And you shall love the L-rd, your G-d, with all your heart and with all your soul and with all your might" (*Devarim* 6:5).

This type of contemplation (thinking about G-d's greatness and goodness) that results from meaningful prayer enables a person to understand the importance of connecting to G-d through Torah and *mitzvot*-which is the higher *teshuvah*. But, as we explained before, it has to be preceded by the lower *teshuvah*, which is done through crushing the ego *before* we begin to pray.

First we contemplate our smallness and lowliness, humbly preparing ourselves for the *teshuvah ilah* that comes during prayer.

Teshuvah Tata Once a Week

It may prove too difficult to undergo the entire process of *teshuvah tata* and then *teshuvah ilah*. A person may also be concerned that preceding his prayers by subjugating his sense of self will make it too hard to switch to joy and great love later on.

A solution is to concentrate on the lower level of *teshuvah* during the bedtime *Shema* the night before and then the higher *teshuvah* in the morning before prayer.

Even the lower level of *teshuvah* may prove difficult to do on a nightly basis, particularly in our generation when people are more sensitive and such self-breaking efforts could depress a person. In that case, it's enough to do this one night a week. The most appropriate night is Thursday evening. And if one is doing *teshuvah ilah,* the higher *teshuvah* once a week, the most appropriate time is before the Shabbat morning prayers.

Blemishing One's Sexual Purity

According to the *Zohar*, a person who misuses his *brit milah* (circumcision) by wasting seed or engaging in forbidden relations causes a far-reaching blemish to his soul and not just to that limb or part of the soul. This is because of the seed's uniqueness-it is endowed with the person's own vitality. Since the soul dwells in the mind and serves as the core of a person's vitality, the blemish is experienced in the brain.

For such a blemish, the lower level *teshuvah* alone is insufficient. Certainly the person first has to feel remorse in the depths of his heart for his transgression, but repairing the damage requires moving on to the higher level of *teshuvah*-Torah study saturated with love and awe of G-d. Since the blemish is experienced in the mind, the repair needs to be done through the mind.

Repairing a blemish to the *brit milah*-a disconnection from G-d in the mind-requires studying increasing amounts of G-d's Torah in a way that unites the mind with the Torah and melds them into a whole.

In Conclusion

Teshuvah ilah is when we restore the first letter *hey* (which represents the *sefirah* of *Binah*) in the Divine Name *Havayah*. It is not *teshuvah* from sins, but rather it is the *teshuvah* we do for feeling that we are separate from the Creator.

Teshuvah tata needs to be done before *teshuvah ilah* can happen. Though it's worthwhile to do *teshuvah tatah* and *teshuvah ilah* every day, if that's too difficult, it can be done at least once a week. The most appropriate night for *teshuvah tata* is Thursday evening. And if one is doing *teshuvah ilah* once a week, the most appropriate time is before the Shabbat morning prayers.

Chapter Forty-Five

Teshuvah
Inspired by Joy

G-d always accepts our teshuvah, and it draws
us closer to Him-what could be more joyful?

(Tanya, Iggeret Hateshuvah, chaps. 11–12)

Joyful *Teshuvah*

Teshuvah ilah should be done joyfully. The fact that it is preceded by the bitterness felt in *teshuvah tata* (see chapter 43) is not a contradiction: the bitterness derives from the Animal Soul, and the joy comes from the G-dly Soul.

Moreover, the entire process of *teshuvah* is undertaken with total trust and confidence that G-d will indeed forgive us. Our deep appreciation that G-d is compassionate, merciful, abundantly forgiving, and-unlike humans-never tires of granting forgiveness is enough to bring us great joy.

When we hurt someone else, or let him down, he may not be willing to forgive us. And when someone hurts us, especially if it's more than once, we may not be willing to forgive him. Even when we sincerely ask for forgiveness from the person we wronged, there's a limit to how many times we can repeat the process and expect to be forgiven. We are limited by human nature, and after being harmed several times by the same person, our willingness to be forgiving fades.

The Creator, however, is not limited. Even if we repeatedly sin, He will always take us back. Our confidence that He will welcome us our return and accept our repentance fills us with feelings of great joy.

A Joyful Confession

The Baal Shem Tov once spent Yom Kippur in a particular city. He noticed that the cantor who led the service used an upbeat, joyful tune during Vidui-the pensive confessional prayer said when we repent for all our transgressions.

After Yom Kippur, the Baal Shem Tov approached the cantor and asked him about his unusual choice of tunes.

"When a simple servant of the king has to clean the palace, he is so moved by the privilege of being a servant of the king that he sings

joyfully as he cleans. Here we are on Yom Kippur, cleansing our souls by the request of our King-shouldn't we do it with great joy?"

The Blessing of Forgiveness

Every day, in the silent *Amidah*, we ask G-d for forgiveness of our sins. We say, "Blessed are You, G-d, the gracious One Who pardons abundantly." We recite a full blessing that uses one of G-d's Names and state that G-d truly forgives us.

We are always very careful never to say one of G-d's Names without reason, so if it weren't true and G-d didn't actually grant us forgiveness, it would be forbidden to make this blessing using G-d's Name. The fact that this blessing is part of our daily prayers demonstrates our unshakable confidence that G-d forgives and pardons us.

A Blessing in Vain

On Yom Kippur, the Ruzhiner Rebbe's Chassidim noticed that the Rebbe paused thoughtfully during Vidui before finishing the blessing "The King who forgives and pardons" before moving on to the next blessing.

Later they asked the Rebbe what he was thinking at that moment.

"In the middle of the blessing, I suddenly wondered, Will G-d truly forgive us this year? And I was afraid to finish the blessing. But then I remembered something I used to do when I was a child.

"If I saw my father holding a delicious red apple, and I wanted him to give it to me, I would say out loud the blessing for fruits grown on trees, 'Blessed are You, G-d, King of the universe, Who created the fruit of the tree.' And my father had no choice but to give me the apple. Otherwise, I would have made a blessing in vain.

"I realized that it was the same now: by reciting the blessing that G-d forgives and pardons, He would have no choice but to forgive and to pardon, lest we be making a blessing in vain!"

Between Joy and Bitterness

The joy we feel when we do *teshuvah* doesn't diminish the bitterness and remorse over the sin that was committed. On the contrary, the sin has to be leveraged and used for a good purpose. We have sinned, and this recollection needs to always be close to our consciousness, as King David wrote, "My sins are always before me" (*Tehillim 51:5*). Bearing in mind our previous sins is our way of admitting that we are imperfect.

However, recounting our sins shouldn't be done in order to make us depressed, but rather in order to keep us focused on who we are and where we came from. This awareness will help us stay far from the arrogance of believing that we're better than others. We acknowledge that we are also imperfect.

Joy in Suffering

The Alter Rebbe concludes this section by teaching us another way to leverage sins and use something that appears bad for a good purpose.

In the previous chapters, we explained that in addition to the process of *teshuvah* returning us to the Creator, there is also a need to rectify what was damaged. G-d's will was transgressed; a sin was committed. Even though it was forgiven, something needs to be done to restore the trust that was breached.

Part of this atonement process could be done by fasting, but as we mentioned before, our generation isn't physically strong enough to handle fasting. The alternative is to realize that when we experience difficulties and suffering, they can be viewed as an atonement. Suffering actually accomplishes what fasting (and before that, bringing sacrifices in the *Beit Hamikdash*) does by cleansing us of our *aveirot*.

Above we said that recollecting our past sins keeps us humble. In the light of the fact that suffering provides atonement, we see another reason to remember our sins. When we experience unpleasant events and challenges in life, the recollection of previous sins helps us reframe the suffering as something positive. Perhaps this difficulty is meant to be a purification of the soul, cleansing away the blemishes that the sins caused.

With this perspective, we can rise above our limited view in order to deeply appreciate the fact that painful suffering in this physical world reduces much more painful spiritual purification in the next world.

Like the Movement of a Shadow

Let's illustrate this concept with a shadow. In order for us to see a shadow move an inch down here on Earth, the Earth must have rotated thousands of miles. Similarly, every small pain, challenge, and trial that we undergo in life saves us from a vast amount of difficult spiritual purification that the soul would need to undergo when it returns to *Gan Eden*.

As human beings we understandably want our pain to end, and we obviously long to understand why it's happening-i.e., to learn the reason for the suffering. But even if we don't yet have these answers, we can still have the clarity to know that as long as the suffering is happening, we can remember that it's for our good.

By deeply internalizing this principle, we can find joy in the fact that "G-d rebukes the ones He loves" (*Mishlei* 3:12) and that our suffering is in fact proof that G-d loves us so deeply.

In Conclusion

Teshuvah means returning to G-d. This applies to both the lower level, where we repair our misdeeds, and the higher level, where we repair our ego-driven feelings of separateness from G-d. The work of doing *teshuvah* can be done joyfully, accompanied by confidence that G-d will surely forgive and pardon us.

Of course, this doesn't grant us permission to sin and then rely on the gift of *teshuvah* to fix what we did. The *Talmud* explicitly teaches us that one who says, "I will sin and then repent," is not assisted in his efforts. Anyone who takes advantage of the ability to do *teshuvah* to allow himself to go sin doesn't understand that *teshuvah* requires deep remorse and a firm resolution not to continue transgressing.

It can't possibly be true, deep remorse if we were already planning to do *teshuvah* before the sin!

Nevertheless, the *Talmud* only says that such a person is "not aided in his efforts to do *teshuvah*"-he can't rely on receiving any Divine assistance to do so. But if he truly feels deep remorse, then even he can repent and be forgiven.

"To the perceptive, this knowledge is basic. And those who grasp this subject will uncover good [things]."

With this quote, the Alter Rebbe concludes *Iggeret Hateshuvah*. These words hint at the ten *sefirot*: "this knowledge" to *Da'at*; "perceptive" to *Binah*; "those who grasp" to *Chochmah*; "the subject" to *Malchut*; and "good" to *Yesod*, which includes the six emotional attributes of *Chesed*, *Gevurah*, *Tiferet*, *Netzach*, and *Hod*. When we do *teshuvah* properly, we achieve *sheleimut*-perfection in all of our ten attributes.

On a deeper level, by featuring *Da'at* first, this statement summarizes the *Tanya*'s first three sections. *Da'at* is the most important of the *sefirot*, because it connects the intellect with the emotions. Being very learned and full of understanding alone is not enough in serving G-d, just as being tremendously emotional is not enough.

The focus of the *Tanya* is to forge a connection between these attributes, which is the specialty of *Da'at*. To achieve deep, thoughtful, meditative contemplation, understanding is not enough-one needs to *know*, to be "enmeshed" within these concepts.

Da'at is responsible for helping us deeply internalize what we know, generating real emotional changes and leading to improved character traits and-our ultimate goal-a deeper connection to G-d. Through the teachings of the *Tanya*, we can achieve all this and bring about lasting and powerful changes on the soul level.

Glossary

This book is meant to help all students of the *Tanya*, regardless of gender. Though the pronoun "he" is often used for convenience, this term generally includes both men and women.

In this *sefer* there are terms that that we use frequently:

ahavah — love (of G-d); the soul's desire to draw closer and be connected to G-d.

Alter Rebbe — Rabbi Shneur Zalman of Liadi, author of the *Tanya*.

Atzilut — the World of Emanation, highest of the four worlds, nearest to the source of creation.

Asiyah — the World of Action, fourth of the spiritual worlds and the final stage in the creative process.

Baal Shem Tov — founder of the Chassidic movement.

beinoni (pl. *beinonim*) — literally, "intermediate"; a person whose state of personal development lies between that of the *Tzaddik* and the *rasha*.

Beriah — the World of Creation, second of the four worlds.

Binah — understanding, second of the ten *sefirot*.

Chesed — kindness, first of the seven *middot*, fourth of the ten *sefirot*.

Chochmah — wisdom, the first of the ten *sefirot* and first of the intellectual powers of the soul.

Da'at — knowledge, the third of the ten *sefirot*, completing the intellectual process together with *Chochmah* and *Binah*.

emunah — faith.

gematria — the numerical value of the Hebrew letters by which deeper meanings are extrapolated.

geulah sheleimah — the complete redemption, which will occur with the coming of Mashiach.

Gevurah — might, restraint, restriction, second of the seven *middot*, fifth of the ten *sefirot*.

kabbalat ol Shamayim — accepting the rule and authority of G-d as King, i.e., fulfilling the commandments.

Kabbalah — literally, "tradition"; mystical teachings of the Torah.

kedushah — holiness.

kelipah (pl. *kelipot*) — shell or peel, the term frequently used in *Kabbalah* to denote evil and the source of our animalistic desires, which are merely a concealment of the G-dly reality in all things.

kelipat nogah — "translucent shell," an incomplete concealment of G-dliness that allows some holiness to shine through and be accessed.

Malchut — royalty, the tenth and lowest of the ten *sefirot*.

memalei — the light that fills the world

middot — emotional attributes and character traits.

Mishnah — the six tractates of the Oral Law.

mitzvah (pl. *mitzvot*) — a commandment, which is part of the Torah way of connecting to G-d.

rasha (pl. *resha'im*) — one whose life is dominated by his Animal Soul and therefore does mostly evil in his thoughts, speech, and actions.

sefirot — the Divine attributes, or emanations, often referred to as the "ten *sefirot*," which manifest themselves in each of the four worlds.

shechitah — ritual slaughter of kosher animals according to Jewish law.

simchah — joy, one of the main fundamental ways of serving G-d.

sitra achra — literally, "the other side," i.e., not the side of holiness; a term for evil that conceals G-dliness.

sovev — the all-encompassing light surrounding the worlds that gives life from a distance,.

Talmud — the Oral Law as recorded in the Mishnah and expanded with commentary (as opposed to the Written Law — i.e., the Five Books of Moses).

Tanya — literally, "it has been taught"; the popular name of *Likutei Amarim* written by Rabbi Shneur Zalman.

teshuvah — literally, "returning"; repentance, returning to G-d's will.

tefillah (pl. *tefillot*) — prayer.

Tiferet — beauty, third of the seven *middot*, sixth of the ten *sefirot*.

timtum halev — literally, "heart congestion"; spiritual blockages that keep a person from advancing.

Tzaddik (pl. *Tzaddikim*) — a righteous, holy person, who has succeeded in transforming his Animal Soul to good.

tzimtzum — contraction; a kabbalistic term explaining the creative process by which G-d made the worlds.

Torah — G-d's will; the Torah that G-d gave to the Jewish people.

yesh me'ayin — something from nothingness; creation.

Yetzirah — the World of Formation, third of the four worlds.

yirah — awe (of G-d).

yirah ilah — the higher level of awe.

yirah tata — the lower level of awe.

Zohar — the major kabbalistic work attributed to Rabbi Shimon bar Yochai.

הודפס
לעילוי נשמת
אברהם בן משיח
הנולד מן תמר
אברמשוילי
ת.נ.צ.ב.ה.

ולעילוי נשמת
אבי אהרון בן מנחם
הנולד מן רבקה
דברשוילי
ת.נ.צ.ב.ה.